C000109361

CRITICAL PERSPECTIVES ON TEACHING IN PRISON

This volume makes a case for engaging critical approaches for teaching adults in prison higher education (or "college-in-prison") programs. This book not only contextualizes pedagogy within the specialized and growing niche of prison instruction, but also addresses prison abolition, reentry, and educational equity. Chapters are written by prison instructors, currently incarcerated students, and formerly incarcerated students, providing a variety of perspectives on the many roadblocks and ambitions of teaching and learning in carceral settings. All unapologetic advocates of increasing access to higher education for people in prison, contributors discuss the high stakes of teaching incarcerated individuals and address the dynamics, conditions, and challenges of doing such work. The type of instruction that contributors advocate is transferable beyond prisons to traditional campus settings. Hence, the lessons of this volume will not only support readers in becoming more thoughtful prison educators and program administrators, but also in becoming better teachers who can employ critical, democratic pedagogy in a range of contexts.

Rebecca Ginsburg is Associate Professor of Education Policy and Director of the Education Justice Project at the University of Illinois, USA.

CRITICAL PERSPECTIVES ON TEACHING IN PRISON

Students and Instructors on Pedagogy Behind the Wall

Edited by Rebecca Ginsburg

Routledge
Taylor & Francis Group

NEW YORK AND LONDON

First published 2019
by Routledge
52 Vanderbilt Avenue, New York, NY 10017

and by Routledge
2 Park Square, Milton Park, Abingdon, Oxon OX14 4RN

Routledge is an imprint of the Taylor & Francis Group, an informa business

© 2019 Taylor & Francis

The right of Rebecca Ginsburg to be identified as the author of the editorial material, and of the authors for their individual chapters, has been asserted in accordance with sections 77 and 78 of the Copyright, Designs and Patents Act 1988.

Library of Congress Cataloging-in-Publication Data
A catalog record for this title has been requested

ISBN: 978-0-8153-7906-5 (hbk)
ISBN: 978-0-8153-7943-0 (pbk)
ISBN: 978-1-351-21586-2 (ebk)

Typeset in Bembo
by Taylor & Francis Books

Visit the eResources: www.routledge.com/9780815379430

Dedicated to Education Justice Project and to incarcerated scholars everywhere

CONTENTS

CONTRIBUTORS

Jerrad Allen brings to the table fourteen years of experience within the California correctional system. He is a vegetarian and a yoga teacher who has earned an associate's degree in Business Management and aspires towards an MBA. He hopes to apply his entrepreneurial skills to develop a successful business of his own.

Osvaldo Armas is an operations manager at Clifton's Cafeteria in Downtown Los Angeles. It is one of the oldest establishments in the city, with deep connections to authors such as Ray Bradbury, Jack Kerouac, L. Ron Hubbard, and many others. He writes, "it is safe to say I'm in good company." His aspirations are to one day publish a book of poetry and a memoir of his encounters.

Victoria M. Bryan teaches English at Cleveland State Community College and teaches composition to incarcerated students at Turney Center Industrial Complex in Tennessee.

Susan Castagnetto, the coordinator of the Intercollegiate Feminist Center for Teaching, Research, and Engagement at Scripps College, received her PhD in Philosophy from Stanford University. She runs writing workshops for incarcerated women at the California Institution for Women.

Jody Cohen coordinates the Bryn Mawr College–Riverside Correctional Facility partnership and has made several conference presentations on that work. She is Professor of Education at Bryn Mawr/Haverford College.

Anne Dalke teaches English and Gender Studies at Bryn Mawr College, where her interests include disability studies and classroom ecologies. She has published and presented often on her teaching with the Bryn Mawr College–Riverside Correctional Facility partnership.

Kimberly Erbe began college after being released from prison. She is currently a doctoral student at the University of Illinois at Urbana Champaign.

Thomas Fabisiak directs the Chillon Project, an initiative of the Center for Compassion, Integrity, and Secular Ethics at Life University to provide college degree programs to people in prison and correctional staff in Georgia. He completed his PhD in Comparative Literature and Religion at Emory in 2014, and he has published a regrettably arcane book that focuses on romantic medical accounts of ghost-seeing and demon possession. His current research critically evaluates moral discourses of rehabilitation and punishment in and around prisons.

Margaret Garb is the author of three books on urban history. She received her PhD in History at Columbia University and was a professor at Washington University in St. Louis, where she co-established a prison higher education program. Sadly, she passed away during the production of this volume.

Raphael Ginsberg is Associate Director of the Correctional Education Program at the University of North Carolina at Chapel Hill, where he is also a lecturer in the Department of Communication Studies. He is a former investigator with the King County (Seattle, Washington) Public Defender. His research interests include critical legal studies and queer theory.

Rebecca Ginsburg is co-founder and Director of the Education Justice Project at the University of Illinois, a comprehensive college-in-prison program that also publishes reentry guides. An architectural historian, she teaches courses on the history of the prison and carceral landscapes. She earned her PhD in Architecture from the University of California, Berkeley, and a JD from the University of Michigan Law School.

James Kilgore is the author of four novels and *Understanding Mass Incarceration: A People's Guide to the Key Civil Rights Struggle of Our Time*. While incarcerated in California, he served as a peer instructor within various prison education programs. He has written widely on mass incarceration.

Doran Larson has been teaching in prisons since 2006. He is Wolcott-Barlett Professor of Literature and Creative Writing at Hamilton College. He is the editor of *Fourth City: Essays from the American Prison* and "The Beautiful Prison," a special issue of *Studies in Law Politics, and Society*.

Malakki (Ralph Bolden) is a published poet and author who is currently serving his twenty-fourth year of a life sentence in Pennsylvania. In the 2016 PEN Prison Writing Awards he won the Dawson Prize in Fiction & Honorable Mention in Nonfiction. He has finished several novels, a few one-act plays, and many poems, and has also displayed his artwork in artists' showcases in the Pittsburgh area.

Stacy Bell McQuaide directs the Writing Center at Oxford College and has taught at Lee Arrendale State Prison, in Georgia, since 2011. She has frequently presented on her work with incarcerated writers at academic conferences.

Tessa Hicks Peterson is Assistant Vice President at Pitzer College, California, and Assistant Professor of Urban Studies. Her research interests include the scholarship of community engagement and service learning. She has taught "Healing Arts and Social Change" at a prison.

Anna Plemons began teaching through Arts in Corrections at New Folsom Prison in 2009. Any summary of her work requires a word of thanks to the writers there whose participation and prose continue to help illuminate both the complications and rewards of educational justice work. Additionally, Anna teaches through the Lake Tahoe Community College *Incarcerated Students Program* and is a faculty member at Washington State University. She has published work related to prison education with *Teaching Artist Journal, Community Literacy Journal,* and the edited collection *Prison Pedagogy: Learning and Teaching with Imprisoned Writers.*

Romarilyn Ralston received her master's in Liberal Arts from Washington University in St. Louis following her release from prison. She currently works for Project Rebound in California.

Mary L. (Molly) Shanley, Emerita Professor of Political Science at Vassar College, has led a women's writing group at the county jail for almost ten years. She is the author of dozens of chapters and journal articles and seven books and edited volumes, primarily on feminism and political theory.

Maggie Shelledy is Assistant Professor of Writing and Language Studies at the University of Texas Rio Grande Valley and a faculty affiliate of the Education Justice Project. Her current research investigates the relationship between literacy and the experience of reentry.

Sarah Shotland teaches creative writing at Chatham University in Pittsburgh. She is co-founder of Words Without Walls, a creative writing program at Allegheny County Jail, which has been expanded to State Correctional Institution Pittsburgh, a medium-security prison. She has also developed weekly creative writing workshops to support students post-release. Sarah Shotland has written and spoken frequently about teaching incarcerated students. Her co-edited volume is *Words Without Walls: Writers on Addiction, Violence, and Incarceration*.

Dennis R. Simpson II, currently incarcerated in the North Carolina Department of Public Safety, is a student of the University of North Carolina at Chapel Hill. A Black Lives Matter movement activist, he fights to end mass incarceration with the goal of prison abolition. He is also a U.S. Army veteran.

Russell X is serving a life sentence in Pennsylvania. The prison administration will allow him to be identified only as "Russell X" and has forbidden him from providing a bio.

ACKNOWLEDGEMENTS

I wish to thank all the contributors to this volume, especially those who spent several days at a writing retreat in Illinois in December 2017, during which we built our own learning community and, in the process, helped to make this a better book.

Warm thanks to the Andrew W. Mellon Foundation for supporting the retreat and for funding to create the editor's website associated with this volume.

Finally, special thanks to Anne Dalke, Anna Plemons, and Maggie Shelledy, the contributors who served as a "mini editorial team" that helped me sort through submissions and make key editorial decisions.

INTRODUCTION

Rebecca Ginsburg

This volume celebrates the enterprise of teaching and learning alongside incarcerated students. It also offers a realistic appraisal of how very challenging that enterprise is. Higher education in prison is not for the fainthearted, and *Critical Perspectives on Teaching in Prison* is meant to help instructors and administrators of college-in-prison programs (a term I use interchangeably with "prison higher education programs") better understand the terrain they must navigate and how others have tackled some of the challenges that appear frequently in our work.

There is much at stake. This volume's contributors share the view that college-in-prison is not inherently beneficial and righteous. To the contrary, a poorly designed or badly implemented program can do more harm than good. The contributors developed the following statement to clarify our position on this. It's appropriate to share it at the start, as a declaration of first principles and values.

> We're committed to high quality educational programming in prisons. We believe that higher education in prison can be a radical and humanizing project and we are advocates of such programs, in their rich diversity.
>
> However, there is a darkness to the work of teaching in prison. When instructors who are headed behind the wall are not aware of the challenges and risks of prison teaching, they are more likely to take on the values and imperatives of the carceral state and their classrooms and programs are likely to become yet another repressive force in incarcerated individuals' lives.
>
> We're committed to critical interrogation of the tensions and risks associated with the enterprise, which includes interrogation of the power relationship between free instructor and incarcerated students and themes of power, authority, violence, trauma, complicity, relational accountability, and punishment.[1]

For the past ten years I've directed the Education Justice Project (EJP), a college-in-prison program based within a medium-security men's state prison in Illinois. I can attest that higher education in prison is a fraught endeavor, laden with tension upon tension, starting with the essential tension that is inherent to the gesture of conjoining a learning community with a carceral site.

It is also, as our statement suggests, a praxis that is full of potential and promise, not only for incarcerated scholars but for society as a whole (see Chapter 4).

The essays in this book, written by prison instructors, currently incarcerated students, and formerly incarcerated students, speak to the promises and the pitfalls. As a group, they address the gritty reality of attempting to do liberating work within a place of confinement and constraint, and the soaring ambitions that many of us have, through this work, to create conditions that will produce a more just and loving world. A healthy and critical prison teaching practice will acknowledge the presence of both conditions, while fetishizing neither.

This volume's central argument is that the best prison teaching does not simply replicate the teaching that occurs on traditional campuses. Instead, effective prison college teachers and college-in-prison programs must take care to manage the particular dynamics and the inherent violence of carceral settings. At its best, higher education in prison is a liberating and transforming force. However, when college-in-prison programs lose sight of their mission, and when prison educators become stand-ins for correctional officers, college-in-prison reinforces the regression of incarceration.

Fortunately, the habits of quality prison instruction are transferable to traditional campus settings. Many of the essays in this volume will not only support readers becoming better prison educators, but better teachers, period. I hope that they bolster instructors' familiarity with and comfort in employing critical, democratic pedagogy of the sort advocated for in this volume.

A major aim of the volume is to excite interest in college-in-prison programs among individuals and institutions not currently engaged in the work, and to prompt critical reflection upon the work by those who already do it. The current practice in many programs is for adjunct instructors to be hired to teach a given course at the prison, provide them a brief training on security matters, and then let them loose on the incarcerated students. There is no feedback loop to campus or ongoing teacher training or assessment. This volume presents college-in-prison as an enterprise that deserves more thought, attention, and support.

This introduction sets out some of the themes that run through the essays in the volume and provides a brief orientation to its structure and contents. It concludes by reiterating the book's primary purpose—encouraging those who can teach to become engaged in delivering quality higher education to people in prison.

Incarceration in the U.S.

Many people come to higher education in prison because they are critical of the American penal system or our criminal justice system more generally. A lengthy discussion of those structures is beyond the scope of this volume (but see e.g., Alexander, 2010; Dole II, 2015; Foreman, 2017; Gottschalk, 2006, 2014; Hayes, 2017; Kilgore, 2015; Longworth, 2016; Pfaff, 2017; and Stevenson, 2015, for an entry into that subject). However, it's not possible to have a thoughtful discussion of college-in-prison without addressing the environment in which it, by definition, operates. An honest conversation about U.S. prisons, how they have failed us, and what to do about them must take into account the pernicious mix of forces that have shaped penal incarceration in the U.S.—income and wealth inequality; implicit racial bias in policing and the court system; zero-tolerance disciplinary codes in schools; lack of affordable quality health care; over-militarized policing; impoverished public school systems; longstanding but ever-transforming patterns of racism, sexism, homophobia, and other ideologies; the U.S. penchant for glorifying punishment and violence; and draconian sentencing guidelines. That incomplete list begins, at least, to scratch the surface.

We'd also want to address current conditions of imprisonment, including the siting of prisons far from families and communities, solitary confinement, the death penalty, life without parole, limited availability to health services of all types, overcrowding, and the difficult conditions under which prison staff strain to work.

Removing mandatory minimums and decriminalization—for example, of drug-related offenses—are often cited as necessary paths to meaningful reform (see e.g., Illinois State Commission on Criminal Justice and Sentencing Reform, 2016). So are creating more checks on prosecutors, increasing funding for public defenders (on both, see e.g., Pfaff, 2017), and creating more alternatives to incarceration (see e.g., United Nations Office on Drugs and Crime, 2007).

Efforts to establish community-based restorative justice programs are even more ambitious, and ambitious is what we need to be in light of the high social and financial costs of incarceration and the psychic harms it imposes on society (see e.g., Comfort et al., 2017; McLaughlin et al., 2016; Price, 2015). Such restorative justice initiatives often form part of deep-seated reappraisals of the purposes and values of the criminal justice system. Efforts to place more mental health resources in communities, change school funding models, and abolish policing as we know it also support visions of fundamental, structural changes. Advocates hope such moves will significantly reduce the amount of harm and violence in our communities and produce a more just society. While, as Fabisiak (Chapter 8) notes, there is no shared platform among them for achieving this end, proponents of comprehensive structural change typically share an understanding of prisons as part of a larger system of punitive-oriented institutions that maintain social inequality. They accordingly work to achieve progressive change in policy realms as seemingly diverse as immigration, disability rights, and environmental sustainability.

Where in the conversation does college-in-prison belong?

It's not clear that it comes up at all.

For those of us who currently teach in, administer, and support college-in-prison programs, or aim to do so, let's break down the implications of what that means.

Humility Is in Order

Higher education in prison is a relatively modest intervention. Even as I hope this volume will generate interest and enthusiasm for the enterprise of offering post-secondary academic programs to people who are locked up, I'm apprehensive about the danger of institutions of higher education and academics making too much of their contributions and the impacts of their teaching. Like Harkins and Meiners (2016, p. 406), I'm cautious about the tendency of faculty members, of which I'm one, to treat the prison as a removed and exotic site of charitable giving. In the words of Malakki, an incarcerated scholar, "it's not about you" (this volume, p. 17).

Making college courses available to people serving prison sentences does not hold promise to redress what ails the U.S. system of criminal punishment. College-in-prison is not an intervention that will put the system right, and this volume is not offered in that spirit.

Granted, you would not have that impression if you followed popular media. Higher education in prison has of late received increasing attention. That's in part because the Department of Education in 2015 approved the use of Pell Grants on a pilot basis to fund such programs. That was news in itself and, then, because the Grants incubated so many new programs, and because some of the players behind the existing and emerging college-in-prison initiatives are large institutions that energetically self-promote what they characterize as their "public engagement" work, college-in-prison has had a higher profile in recent years. Furthermore, talk of "prison reform" has become more mainstream, bipartisan, and urgent. For that reason, too, the media has shown more interest lately in prison education initiatives, as they are often promoted as reformist ventures.

However, the press attention is misleading.

For one thing, most people in the U.S. are locked up without a high school degree or equivalent. Accordingly, the greatest educational need in American prisons is not for college, but GED (General Education Development) and ABE (Adult Basic Education) instruction. Sadly, those programs, which are typically administered by state departments of correction, get little attention. In the college program that I direct, in a typical semester only around 70 of the 1,800 people incarcerated at the prison qualify for our courses, though we try to leverage our presence in the facility by training our students to teach individuals in the general population. At the same time, there is a waiting list to get into the GED program. Tyrone Werts, formerly incarcerated at Greaterford Prison in Pennsylvania, reminds us that those who lack the qualifications or confidence to get a college education are in the majority.

They are what I think of as the "throw-away people"—men and women who recidivate because no one showed them compassion or kindness or demonstrated a belief that they could survive the rigors of a higher education. I was one of those people (Werts, 2013, p. 160).

Not with standing my calls for humility, there is much that is good and just about higher education in prison. By providing opportunity for accreditation, leadership development, and the accumulation of cultural capital (among other benefits) for incarcerated scholars; and by creating pathways that can lead to enrollment in college upon release, college-in-prison programs can play a role in those comprehensive efforts to change the American system of incarceration that I referred to above. The goal of such efforts is not better prisons. It is a reorientation to criminal justice. It is a long-term struggle to recast the way we as a society respond to social harms and the people who are hurt by them, and in so doing redefine what Americans understand to be productive, efficient, moral, and just in the realms of crime and punishment. It's essential that people who have been in prison play leading roles in those struggles, and college-in-prison programs can smooth the way to their engagement.

By exposing instructors to issues and conditions surrounding penal incarceration, these programs can contribute as well towards creating a better-informed public, one that knowledgably supports calls for change. I encourage instructors to take seriously the need for us to share what we have seen and learned about prisons and people in prison.

Finally, educational programming at its best creates spaces of humanity and dignity that invite incarcerated scholars to breathe, build community with one another, and to produce and create.

Higher education in prison can play a productive role in the struggle for a more just approach to criminal wrongdoing, but only if we get it right. This involves maintaining a due modesty about the numbers of people impacted by our programs, and modesty regarding our role as instructors.

It's Not about Rehabilitation

This leads to the second lesson. We might start by stipulating that high rates of crime and violence in the U.S. have structural roots, and that the problems associated with penal incarceration are structural as well. Systemic changes in education, health care, income distribution, just to name a few, are required to remedy them. This is not a case of a few rotten apples. The barrel itself is moldy and cannot hold. Fortunately, organizations and scholars provide insight into the ways that historical forces, economic trends, political agendas, and even culture and ideology contribute to high levels of interpersonal violence in the U.S. and to our often-misguided institutional responses to that violence.

In brief, it's not about rehabilitation. Our job is not to reform our incarcerated students, any more than faculty on traditional campuses think of ourselves as engaged in student reform. When we think of our presence in a prison as having mainly rehabilitative functions, there are a few things that can go wrong. First, seeing our students as defective or otherwise in need of restoration can lead to lowering academic standards. After all, they're broken; how can we expect them to do the same quality of work as "normal" students? Lowering standards cheats the students of their education and compromises our relationship with them, because they will almost certainly pick up on our condescension.

Second, we are more likely to align our programs with the rehabilitative agendas of departments of correction if we have convinced ourselves that rehabilitation is our task. Our work requires us to work closely with our partners in prison administration, but integrity of purpose should compel us to be clear in our own minds, and to be able to explain to our students, how the university differs from the prison. Indeed, a little creative tension between a college-in-prison program and the prison that hosts it is probably a good thing. For logistical, political, and pragmatic reasons, not to mention fidelity to mission, a campus would be unwise to confuse its agenda with that of its contractual partner. Universities educate; prisons confine.

It is easy and tempting to adopt the rhetoric of criminal justice reform and crime prevention. After all, it's often what donors and funders wish to hear. I encourage instructors and program administrators to stay in our own lane. There is more than a sniff of instrumentalism when a college-in-prison program adopts an implicit or explicit orientation of teaching "to lower recidivism." Not only is recidivism an exceedingly complex and therefore easily misleading metric (Castro and Zamani-Gallaher, 2018, pp. 14–15; Maltz, 1984), but viewing our students as potential dangers to society, but for our intervention, returns us to the dangers of holding an inflated sense of our role and losing their trust. Howard S. Davidson acknowledges the trickiness of dismissing a possible education–recidivism link. It is "not because we have no concern with crime and the harm it creates, nor is it a sign that we are callous to students' conditions and their desire to leave prison and live creative lives" (Davidson, 1995, p. 11) that we decline to characterize our programs as aimed towards lowering recidivism. It's because doing so will put us in a frame of mind that is counter-productive and misplaced.

There is a demographic reality at play that complicates matters, and makes it more likely that people engaged in this work will slide easily into a rehabilitative orientation towards teaching people in prison. Those incarcerated are disproportionately African American, Latinx, and indigenous Americans. In some states, including Illinois, where I work, the majority of people in prison are African American. For instance, the majority of EJP students are black. And, as is the case for most college-in-prison programs, the majority of our instructors are white.

EJP is actively trying to increase the proportion of our instructors of color through affirmative hiring. We're doing this for many reasons, including the express request of our students and research that suggests that learning is enhanced when students and teachers share common backgrounds. For the purpose of this conversation, though, the issue is the literally centuries-long legacy of racial domination that makes it difficult for middle-class whites to avoid approaching poor African Americans, in particular, without a gloss of paternalism and what has come to be called a "white savior" mindset. A rehabilitation framework slides easily onto the narrative that people of color are almost by definition in need of help, and that white people can and should provide it.

This is complicated and hard. Class clearly comes into play, too, as I can personally attest as a middle-class African American woman. Our students, at the same time, bring their own baggage around race, gender, class, and sexuality. EJP has had more than one white instructor who endured homelessness growing up, and who shattered assumptions among our students about where we, as instructors, come from and what we bring into the space of the classroom.

Our queer and non-gender conforming instructors endure the hyper-masculine, homophobic atmosphere, not only of the prison in general, but of some EJP classrooms. The climate is better since we started to bring these complex dynamics intentionally to the surface through readings and discussions, and it is a long process.

As the readings in this collection make clear, an honest appraisal of one's assumptions, prejudices, and biases will contribute to better classroom experiences, and a more trusted and sustainable program. It is, in any event, a worthwhile thing for all who live in this country to reflect on our relationship to race and privilege, and how these things can get in the way of the relationships we seek to build with one another.

Finally, a rehabilitation mindset gets in the way of seeing students in their full-bodied wholeness. This is not just demeaning, it's a lost opportunity.

> A powerful shortcoming in the dialogue about higher education and prison is the consideration of those behind bars solely as passive objects … People behind bars are discussed only as recipients, able only to take in knowledge and benefits from education. Little attention is ever provided to these folks as resources. This mindset reflects an undercurrent of the very one-dimensional stereotype that reformers and researchers seek to overcome: that those in prison cannot offer society anything (Mahon-Haft, 2019).

Adult students, of the sort we teach in our programs, are capable of being partners in the design and administration of college-in-prison, to the extent the security apparatus of the facility allows. Even if formal structures such as student advisory boards are not possible, acknowledging the capacity of students as well-considered and thoughtful contributors can lead to discussions that usefully shape the work. Many of EJP's programs, for instance, have come as a result of proposals our students brought to us, and EJP is the stronger for them. Students are expert in how the institution works and who your programs' allies are among staff and administration. They're familiar with other programs that enter the facility and can direct you to allies on the outside.

Beyond these practical considerations is the interest we should always have in seeing things as they are. Incarcerated students are, on the whole, older, wiser, and more sophisticated than students on traditional campuses. Because we might not proactively seek the counsel of typical nineteen-year-old undergraduates, it can be an adjustment to consider our students at the prison as resources. And, certainly, if our mindset is that we are there to redeem them, rather than to engage in building a community of learning with them, there is yet another obstacle to recognizing the gifts that they bring.

As Daniel Karpowitz from the Bard Prison Initiative in New York explains, in relation to the rehabilitation mindset, "if there is a connection between 'change' and the justifications for college in prison, our foremost goal must be not to change people in prison, but to change the landscape of the prison itself" (Karpowitz, 2017, p. 12).

Embrace Complexity

A college-in-prison program is not just another extension of the university campus, and it never will be.

College-in-prison is enmeshed in a web of tensions—between incarcerated individuals and the prisons that confine them; between the interests of administrators of institutions of higher education and the idealistic visions of prison instructors; between competing rhetorics of punishment, rehabilitation, abolition, and public safety; and between instructors and students, just to name a few.

This is not to suggest that the project of higher education on traditional campuses is straightforward and easy. Of course not. It's only to explain that when prisons and incarcerated students are added to the mix, the enterprise of higher education becomes even more challenging. A college-in-prison program is a significant intervention into the operations of a given institution, the lives of incarcerated scholars, and the workings of a college campus. It is likely to involve work with state legislators and the media, connecting to community-based organizations that work in the field of reentry and supporting families with incarcerated loved ones, and explaining the effort to alumni and boards of regents.

On the prison side, corrections officers will probably find themselves sorting through boxes of books, escorting guest speakers, and walking lines of students through the rain to events that the college-in-prison has scheduled. The program's operations will likely disrupt the regular operations of a prison, and represent a shift away from what many, especially old-school officers, consider the mission of the facility to be. Some welcome the change and the challenge, and others will resent it.

Innocence is not attractive in this work, nor a willful denial of the hard realities that our incarcerated students and those they love live with, nor a reluctance to face what it means for our students, for those who are incarcerated with them but who are not our students, and for prison staff and prison administrators when we and our programs enter their worlds. We can harm them when we operate in a way that compromises the safety and security of our students. Simpson (Chapter 4) argues that instructors should seek to better understand the home communities from which our incarcerated students come. I would add that it's imperative for us to learn as well about the current contexts of their lives. When we fail to appreciate the implications of our program's policies and operations for their daily lives, or to understand the position we put them in by virtue of what we ask of them, we are more likely to make missteps that inconvenience and perhaps even endanger them.

In short, teaching in prison is a messy business. Jim Thomas, who taught for many years in an Illinois prison, explains that there are so many obstacles associated with running college-in-prison programs, from prison staff arbitrarily disciplining students, to lock downs that interrupt class schedules, that prison higher education can't in fact be truly or fully implemented (Thomas, 1995).

From his perspective as an incarcerated student, Eli Davis warns that

> you educators who come into prison to truly teach need to know that you are not wanted by the administration. Having this knowledge will help to keep you from getting frustrated, from asking why prison officials are not meeting your smallest demands, why there's no consistency between how things went last week and this week, why students fail to give their all in class (Davis, 2018, p. 2).

Directly transplanting existing campus programs and classes into prison settings would be easier. However, as many of the essays in this volume suggest, considering the appropriateness of program content and procedures for the prison setting is more productive. Nothing in that statement should be construed as implying that courses should be "dumbed down" for incarcerated students. To the contrary, this recommendation speaks to their interests in having college-in-prison be responsive to the contexts of their current and future lives, and to the challenges of faithfully implementing our programs with that in mind.

In This Volume

The volume contains an introduction and nineteen chapters written by prison educators and students. Almost half of the essays are by currently or formerly incarcerated individuals. The focus is on post-secondary academic education, what is sometimes referred to as higher education or, in the prison context, college-in-prison. It does not address vocational or technical education. This clearly has a useful place in prisons, and is long due for the sort of critique that has been part of higher education in prison since at least the 1970s, but that is beyond the scope this volume. (For a discussion of the dangers of stressing vocational education in prison at the expense of academic offerings, see Graves, 2015).

I would have liked to include even more essays by people in prison. However, it proved difficult to manage the delivery of manuscripts and revisions in and out of the various prisons where our would-be contributors lived, and it took too long. (Within EJP we have a specially-designated coordinator who works with students on their publishing efforts, but most programs don't have such personnel. I'm very grateful to the several individuals who ushered manuscripts and correspondence in and out prisons across the U.S., and facilitated my efforts to involve incarcerated contributors to the extent we were able.) Many pieces written by currently incarcerated individuals can be found on the eResources page that accompanies this book, along with other materials that I hope will assist with the nuts and bolts of setting up and sustaining a program. They include sample syllabi, Memos of Understanding (MOUs) with Departments of Correction, release forms for students, class ground rules, orientation materials for instructors, state coalition bye-laws, guidelines for talking to media and taking photos, helpful websites and links, and more. Please let me know if there are other resources you would like to see on there by emailing me. I can be reached at www.rebeccaginsburg.net.

The volume itself is divided into two parts. Chapters in the first, "The Context," consider the broader social, historical, and educational contexts of the enterprise of engaging in higher education in prison. They consider questions of why and how educators should engage with college-in-prison programs, and the scope such programs could most usefully assume. The second, larger part called "In the Classroom" contains chapters about teaching practices that acknowledge the context of imprisonment and confinement. Both parts include some highly theoretical chapters and selections that are more "hands on."

The volume opens with "An Open Letter to Prison Educators" by Malakki, an incarcerated scholar imprisoned in Pennsylvania. His appeals for instructors to "come and be with us as we struggle to reach our best us" and to keep in mind that "it's not about you" belong front and center. The importance of retaining humility, and acknowledging the limited role outside instructors play within a large and complex system, runs throughout the collection.

In too many jurisdictions, people serving life sentences are unable to enroll higher education programs (or any programs). Sometimes this is because of explicit rules that forbid their participation; in other instances it is because priority is given to individuals with out-dates, and the shortage of space is such that lifers never make it off the waiting lists. Russell X, a lifer in Pennsylvania (at a different facility than Malakki), argues that educational opportunities for lifers in prison is essential, given their roles as leaders on the inside and their connections to families and communities on the outside. "Hope for Leaving a Legacy" challenges program administrators and instructors to reconsider their own assumptions about who our students should be, and to advocate for changes to department policies.

Answering the "why" question in regards to college-in-prison is not the main focus of this book. Accordingly, there's been no effort to be comprehensive in presenting arguments that justify college-in-prison. At the same time, this volume is meant to be useful to those in the trenches who may find themselves asked to defend or explain these programs. Doran Larson, in "Repairing the Generations: Prison Higher Education as Historical Reparations," suggests that we view higher education in prison as compensation for state-sponsored racial inequality. This requires attention to the historical context in which incarceration and higher education in prison takes place. "When we argue for and practice [college-in-prison programming] ... we pursue reparative justice and healing as concrete, historical resistance not only to the retributive prison but to the structural inequalities that the prison both creates and maintains" (this volume, pp. 27–28).

Dennis R. Simpson II argues that higher education in prison programs' entrance requirements produce marginalization and social stratification in facilities where they operate (this volume). In "Pedagogy of the Offender," he also takes issue with programs whose expressed goals are to rehabilitate individuals, arguing that higher education in prison should be a political act that prepares students to change the communities to which they're returning. "This requires a fundamental shift of focus ... from the micro to the macro" (this volume, p. 34). The goal should not be fixing broken individuals, but equipping formerly incarcerated people to fix a broken society.

As Russell X argued for expanded access to higher education programs for lifers, Kimberly Erbe points to gender disparities in programming and makes a case for offering more academic programs in women's prisons. Incarcerated women are greatly underserved by prison university programs, even as the numbers of women in prison are growing. Notions of femininity and domesticity, Erbe argues, have been an obstacle to offering college-in-prison to women, in favor of programs that are intended to cultivate their assumed nurturing roles within their households. She concludes by noting that it is uncomfortable to advocate for increased prison programming, but that practicalities demand that women receive access to the education that will expand their economic opportunities, and prospects for their families.

In "From Africa to High Desert State Prison: Journeys of an Invisible Teacher," James Kilgore shares his experiences as an educator in Zimbabwe, in South Africa, and in a California prison where he was incarcerated and urges outside prison educators to recognize the contributions of such "invisible educators" who inspire and support other scholars, whether they themselves are enrolled in a college program or not. This is a helpful reminder of the appropriateness of humility. Our university programs are not the only sources of education in prison. Far from it. And when we fail to appreciate the broader prison ecology of formal and informal educational practices that college-in-prison is part of, we fail to do justice and give credit to the people and institutions that make our programs possible.

The "In the Classroom" part opens with Raphael Ginsberg's "The Perils of Transformation Talk in Higher Education in Prison." This essay offers a thoughtful challenge not only to the notion that college programs ought to be in the business of seeking to change their students in fundamental ways but, even more incisively, to the use of critical pedagogy within prison classrooms. This approach to teaching, he argues, locks the incarcerated scholar into the role of "prisoner," an act that amounts to a "psychic invasion on acutely vulnerable students who lack the ability to represent themselves." The solution—treat students as students—is only a partial one, Ginsberg admits, since there are dangers as well in not accounting for the differences between incarcerated and non-incarcerated students—for example, in not acknowledging the power disparities that exist between free instructors and incarcerated students. Ginsberg's uneasy conclusion speaks to what he terms "the darkness inherent in the prison classroom's power dynamics" (this volume, p. 66).

Thomas Fabisiak is attuned to that darkness as well, and to the self-doubt and self-criticism that may result when instructors try unsuccessfully to create liberating spaces in an institution that cannot allow it. In "On the Practice and Ethos of Self-Compassion for Higher Educators in Prisons," he encourages instructors to try to avoid postures of self-judgement, and also the trap of self-praise. (Ginsberg also notes the valorization by self and others that can accompany teaching in prison). Practicing awareness of the complexity of higher education in prison and of one's own role helps us to accept what is, to stay present to it, and be "open to unknown possibilities to which our work might lead" (this volume, p. 77).

Anna Plemons turns our attention back to transformative talk, which she associates with the doctrine of progress, an ideology that assumes an individualistic, linear journey towards self-improvement, however defined. In "Beyond Progress: Indigenous Scholars, Relational Methodologies, and Decolonial Options for the Prison Classroom," Plemons offers decolonizing pedagogies that are based instead in the principle of relationality. "A critique of the ideological primacy of the individual and the idea of progress in prison education opens up some space in which to consider other possible ways … of making meaning of what happens in the prison classroom" (this volume, p. 83). She illustrates what a relational framework might look like in practice by applying the model to a case study around the production of a coloring book in the Arts in Corrections program in which she teaches.

The next four chapters address strategies for teaching writing in prison, the most common form of higher educational programming in the U.S. Sarah Shotland, in "No One Ever Asked Me: Embracing Embodied Pedagogy in the Creative Writing Classroom," discusses how awareness of the prevalence of physical trauma in her female students' lives led her to want to better center writers' bodies and to conceptualize writing, in the workshops she offers in prisons, jails, and rehabilitation centers, as a physical practice. Stacy Bell McQuaide's essay, "'Go Hard': Bringing Privilege-Industry Pedagogies into a College Writing Classroom in Prison," reflects on the tension between the culture of universities, "status factories, where privilege and opportunity are reproduced" (this volume, p. 103), and the punishment industry that is represented by prisons. Explaining that the educational paradigms of the former may not anticipate the needs of incarcerated students, she offers specific practices that she uses in her classroom, including one-on-one consultation, multiple opportunities for revision, and negotiation with students of text selection.

Like Sarah Shotland, Susan Castagnetto and Mary L. (Molly) Shanley also teach writing workshops in prisons and jails. Drawing on reflections from members of their writing groups and published accounts of other writing groups in prison, in "Women's Writing Groups Inside: Healing, Resistance, and Change" they reflect on how such groups can support members' efforts to build community, create solidarity, and create new narratives about themselves through "restorying."

Maggie Shelledy urges teachers to anticipate the sorts of needs their students will have, with respect to writing, after they're released. In "Writing for Reentry: A Few Lessons from Transfer Theory," she argues that instead of assuming that students can automatically, and easily, apply what they've learned about writing in the prison classroom to the very different situations that they will encounter on the outside, instructors strategically employ three practices—creative repurposing, boundary crossing, and hope as critical rhetorical practice—that will foster students' "rhetorical resilience" (this volume, p. 130) in the transition from prison to the day-to-day realities of life on the outside.

Anne Dalke and Jody Cohen ruminate on the experience of prison time— slow, jerky, uncertain, and without forward movement. One way to understand incarceration is as "serving time." Students are confined in space and in time. For outside instructors, encountering the (lack of) rhythms of prison time can be disorienting, almost like an assault. In "Untimeliness; or, What Can Happen in the Waiting," Dalke and Cohen reflect on the meanings that time holds for their students and the implications for their orientation to teaching in prison.

In "Teaching American History in Prison," Margaret Garb recounts what it was like to teach incarcerated students in Pacific, Missouri, an hour away from Ferguson, Missouri, in the same autumn that Michael Brown had been killed by a police officer in that city. That semester, she taught the same history class to traditional students at Washington University in St. Louis. She considers the connections between her two groups of students, the protests in St. Louis, the events they are studying, and her role as instructor in assisting her students to see different futures.

"The Prison Oppresses: Avoiding the False Us/Them Binary in Prison Education" is the only piece in this collection to address the condition of prison employees—in particular, correctional officers (COs). Victoria Bryan, speaking

directly to prison instructors, issues a challenge to them to extend the same sus-
pension of judgement to COs as we do to our incarcerated students. As she notes,
the effort to consider students' current positions, in light of troubling pasts and
trauma, should apply as well to prison workers. She stresses that she is not arguing
for "simply giving corrections officers the benefit of the doubt" (this volume,
p. 163) and characterizes COs as "the people who have stepped up to
administer" the oppressive and brutal policies of the prison. At the same time,
she stakes out a radical abolitionist position, arguing that "we cannot leave
anyone oppressed by the PIC behind."

The next two pieces form a pair. The first, "Learning Inside-Out: The Perspective
of Two Individuals Who Had the Opportunity to Partake in the Soul Journey of
Healing Arts and Social Change," is by two men who participated in an Inside-Out
program in a California prison. (That term describes a classroom in a prison that is
made up of both incarcerated and non-incarcerated students.) Jerrad Allen and
Osvaldo Armas describe their initial suspicions about the class, their experiences in it,
and their current strong advocacy of Inside-Out programming. Poignantly, they
explain their expectation that its impacts will be felt throughout their lives.

The second piece is by the instructor of the course that Allen and Armas
enrolled in, Tessa Hicks Peterson. Like Raphael Ginsberg, Thomas Fabisiak, and
Anna Plemons, she considers the contradictions that inhere in attempting to offer
critical, liberating education in a carceral setting. In "Healing Pedagogy from the
Inside Out: The Paradox of Liberatory Education in Prison," though, she holds
up a new tension, "the limits of internal transformation against a backdrop of
systemic oppression" (this volume, p. 179). Revealing that neither of her two
co-authors have, in fact, flourished following the end of the class, Hicks
Peterson wonders about the ethics of building strong community and sense of
agency inside the classroom, and then ending the course, letting the students
scatter, and leaving them to battle the same old structures. In the end of her
essay, she shares an email that she received shortly before she submitted this
essay from one of her co-authors, revealing that it has indeed been a long
struggle.

Romarilyn Ralston's "Schools, Prisons, and Higher Education" allows us to
end the volume on a more optimistic note. Ralston recounts her educational
journey, from public school student through to university staff, with two stints of
college-in-prison in the middle. Ralston's piece, like that of Jerrad Allen, Osvaldo
Armas, and Maggie Shelledy, reminds us that when we work with individuals
who are likely to be released, we would do well to incorporate into our programs
elements that support them upon reentry. People leaving prison after a stint of
incarceration, as Dennis Simpson also points out, are exceedingly vulnerable. If
identifiable groups of students on our traditional campuses were in danger of
faltering after graduation, to the extent that it endangered their personal well-
being and that of their families, university administrators would find ways to
intervene. We need to be concerned with the realities of our students' lives. How

can our programs, and the resources of our institutions, be used to support students through the challenges of reentry, and how can they better guarantee the fulfillment of the promises of higher education?

Finally, a word about language. The contributors to the volume agreed—indeed, insisted—that the language in this volume should be humanizing and respectful, especially with regard to people who are criminal justice involved. For that reason, we do not use words like "felon," "convict," "prisoner," or "inmate" to refer to incarcerated students. Instead, we call them students, scholars, individuals, and people. As the late community organizer Eddie Ellis, formerly from the Center for Nu Leadership on Urban Solutions, wrote,

> if we can get progressive publications, organizations, and individuals like you to stop using the old offensive language and simply refer to us as "people," we will have achieved a significant step forward in our life giving struggle to be recognized as the human beings we are (Ellis, n.d.).

In conclusion, most U.S. prisons do not host higher education programs. That means that well over a million incarcerated individuals have no practicable access to college, since correspondence programs that charge tuition are beyond the reach of most. This book and the accompanying eResources are meant to encourage teachers who have considered getting involved with higher education in prison, whether you're thinking about setting up a degree-granting program or offering a few classes. We need you to get to work. I encourage you to start slowly and thoughtfully, but to begin, so that more of our family members, friends, and neighbors who are behind bars can avail themselves of a college education. You will be joining a community of committed educators. We will help you, and do our best to sustain and support your efforts. I hope this book will help you to venture into the field with humility, energy, a critical spirit, and generosity of heart.

Note

1 This is an abridged version of the Statement of Principles Agreed to by *Teaching College in Prison* Contributors in Urbana, IL on December 10, 2017.

References

Alexander, M. (2010). *The new Jim Crow: Mass incarceration in the age of colorblindness*. New York: New Books.

Castro, E. and Zamani-Gallaher, E. (2018). Expanding quality higher education for currently and formerly incarcerated people: Committing to equity and protecting against exploitation. *ASHE-NITE Paper Series*.

Comfort, M. *et al.* (2017). The costs of incarceration for families of prisoners. *International Review of the Red Cross*, 98(3), 783–798. Retrieved at doi:10.0.3.249/S1816383117000704.

Davidson, H. S. (1995). Possibilities for a critical pedagogy in a "total institution": An introduction to critical perspectives on prison education. In H. S. Davidson (ed.), *Schooling in a "total institution": Critical perspectives on prison education*, pp. 1–23. Westport, CT: Bergin & Garvey.

Davis, E. (2018). *Just teach* (unpublished manuscript).

Dole II, J. R. (2015). *A costly American hatred.* Berryville, AR: Midnight Express Books.

Ellis, E. (n.d.). An open letter to our friends on the question of language. Retrieved at http s://cmjcenter.org/wp-content/uploads/2017/07/CNUS-AppropriateLanguage.pdf.

Foreman, J. (2017). *Locking up our own: Crime and punishment in black America.* New York: Farrar, Straus and Giroux.

Gottschalk, M. (2006). *The prison and the gallows: The politics of mass incarceration.* Cambridge: Cambridge University Press.

Gottschalk, M. (2014). *Caught: The prison state and the lockdown of American politics.* Princeton: Princeton University Press.

Graves, D. (2015). A call for cultural democracy. In R. Scott (ed.), *Bringing college education into prisons*, pp. 51–55. New Directions for Community Colleges, 170. San Francisco, CA: Wiley.

Harkins, G. and Meiners, E. R. (2016). Teaching publics in the American penalscape. *American Quarterly*, 68(2), 405–408.

Hayes, C. (2017). *A colony in a nation.* New York: W.W. Norton.

Illinois State Commission on Criminal Justice and Sentencing Reform (2016, December). Final Report (Parts I and II). Retrieved at http://www.icjia.org/cjreform2015/pdf/ CJSR_Final_Report_Dec_2016.pdf.

Karpowitz, D. (2017). *College in prison: Reading in an age of mass incarceration.* New Brunswick: Rutgers University Press.

Kilgore, J. (2015). *Understanding mass incarceration: A people's guide to the key civil rights struggle of our time.* New York: The New Press.

Longworth, A. (2016). *Zek: An American prison story.* Seattle: Gabalfa Press.

Mahon-Haft, T. J. (2019). Higher education behind bars: Elevating participants, communities, and culture beyond dollars and recidivism (forthcoming).

Maltz, M. (1984). *Recidivism.* Orlando, FL: Academic Press.

McLaughlin, M. *et al.* (2016, July). The economic burden of incarceration in the U.S., Working Paper #CI072016. St. Louis: Washington University in St. Louis. Retrieved at https://joinnia.com/wp-content/uploads/2017/02/The-Economic-Burden-of-Inca rceration-in-the-US-2016.pdf.

Pfaff, J. (2017). *Locked in: The true causes of mass incarceration and how to achieve real reform.* New York: Basic Books.

Price, J. M. (2015). *Prison and social death.* New Brunswick: Rutgers University Press.

Thomas, J. (1995). The ironies of prison education. In H. S. Davidson (ed.), *Schooling in a "total institution": Critical perspectives on prison education*, pp. 25–41. Westport, CT: Bergin & Garvey.

Stevenson, B. (2015). *Just mercy: A story of justice and redemption.* New York: Spiegel & Grau.

United Nations Office on Drugs and Crime (2007). *Handbook of basic principles and promising practices on alternatives to incarceration.* New York: United Nations. Retrieved at http:// www.unodc.org/pdf/criminal_justice/Handbook_of_Basic_Principles_and_Promising_ Practices_on_Alternatives_to_Imprisonment.pdf.

Werts, T. (2013). Access for whom? In S. W. Davis and B. S. Roswell (eds.), *Turning teaching inside out: A pedagogy of transformation for community-based education*, pp. 157–162. New York: Palgrave Macmillan.

1

AN OPEN LETTER TO PRISON EDUCATORS

Malakki (Ralph Bolden)

To Whom It May Concern,

I'm sorry for your loss. Any divine plan you may have concocted in relation to the grand scheme of prison education is dead. I'm not suggesting you don't prepare yourself for the challenges you will face when visiting the incarcerated. Please come through with all of your bells and whistles. But just know that it's not all about you and your agenda any more.

Not that it was ever really about you anyway. For to be an educator is like being a needle and thread, while the students are the fabric. When people remark on an exquisitely designed quilt, no one asks about the needle. Although most crucial for the finished product, it's just not about you.

And the incarcerated are a different breed of cloth than the average entitled, whiney college students you're used to. Added to the typical educational matrix is the fact that you can come and go as you please. And once you leave the prison, you can go on a date, eat what you want, wear whatever closes you like and bathe and use the restroom in private. Some of us may secretly hold this against you.

And there will be times when, due to the rigors of our environment, we may miss class because of things you can't comprehend—even when we explain to you that our cellie (in our language it means "cell mate") *finally* left the cell and we had a chance for some alone time. You may consider this not only a measure of insincerity in regards to this person's academic goals, but you may also consider it a bit disrespectful. In no way can you truly comprehend how coveted this alone time is. Don't take it personal; it's not about you.

When you first meet us, the social inequity may cause a heart break hard to stomach. It may be a bit much. But you must divorce yourself from trying to save us. You can't.

Missiles have been hurled from academia that have toppled certain carceral fortresses. But unless you are willing to sacrifice your cushy, tenured safety net for a lengthy administrative war against an unyielding, bureaucratic foe, leave it be.

We just need you to come and be with us as we struggle to reach our best us. And please keep in mind that rushing to pounce on every mistake in grammar—especially in our poorly conjugated verb choices—is ill-advised. You may at first consider it the responsibility of your superior intelligence to sternly enforce the rigors of the King's English, especially when it comes to the unwashed lumpen-proletariat masses. But please know that we are not butchering what you hold most dear purposely, just to harass you.

It is hoped that, in time, you will come to understand that we have our own language, so to speak. It is comparable to the rich, rhythmic patois of the colonized oppressed. For, like them, we are forced to self-define ourselves in the words of those who conquered us.

Your role as a facilitator is key. For when you appear, a special place comes into existence that allows us to be a different us than the cell, chow hall, yard, and day-room us. And what's beyond your purview is that the place where you have your class becomes defined and sanctioned by the group as a sort of sacred space.

This is so because, in that classroom, we sit beside and conversate (a word that exists in our language) with people we may not generally speak to or even want to be around. Prison has strict social circles based on numerous criteria that most certainly may not be violated for any reason.

But classrooms constitute a loophole. Don't ask why, just take advantage of the opportunities this provides. And keep in mind that, if we are hesitant to partner up or engage in certain group activities, it's not because we don't respect your curriculum. Because, like I said, it's not about you.

You must always remember that, in the work it takes for this quilt to be built, each seemingly random piece of rugged-edged material—each student—will only be able to join together by virtue of what you bring to the table.

So don't lose hope. And I guarantee you that there will come a time when you get that "tingle" of achievement. It's kind of hard to explain, but it's when you receive a verification that your altruism bred something good. A lot of prison educators have stories about how something magically came together for a student or a group and a ray of light shone from above to frame and authenticate the relevance of that moment.

But don't spoil it! You will ruin the organic nature of the circumstance when you begin using too many words and arcane allusions that only other academics understand to explain to us what you witnessed and what it meant to you. Don't do this! For, as I keep trying to tell you, it's not about you.

Do your best and be good.

Respectfully,
Brother Malakki

2

HOPE FOR LEAVING A LEGACY

Russell X

As a prisoner who was enrolled in the Swarthmore Inside-Out college course, I was tasked with reading Michelle Alexander's *The New Jim Crow*, and an excerpt from John Pfaff's *Locked In* and with preparing a writing assignment that relied upon those authors' writings. While I was sitting in the lobby area of our block, several young black men walked by me. Observing the reading material, they quickly engaged me in conversation about the authors and the content in their books. Although my time was limited and I didn't wish to be disturbed, as one of the elders on the block, I felt obligated to entertain the young men's curiosity. They asked insightful questions, including what they needed to advance their *education* level so that they could participate in such educational opportunities. A couple even expressed their desire for assisting their children or siblings with their school work and various other endeavors related to learning.

To me, this encounter illustrates that educational opportunities are essential in prisons, particularly for lifers, who are the leaders in such communities and often set the example for the younger generation to follow.

The positive influence of lifers isn't easily measured or even observable by casual onlookers, so it's often overlooked and rarely reported. Yet the sway of lifers can be quite profound and wide sweeping, even on members of society who are not incarcerated. In the Swarthmore course, students from the campus who worked alongside those from *prison* (most of whom were lifers or had exceedingly long sentences) proclaimed how significantly their lives were impacted by our shared educational experience. Some outside students made on-the-spot commitments to a life of serving the least fortunate and incarcerated civilians. Despite our negligible chances of reentering society, lifers can still have an impact upon the younger generation, not simply in prison, but also beyond these walls.

It's easy to envision that those who are locked up with life sentences are buried so far down and away from society that they can't possibly make a positive difference in prison, let alone in the larger world. Prisoners still have families, friends, and close ties to their communities that, if properly equipped and inspired, can aid in the shaping of the next generation of leaders. But education behind the walls is necessary to make this happen. Education allows mentors to mentor, fathers to father, mothers to mother, and even prisoners with life sentences to help all of humanity. Progressive thinking states and prison officials, such as the ones in SCI-Chester, see this potential. They know that equipping prisoners with valuable skills and sound work ethics, in the form of higher education, produces positive results. Education directly enhances the chances of any released prisoner to make a successful transition back into society and contribute to positive change in their home community. Although lifers will not go home, they can work as mentors, an indispensable commodity that can be effectively utilized by prison officials and prison educators.

A life sentence, without the possibility of parole, plus thirty years, has not diminished either my intellectual thirst, or my desire to write another more positive chapter to my life. I am in no way unique in holding such lofty aspiration. Most of us with a life sentence hope to leave a better legacy than the narrative set by our sentence. The Swarthmore College Inside-Out course helped me enormously in moving towards this goal. That's the example of what could and should be the norm in all prisons. Yet such opportunities no longer exist in many prisons in this country.

I was initially incarcerated at Vaughn Correctional Center, in Delaware in the 1990s. The facility offered numerous educational programs, trade courses, treatment options, and life skill programs. These options kept the minds and bodies of much of the prison populace occupied. Men like myself were able to pursue higher education with the help of the Pell Grant, which allowed me to pursue a degree in Computer Science. The knowledge and experience I acquired allowed me to seek higher skilled jobs at that prison, which were in short supply. In one of these I worked as a high school teacher's aide, helping teach computer literacy to younger students. I was able to push them to be not only better students, but also better members of their families and communities. Because of their education and experience, lifers both gain skilled positions and act as role models for the younger generation. Since most of the younger students lacked positive role models in their upbringing they tended to gravitate towards those of us who were either enrolled in higher educational courses or actually teaching the classes they attended.

Nothing has been more gratifying for me than witnessing the young men I have tutored celebrate achievement of their educational goals. At one graduation, a student asked me to sit with his mother, aunt, two young children, and younger brother. He pointed to me and began to heap praises upon me, thanking me for pushing him, not allowing him to take shortcuts or quit when the work seemed insurmountably difficult. With a big grin on his face, he shared his adventure with his family and promised to be that same type of mentor to them. His educational journey wasn't easy. He was bucking trends perpetuated in the media and even degrading misconceptions held by his own family. Yet, his sense of self-worth, as well as that of his family and mentor(s), will have lasting repercussions that can extend to many others.

In the mid-1990s, when President Bill Clinton eliminated the Pell Grant availability, first to lifers like me, and then eventually for all prisoners, he ended my particular dream of obtaining a degree in Computer Science and ended, more generally, the good rehabilitation restoration in prison. Prisons like the one in Delaware, where I was incarcerated then, curtailed nearly every educational course and treatment program, leaving no further chance of pursuing educational ambitions for the strongest advocates of education in prison, the older generation, which no longer invested in it, since it was no longer investing in them. When educational opportunities are denied, idle minds become the devil's shop. During the February 2017 Delaware prison uprising and hostage standoff, which led to the death of one of the guards, the prisoners' primary demand was for more educational and treatment programs. I believe that the uprising would not have happened had Delaware continued to provide progressive higher educational options and treatment programs.

The thirst for knowledge and mental challenge exists within the walls of all prisons. I believe that the desire to learn should be encouraged and provided without limits or limitations. And I am testifying here that when properly motivated and utilized, lifers can be a powerful resource in this endeavor, offering benevolence, change, and inspiration. I know this because several younger men have expressed their gratitude to me for helping them find purpose in their lives.

Just the other day when a young man named "Breezy" and I were discussing his academic pursuits, he asked me to mentor him in my area of expertise, history. I was amazed that such a bright and well-read young man could not distinguish the effects for the American Civil War from those of the American Revolution. As usual, I directed him where to look for the answers to his questions, what books he should check out. Rather than answering his questions myself, I was teaching him how to teach himself. More than that, I was teaching him to question what he learned.

As James Baldwin (1963) explained in "A Talk to Teachers," "The paradox of education is precisely this that as one begins to become conscious one begins to examine the society in which he is being educated." I learned that message in a Swarthmore College writing assignment and was able to pass on its power to a student of my own. In doing so, I learned that lifers, like myself, can have a profound impact on the younger generation, not simply in prison, but also beyond these walls. Young Breezy is now seeking those answers, which he will pass on to his sister, his daughter, and his like-minded friends who are intellectually thirsty too. And so the circle of learning widens, from a lifer to the world.

References

Baldwin, J. (1963, October 16). The Negro child – His self-image (speech). Retrieved at https://www.zinnedproject.org/materials/baldwin-talk-to-teachers.

3

REPAIRING THE GENERATIONS: PRISON HIGHER EDUCATION AS HISTORICAL REPARATIONS

Doran Larson

Effective classroom teaching is an intensely in-the-moment enterprise both made up and shared by the singular minds in any classroom. As a prison higher education teacher and organizer, I have seen how the commitments of instructors and students—despite singular challenges—can mesh in carceral settings and empower everyone concerned. But prison education has been contested ground from its beginnings (Schorb, 2014), and it carries different historical echoes than education outside. My aim here is to trace the origins of one of those echoes, and by doing so to amplify the resonance of prison higher education as a historically grounded reparative justice project.

Since 1854, arguments have been raised for material compensation to those violated and exploited by American chattel slavery. Advocates have included Sojourner Truth and Frederick Douglass, the SNCC's James Forman, and Representative John Conyers, whose proposal simply to study the question has been quashed by congress every year since 1989 (Allen, 1998; Kendi, 2016, pp. 270–271). One of the staples of black reparations demands has been support for education for those once legally barred from literacy and whose descendants' educational achievements continue to trail behind whites' (National Assessment of Adult Literacy, 2018). Predictably, even more deplorable rates of illiteracy persist among the American carceral population (National Center for Education Statistics, 1994; Sainato, 2017).

Recognizing this problem at its roots, the Freedmen's Bureau Act of 1866 allotted much of its attention to building and supporting black schools and colleges (Westley, 1998, p. 461).[1] Despite the short, troubled life of the Freedman's Bureau, formerly enslaved people, according to W. E. B. Du Bois, made a priority of fostering race-blind education (Du Bois, 1983, p. 665; Henry, 2007, p. 52; Westley, 1998, p. 460). Du Bois understood what continues to be true today:

the inequality of black and white education mortars the unequal foundations for black and white life. This pattern, and its exceptions, cross from law into politics and back: The 1954 end of legal segregation in schools evoked white anger that continues in our politics to this day; America's first black president was a graduate of Harvard; and the white backlash we see unfolding at this moment includes a Secretary of Education who is literally clueless regarding struggling public schools (Blake, 2018). Race, education, and the distribution of power are inextricably enmeshed.

Rather than address all the thorny debates surrounding reparations, I want simply to argue that current college-in-prison programming (CIPP), wherever it is seriously undertaken, works like an ad hoc puzzle piece: not built to address reparations, CIPP does so in ways that are singularly well suited to answer both the demands made by reparations advocates *and* the objections brought by their opponents. CIPP cannot be thought of as the sole means of making historical reparations; nor can CIPP end mass incarceration. Yet CIPP is both one of the most effective and well-focused venues for historical reparative work, and a crucial tactic within prison-abolitionist strategy. The aim here is to understand CIPP as a working model for addressing the issues surrounding, the aspirations of, and the legal challenges to historical reparations.

To avoid rehearsing all the issues that emerge in discussion of reparations, I'll begin with a question that aggregates the major objections its advocates have faced, and then offer three questions that devolve from thinking about CIPP as a program of reparations.

Why should white people who have never, and most of whose ancestors have never, owned slaves be required to compensate those who may have slave ancestors but have never been enslaved themselves and indeed might today in some cases be better off financially than those paying the reparations bill?

1. Conceived as a reparations program, how does CIPP avoid punishing white people?
2. How does CIPP obviate the problem of reparations rewarding the rich, and how can CIPP address an ongoing wrong if it is for a practice that legally ended in 1865; that is, how does it identify those directly affected by this practice?
3. What are the greater, shared, *inclusive* social goods that CIPP can serve?

One: Conceived as a reparations program, how does CIPP avoid punishing white people?

As the aggregate question above suggests, the most common objections to reparations start from zero-sum thinking: what slavery's ancestors gain must be at white people's loss. W. James Booth characterizes this thinking's base: "because we [white people] are not one with the perpetrators, because we do not share with them a political identity, we are not accountable for their injustices" (Booth, 1999, p. 249). The moment we frame CIPP as reparations, this thinking dissolves through what we might think of as the CIPP classroom's front and back doors.

First, were such programs funded by state and federal taxes (as virtually all reparations proposals have assumed), the provision of support would be as evenly distributed as current tax burdens. Second, this provision, or "sacrifice" is no sacrifice at all, given that CIPP—like other prison education programs—yields a net return of 400 percent (Davis et al., 2013).[2] Yielding sizable net financial gains, CIPP breaks zero-sum thinking both coming and going; it is not a cost but an investment proven capable of both supporting and perpetuating itself while paying back its investors. Third, and most importantly, the recipients of CIPP benefits are people of all the races and ethnicities and classes represented inside U. S. prisons. These benefits go disproportionately to those with slave ancestry *only to the degree that those with slave ancestry have been disproportionately caught up in the near half-century rise of mass-scale incarceration*—a history that stands on a continuum with the long history of U.S. racial and class disenfranchisement. The same beneficial disproportionality will also reach Native peoples, Latinx peoples, and poor white people—all of whom have been relegated to subaltern positions and to carceral destinies, in large part due to their lack of access to adequate K-12 and higher education.[3]

The carceral histories of poor people—of all colors—becomes here an ironic, practical boon in that CIPP reparations are directed to those who are suffering today inside the most concrete legacy and guarantor of continuing U.S. social and economic stratification. CIPP reparations avoid the problem noted by Mari Matsuda: "Just as affirmative action in employment and college admission—a form of reparations—may impact negatively on the white underclass, monetary reparations to one victim group may result in a new group slipping to the bottom" (Matsuda, 1987, p. 397). CIPP works *from* the bottom up, for all inside. Such programming thus addresses the paradox that Robert Westley claims successful reparations must resolve:

> Blacks should [not] receive reparations either exclusively or even first ... [I]ndigenous peoples should probably be compensated ahead of any others. I believe that the way to avoid the "everyone's been harmed" hierarchy of oppressions game is to coalesce as communities affirming real equality around development of *a legal norm in the United States that mandates reparations to groups victimized by racism that is not group specific* (Westley, 1998, p. 436, emphasis added).

Prisons are arguably the largest state-sponsored institutions that can serve as venues for non-group-specific "reparations to groups victimized by racism." Virtually all the racial and class groups represented in prisons can point to their people's historical subjugation (Larson, 2018, pp. 111–138); and education inside benefits all the members of their outside communities, which enjoy the positive "spillover effects" when the newly educated return home (Lagemann 2016, pp. 75–92). Zero-sum economics and racial side-taking are dissolved into a practice of national, collective self-care. CIPP gives to communities neither often-resented welfare supports nor equally disdained (and today, legally diminished) affirmative action. Instead, CIPP offers enriched human resources—individuals who can become rebuilders of those communities.[4] CIPP is nothing less than an engine driving towards prison abolition—an engine that gives more than it consumes by a factor of four. CIPP benefits support incarcerated people, the communities they will return to, and a nation that can use its resources to renew itself from the bottom up.

Two: How does CIPP obviate the problem of reparations rewarding the rich, and how can CIPP address an ongoing wrong if it is for a practice that legally ended in 1865; that is, how does it identify those directly affected by this practice?

Who ends up in prison is both sadly predictable and predictably not those who enjoy substantial wealth. Implied here are two more questions: What form should benefits take, and who should benefit?

Charles Henry contrasts the cases of reparations claims made by the inhabitants of Rosewood, Florida, and Greenwood, Oklahoma, for white riots that destroyed their respective communities. The successful Rosewood case proceeded as a property claim; Greenwood's failed argument was a plea for racial justice. Henry draws the conclusion that reparations claims in general fail when framed as racial justice; they succeed when they make concrete claims to loss of property (Henry, 2007, p. 90). (Like other advocates for reparations, Henry places failed slavery-based reparations claims beside the successful suits for Jewish and Israeli claims upon the German nation, and Japanese-American claims for losses to internment.) If reparations come, they will come (via litigation or legislation) on the basis of a property claim that can be shown to have evolved directly from chattel slavery. They will succeed when links can be traced from enslavement to black poverty today as a property claim.[5]

The popular controversy around Ta-Nehisi Coates' 2014 essay, "The Case for Reparations," lies precisely in that Coates makes these linkages in numerical terms of slave-based export revenue that set the grounds for the U.S. becoming the economic power that it is, while tracking state and federal policies and practices that guaranteed people of color an unequal share of national wealth (Coates, 2014). Coates and others write numbers into the bounced check that Martin Luther King spoke about in 1963. Without such numbers, recent state and federally legislated "apologies" for slavery are not merely cheap racial-justice lip-service; they can actually stymy claims for material reparations (Davis, 2012). A property claim can be tailored—as most successful claims have been—to benefit those in direct and demonstrable need (King and Page, 2018, pp. 752–753). In law, as determined by the Supreme Court in 1975, education is property;[6] and there are few people in such need of the property benefits attached to academic credentials as those who will eventually enter the job market with a felony record.

The other part of this question, of who benefits, is the question of who holds "standing," a common legal obstacle to reparations litigation. As determined by the Supreme Court in Lujan v. Defenders of Wildlife (1992) standing requires from those seeking reparations proof that they have suffered a concrete, particular, and/or immanent injury; that the injury is causally linked or "fairly traceable" to an action taken by the defendant (i.e., state sponsorship of slavery, convict leasing, Jim Crow, and mass incarceration) and it must be an injury that is "likely to be redressed by a favorable decision" (Martin, 2008, p. 113).

Over the past fifty years, research has made truism of the causal links implied above: from the Constitution's ground-up accommodation of slavery (Waldstreicher, 2009), to the criminalization of aid to escaped slaves in the Fugitive Slave Law of 1850 (a re-enforcement of Article IV, section 2, clause 3 of the Constitution), to Judge Taney's infamous decision that neither Dred Scott nor any other black person could claim U.S. citizenship, to the continuation of slavery through a subclause of the Thirteenth Amendment and the resulting convict leasing system that lasted until WWII (Blackmon, 2008), to Jim Crow and the legal and de facto segregation that continues today, to the targeting of poor people of color by mass-scale incarceration (Alexander, M., 2010, Wacquant, 2006). As Robert Allen writes:

> Underdevelopment manifests in the restriction of black labor to certain functions: chattel slavery, sharecropping, low-paid industrial work, a reserve army of labor … in the restricted and distorted development of black landownership, home ownership and black business enterprises. It manifests in chronic impoverishment, the fostering of retrograde political leadership, *the destruction of black education*, the spread of racist violence, and *the wholesale incarceration of black youth* (Allen, 1998, p. 14, emphasis added).

The children of rich people do not inherit poverty any more than the children of the poor inherit wealth, while all people of color inherit suspicion of inherent criminality. The distribution of inequality is itself unequal, and it is color coded; and that coding marks bodies for prison. It is thus virtually inevitable, when 60 percent of poor black male high school drops outs will go to prison (Western, 2006), that our incarcerated students are often those suffering generational, state-sponsored imposition of poverty and educational deprivation, reaching back to 1619. Who then should benefit? Allen continues, "In my view, such transfers must first and foremost benefit the black working class and the poor" (Allen, 1998, p. 21). He goes on to name the perpetrator: "In the modern era, as in the slave era, the state has been the chief instrument shaping the exploitation of black labor and blocking the accumulation of capital assets by black people" (Allen, 1998, p. 18).

Coates' recent essay makes this quite clear; but the fact that black poverty is intergenerational and that legal bars (or nonenforcement of laws intended to foster equality) and legislative policy have perpetuated this inheritance has long since become an axiom of both scholarly and popular literature.[7] And where poverty is inherited, so is incarceration. As Bruce Western notes in his study of the prison's place in the lives of poor people of color, "Convict status adheres now, not in individual offenders, but in entire demographic categories" (Western, 2006, p. 31). And it is the ability to identify categories of the materially injured— Jews robbed in the Holocaust, Japanese heritage internees, Rosewood residents— that has set the legal grounds for successful reparations claims.

The research noted above establishes the first two points of legal standing: the injury is real and a causal history can be traced to state actions. Point three, that a decision in the complainant's favor is "likely" to redress the problem, brings us back to CIPP. The history of unequal educational opportunities stretches from legal and terrorist bars against teaching slaves to read, to the "savage inequalities" that Jonathan Kozol so powerfully described (Kozol, 1991), to the seemingly intractable racial gaps in education, wealth, and social capital we see today. It is no accident that the poorest of the poor, of all colors, contribute to a prison population plagued by illiteracy. The intersection of poverty, race, and educational deprivation, however, also fixes the prison as a focused site for "likely redress" of harms in the form of at least four types of justice: remedial, transitional, reparative, and restorative.

Desmond King and Jennifer Page define remedial and transition justice as follows:

> Remedial justice consists of policies and programs designed to remedy the harmful effects of past injustice. Transitional justice, by contrast, is more focused on the causes that gave rise to the harmful effects, particularly rights violations, abuses of power, and atrocities … This is not to say that transitional justice is only concerned with blame and unconcerned with repairing harms. But, for the transitional justice practitioner, coming to terms with past abuses and repairing harms go hand-in-hand (King and Page, 2018, pp. 746–747).

When we teach in prisons we are not only helping by "repairing [the] harms," of state-sponsored racial inequality; we are addressing one of racial inequality's founding causes, unequal education. In so far as we support incarcerated people to become contributors to the communities to which they will return, CIPP is also restorative. CIPP reparative justice achieves restorative results by practicing remedial and transitional justice. The prison's historical roots and current branches are partially cut and trimmed. Prisons become (for far too few) places to learn and grow, on their way to shrinking both the number of people who return and supporting the communities most likely to send more people inside. Just one tool in the abolitionist tool kit, CIPP gives those at the bottom of race and class history the boots and the straps to pull up both themselves and their neighbors. When we argue for and practice CIPP, and *when we understand the historical context in which we labor*, we pursue reparative justice and healing as concrete, historical resistance not only to the retributive prison but to the structural inequalities that the prison both creates and maintains.

Three: What are the greater, shared, *inclusive* social goods that CIPP can serve?

You walk into the first meeting of a college-in-prison program. The room, like so many utilized for the same purpose, evokes all the challenged K-12 classrooms you have ever seen or imagined. Curling motivational posters (circa 1985) hang between multiplication tables, and explanations of what happens (as has already to the lives of those who pass through the room) when a positive is multiplied by a negative. This is the modern one-room schoolhouse, which, despite its quaint associations, was always a scene of diminished resources trying to serve excess need. Such rooms were once outposts of hope against white terror; now, in cities across the nation, they are simply called "struggling." This is space intended to nurture, to mature, to empower with knowing, yet that succeeds only in spite of the conditions in which it must do its work: in barns and cellars in defiance of slave law; in the shadows of crosses burning since the end of Reconstruction; despite white mobs screaming at children across National Guards rifles; despite deputized security officers today, just one phone call from poor children's collars to the county jail; and despite the political winds that will drop higher education as the first line of defense against public outrage over caring for incarcerated people at tax payers' expense (Lagemann, 2016, p. 154).

Such rooms have held those beleaguered throughout U.S. history, and who have historically felt resurrected from beleaguerment by the hope of education. Abolitionist reparations are alive every time such a prison space is animated by living, engaged voices and minds bound by the common purpose of learning, of peeling mystification bare, and rebuilding on the foundations of things known, and yet to be understood. Simply by treating convicted people as students first, CIPP, as Daniel Karpowitz notes, intervenes in "the moral economy of punishment" (Karpowitz, 2017, p. 82), an economy older than a nation built on the backs of enslaved and indentured people, on grounds cleared by genocide. CIPP also intervenes in the literal economies of states that have, for decades, been shifting funding for education into funding for prisons (Ingraham, 2016). CIPP meets this trend at its intersection, where the education-deprived are afforded education in prison—*without ever assuming that this is where they should first meet such opportunities.* We are not here to repair our students, and certainly not to repair prisons; we are here, in a reparative spirit, to offer what has been denied, and to aid students in making of this offering what they choose, hoping that the choice will include restoration and de-carceration of the communities they come from.

The question is not whether our students have standing on our national moral compass. To deny that is to deny the very manner in which American history has shaped, enforced, monetized, and moralized the lines of race and class. It is also to deny the heritage that all who teach inside prison share with those one-room teachers, and the newly college-trained black teachers who taught the children and grandchildren of slaves, and public school teachers today working without public investment. Education cannot repair all troubles. But it is the place where we prepare people to find all the solutions they can. Whatever their ancestry, the bodies with whom we share prison classrooms are the current incarnations of every moral error we have made in the name of racial exploitation or profit. CIPP reparations benefits all, and it benefits most those who historically have most severely and longest suffered our history's racial and for-profit assaults on civic equality. This is where America's unceasing race and class wars, which are both concretized and silenced within prison walls, can find a model of how to reach their ends: one night, one class, one semester at a time. It is a quiet revolution, conducted primarily beyond our view, in the hours when incarcerated students commit themselves to their studies.

"The call for racial reparations," Charles Henry writes, "challenges the official histories that ignore, explain away, or trivialize mass cruelties. Reparations thus are a way of democratizing history and hearing those voices that were silenced in the past" (Henry, 2007, p. 7). Incarcerated people are always the vanguard witnesses to the true human costs of the current legal order. We see this in the rich American history of writing by incarcerated people, from the prison's founding to the enormous volume of prison witness being produced by people incarcerated in the U.S. today (Franklin, 1989; Larson, 2014, 2018). Like other pedagogical revolutions, the work of CIPP seeks to upend existing hierarchies by bringing to prominence the voices of those who know the current state of concrete social and power relations from the bottom up, for "Those who are oppressed in the present world can speak most eloquently of a better one" (Matsuda 1987, p. 346; Freire, 1996). If it is possible to imagine a post-carceral world, it is incarcerated people, many of them armed with the skills fostered by abolitionist reparations in college-in-prison programs, who will show us the way.

Notes

1 On the place of education supports among reparations proposals, see Allen (1998), Bouie (2014), Du Bois (1983, pp. 621, 665), Henry (2007, p. 159), King and Page (2018, p. 743), Magee (1993, p. 882), Matsuda (1987, p. 391), Munford (1996, pp. 57–58), Robinson (2000).
2 This fact has legal ramifications. Were a case ever brought for reparations via CIPP, the law of restitution states that benefits cannot unjustly damage others (Henry, 2007, p. 22).
3 The connection between educational achievement and class mobility is well established: e.g., Bathmaker et al. (2013), Bledstein (1976), Knapp and Woolverton (1995). On disproportionate incarceration of the poor and poorly educated, see Alexander, M. (2010), Wacquant (2006), and Western (2006). Sampson and Loeffler's work (2010) maps neighborhoods most deeply affected by incarceration, where general disadvantage is concentrated—neighborhoods where people of color live. And yet, even if all black and Hispanic people were released from prison today, the U.S. would still have one of the highest incarceration rates in the world at 450 for every 100 citizens (Sakala, 2014). Buzz Alexander calls mass incarceration "perhaps a crime against humanity" that "will not be brought to court" (Alexander, B., 2010, p. 50). This is, of course, all the more reason to foster CIPP and other prison education efforts, which deliver the benefits of a legal verdict never proclaimed.

4 This statement should not be read as critique of those programs; I simply point out one political obstacle that CIPP can be understood as sidestepping.
5 Thomas Craemer sets "the present value of U.S. slave labor in 2009 dollars to range from $5.9 to $14.2 trillion" (Craemer, 2015, p. 639).
6 See Goss v. Lopez (1975) and Bullock (2017).
7 Adamson et al. (2016), Alexander, M. (2010), Allen (1998, p. 20), Davis (2003), Henry (2007, pp. 101–106), Jackson (1994), Rothstein (2014), Shakur (1987), Sharkey (2008), Westley (1998, pp. 439, 465), Winter (2007, pp. 379, 382). The starkest contrast between white and black financial conditions is that which indicates persistent, multi-generational disadvantage: the difference in household wealth; see Center on Poverty, Work and Opportunity (2011).

References

Adamson, R. *et al.* (2016, June 21). Why the racial wealth gap harms everyone—Even whites. Retrieved at https://slate.com/news-and-politics/2016/06/whats-the-cost-of-being-black-in-america-an-excerpt-on-racial-wealth-inequality-and-discrimination-from-the-co lor-of-wealth.html.

Alexander, B. (2010). *Is William Martinez not our brother? Twenty years of the prison creative arts program*. Ann Arbor, MI: University of Michigan Press.

Alexander, M. (2010). *The new Jim Crow: Mass incarceration in the age of colorblindness*. New York: The New Press.

Allen, R. L. (1998). Past due: The African American quest for reparations. *The Black Scholar*, 28(2), 7–28.

Bathmaker, A. *et al.* (2013). Higher education, social class and the mobilisation of capitals: recognising and playing the game. *British Journal of Sociology of Education*, 34(5–6), 723–743.

Blackmon, D. (2008). *Slavery by another name: The re-enslavement of black Americans from the Civil War to World War II*. New York: Anchor Books.

Blake, A. (2018, March 12). Betsy DeVos's botched '60 Minutes' interview, annotated. *The Washington Post*.

Bledstein, B. (1976). *The culture of professionalism: The middle class and the development of higher education in America*. New York: W. W. Norton & Company.

Booth, W. J. (1999). Communities of memory: On identity, memory, and debt. *The American Political Science Review*, 93(2), 249–263.

Bouie, J. (2014, May 22). Reparations are owed: Here are a few ways to pay the bill. Retrieved at https://slate.com/news-and-politics/2014/05/reparations-should-be-pa id-to-black-americans-here-is-how-america-should-pay.html.

Bullock, E. C. (2017). Only STEM Can Save Us? Examining Race, Place, and STEM Education as Property. *Educational Studies*, 53(6), 628–641.

Center on Poverty, Work and Opportunity (2011, May 31). Tracing the causes of racial wealth disparity: A report for the Z. Smith Reynolds Foundation. University of North Carolina at Chapel Hill. Retrieved at http://www.law.unc.edu/documents/poverty/p ublications/tracingcauses_povertycenter.pdf.

Coates, T. (2014, June). The case for reparations. *The Atlantic*. Retrieved at https://www. theatlantic.com/magazine/archive/2014/06/the-case-for-reparations/361631/.

Craemer, T. (2015). Estimating slavery reparations: Present value comparisons of historical multigenerational reparations policies. *Social Science Quarterly*, 96(2), 639–655.

Davis, A. M. (2012). Racial reconciliation or retreat? How legislative resolutions apologizing for slavery promulgate white supremacy. *The Black Scholar*, 42(1), 37–48.

Davis, A. Y. (2003). *Are prisons obsolete?* New York: Seven Stories Press.

Davis, L. M. *et al.* (2013). Evaluating the effectiveness of correctional education: A meta-analysis of programs that provide education to incarcerated adults. RAND Corporation. Sponsored by the Bureau of Justice Statistics. Retrieved at https://www.rand.org/pubs/research_reports/RR266.html.

Du Bois, W. E. B. (1983). *Black reconstruction in America: An essay toward a history of the part which black folk played in the attempt to reconstruct democracy in America, 1860–1880.* New York: Harcourt Brace.

Franklin, H. B. (1989). *Prison literature in America: The victim as criminal and artist.* New York: Oxford University Press.

Freire, P. (1996). *Pedagogy of the oppressed.* Translated by Myra Bergman Ramos. New York: Penguin.

Goss v. Lopez (1975). 419 U.S. 565.

Henry, C. P. (2007). *Long overdue: The politics of racial reparations.* New York: NYU Press.

Ingraham, C. (2016, July 7). The states that spend more money on prisoners than college students. *The Washington Post.* Retrieved at https://www.washingtonpost.com/news/wonk/wp/2016/07/07/the-states-that-spend-more-money-on-prisoners-than-college-students/?utm_term=.44d67abc991f.

Jackson, G. (1994). *Soledad brother: The prison letters of George Jackson.* Chicago: Lawrence Hill.

Karpowitz, D. (2017). *College in prison: Reading in an age of mass incarceration.* New Brunswick, NJ: Rutgers UP.

Kendi, I. X. (2016). *Stamped from the beginning: The definitive history of racist ideas in America.* New York: Nation Books.

King, D. S. and Page, J. M. (2018). Towards transitional justice? Black reparations and the end of mass incarceration. *Ethnic and Racial Studies,* 41(4), 739–758.

Knapp, M. S. and Woolverton, S. (1995). Social class and schooling. In J. A. Banks and C. A. McGee (eds.), *Handbook of research on multicultural education.* 2nd edition, pp. 548–569. New York: Jossey-Bass.

Kozol, J. (1991). *Savage inequalities: Children in America's schools.* New York: Harper.

Lagemann, E. C. (2016). *Liberating minds: The case for college in prison.* New York: New Press.

Larson, D. (2014). *Fourth city: Essays from the prison in America.* East Lansing, MI: Michigan State University Press.

Larson, D. (2018). The American prison writing archive. Retrieved at http://www.dhinitiative.org/projects/apwa.

Lujan v. Defenders of Wildlife (1992). 504 U.S. 555.

Magee, R. V. (1993). The master's tools, from the bottom up: Responses to African-American reparations theory in mainstream and outsider remedies discourse. *Virginia Law Review,* 79(4), 863–916.

Martin, M. A. (2008). "Standing": Who can sue to protect the environment? *Social Education,* 72(3), 113–117.

Matsuda, M. J. (1987). Looking to the bottom: Critical legal studies and reparations. *Harvard Civil Rights—Civil Liberties Review,* 22(Spring), 323–399.

Munford, C. J. (1996). *Race and reparations: A black perspective for the 21st century.* Trenton, NJ: Africa World Press.

National Assessment of Adult Literacy (NAAL) (2018). A first look at the literacy of America's adults in the 21st century. Retrieved at https://nces.ed.gov/NAAL/PDF/2006470_1.PDF.

National Center for Education Statistics (1994, October). Literacy behind prison walls. Retrieved at https://nces.ed.gov/pubs94/94102.pdf.

Robinson, R. (2000). *The debt: What America owes to blacks*. New York: Dutton.

Rothstein, R. (2014, January 7). The urban poor shall inherit poverty. *The American Prospect*. Retrieved at https://prospect.org/article/urban-poor-shall-inherit-poverty.

Sainato, M. (2017, July 18). US prison system plagued by high illiteracy rates: Inability to read traps inmates in the criminal justice system. *The Observer*. Retrieved at https://observer.com/2017/07/prison-illiteracy-criminal-justice-reform/.

Sakala, L. (2014, May 28). Breaking down mass incarceration in the 2010 census: State-by-state incarceration rates by race/ethnicity. *Prison Policy Initiative*. Retrieved at https://www.prisonpolicy.org/reports/rates.html.

Sampson, R. J. and Loeffler, C. (2010). Punishment's place: The local concentration of mass incarceration. *Daedalus* (Summer), 20–31.

Shakur, A. (1987). *Assata: An autobiography*. Westport, CT: Lawrence Hill.

Sharkey, P. (2008, January 1). Ending urban poverty: Understanding the persistence of racial inequality. *Boston Review*. Retrieved at http://bostonreview.net/patrick-sharkey-inherited-ghetto-racial-inequality.

Schorb, J. (2014). *Reading prisoners: Literature, literacy, and the transformation of American punishment, 1700–1845*. New Brunswick, NJ: Rutgers University Press.

Wacquant, L. (2006). *Punishing the poor: The neoliberal government of social insecurity*. Durham, NC: Duke University Press.

Waldstreicher, D. (2009). *Slavery's constitution: From revolution to ratification*. New York: Hill and Wang.

Western, B. (2006). *Punishment and inequality in America*. New York: Russell Sage.

Westley, R. (1998). Many billions gone: Is it time to reconsider the case for black reparations? *Boston College Third World Law Journal*, 19(1), 429–476.

Winter, S. (2007). What's so bad about slavery? Assessing the grounds for reparations. *Patterns of Prejudice*, 41(3–4), 373–393.

4

PEDAGOGY OF THE OFFENDER

Dennis R. Simpson II

Introduction

> We must accept the reality that to confine offenders behind walls trying to change them is an expensive folly with short-term benefits—wining battles while losing the war.
>
> *Warren Burger, U.S. Supreme Court Justice*

Studies demonstrate that recidivism rates are substantially lower for individuals who have participated in prison higher education programs as compared to those who have not (see e.g., Davis, 2014; and Contardo, 2005). It would seem that celebrations are in order, complete with champagne and confetti.

However, unfortunately, the philosophy surrounding prison education is fatally flawed. Programs claim to "fix" individuals by showing them how abnormal their past behavior and thought processes were and introducing them to an alternate way, the "normal" way of thinking about themselves, their peers, and their world. They are made fit for companionship with other "like-minded" individuals. They are made "sociable." They become "good."

Then, newly released individuals are thrust into a society and economy that's not prepared or able to accommodate them. Although unemployment has held at 4 percent, it remains extremely difficult to find employment in general, even after obtaining a college degree. To further complicate matters, with felon disenfranchisement and employment discrimination an issue, many employers are unwilling to hire formerly incarcerated people for fear of losing their clientele. Faced with the many responsibilities that accompany freedom, unable to find employment, facing familiar obstacles to self-respect and self-esteem, not finding society welcoming or "respecting the human potential of the offender," many begin feeling betrayed by the very society they've placed their faith in.

Thus, the current philosophy and dominant narrative about prison education is not based in reality.

This essay seeks to redefine the narrative surrounding higher education in prison. It is about shifting the focus from merely treating symptoms to curing an illness. It is about avoiding "reactionary" policies and bringing about "revolutionary" change. This discussion is not about how we are winning battles; it's about how to win the war.

Redefining Higher Education in Prison

Prison education should be geared towards the full development of students. It must acknowledge the larger environment from which students come and equip them with the ability to do for themselves what society is not prepared to do. Can we expect correctional education to effectuate change to the current social order, for the good of incarcerated students as well as society as a whole? When it comes to higher education in prison, not only should we expect these programs to prepare their students to think about and engage in programs for social change, we must demand it! In fact, prison education would be absolutely worthless unless it accomplishes this very task.

Higher education in prison should therefore be a political act, responsive to the economy and social conditions. It should incorporate a vision or overall plan for society, still to be realized in the future (Freire, 1970). This will require a fundamental shift of focus, from the micro to the macro.

With such issues as poverty and unemployment facing our communities, higher education programs should allow us to take up subjects that concern our communities, and not just abstract theory. For instance, African Americans are incarcerated in America's state prisons at five times the rate of whites (Nellis, 2016). Most come from the lowest socioeconomic rungs of society. Additionally, punitive policies (called collateral consequences) attached to felony convictions, such as voter disenfranchisement, denial of welfare, and so on, destroy these very communities politically, economically, and socially, reducing the successful reintegration of people back into society and increasing the chance of recidivism. In prison, educators must identify the "reality" of their students' backgrounds, who they are today, what their possibilities are, and how to begin to develop these students where they are.

Therefore, educators need to submerge themselves in the contexts of the students' life experiences, primarily to be able to listen while encouraging students to unveil and un-package their lives and problems. "Listening" does not mean literally "hearing" them, but listening in order to create a curriculum out of what's been discussed. For example, after listening to certain issues raised by her students, an educator offers an economics class that reflects the issues raised, working out solutions to lack of capital, cooperative entrepreneurship, and building long-term establishments in their communities.

Courses in Sociology and Criminology are vital, aiding students to identify many of the issues, theories, and possible remedies for issues like crime, poverty, hunger, and unemployment. Courses in History and Anthropology would develop understanding of the exact state of their communities and of the inner workings of institutions and their processes, which are currently foreign to students; Public Speaking and English enable to help them to become effective communicators. Courses in Business Law and Administration would continue to build upon any vocational training acquired, while allowing students the opportunity to not just enter the job market as entry-level workers, but to eventually develop their own enterprises which would also create employment opportunities for other returning citizens.

The main curriculum should be uniquely designed to address issues that affect the daily lives of people who are in prison.

Thanks to the skills, information, and lessons learned through correctional education programs, students return to their communities prepared and equipped to challenge systems of rank and privilege, oppression and repression, structures of hierarchy and bureaucracy, exploitation and inequality, and selfishness and individualism. They return promoting new moral and ethical visions, based on democratic participation in which even "ex-felons" are welcome, cooperation, and collective decision-making.

They return to their communities prepared to combat poverty and unemployment. They create cooperatives in which the needs and interests of the community are served, addressing issues like property and economic divestment, and providing growth and development and infrastructure. As they gain valuable experience serving the needs of their communities, they become even more politically active, allowing them to change the political culture of their communities, cities, counties, maybe even their state and nation, all from the ground up.

Higher education can also have a "liberating" effect on society. These individuals are not putting such a burden on society's institutions. New business and employment opportunities that are created by people leaving prison can significantly reduce the demand on social services like welfare and public housing, while also developing much-needed faith in these same institutions. This develops trust and confidence while increasing social participation and interaction. A demand for change is created and supported publicly, not just a change in public policy but a cultural change as well. As the "penal" culture of our governments and courts begin to fade, the need to house people convicted of committing crimes begins to decline. With a change in culture and a steady decline in crime, prisons begin to close their doors ... forever.

Fixing a Broken Society

In fact, when we think about the rehabilitation of society, we should start with the prison. Not with the offender, however, but with correctional administrators! With prison overcrowding as the result of punitive sentencing policies, prison administrators are working overtime simply to "manage" their populations. In doing so, administrators "track" offenders in their facilitates. This administrative culture is counter-productive in general, and especially when applied to education.

Many people in prison who are interested in education are ruled ineligible or simply not selected. Correctional educational programs have a tendency to select the most capable and well-behaved individuals, sending the message that only socially acceptable men or women will be considered. The problem is, it is those who are deemed "socially unacceptable," those most in need of educational services, who are being turned away! The rejection of these people and the denial of these services reinforce their feelings of alienation from the larger society.

What's needed is an "about face" in attitudes towards these individuals. Correctional education should not just be made "available" but "accessible" to entire prison populations. Allowing certain types of programming to be accessible to only certain groups creates a form of social stratification reminiscent of what's present in many of the communities from which these individuals come. In effect, those who are labelled as ineligible and those who are not selected are told to "stay in their place" by society, while they watch others being given a chance at upward mobility.

They begin to be disenchanted with correctional authorities, who represent society at large. Opportunities that are generally available to all are once again withheld from them, just as in the communities they come from. Bitter towards a society that continues to alienate them, these men and women are released back to these communities more "broken" than before. It's from these that the 67.5 percent recidivism rate comes.

Conclusion

Correctional education should not be designed just to return and restore students to their former positions in society. Higher education in prison should actually seek to elevate them. This type of education is not "punitive"—as in where access to programming is used as a form of behavioral control, something to be taken away when societal norms are not being observed—but "transformative." The ideas, subjects, and lessons learned transform not only students and the community they come from, but society itself. The change being discussed isn't just about crime or recidivism rates, but something far more significant.

If this sounds utopian, it's because narratives painting "offenders" as socially dysfunctional make it so. It's practical to take socially disadvantaged individuals intimately aware of the issues that plague our society, educate and equip them with the skills and knowledge necessary to combat the issues leading to criminal activity, and release them to their communities as agents of change. With severely crowded court docks; dangerously overcrowded prison; billions spent on prisons annually; and a national recidivism rate of 67.5 percent—it's evident that this sort of correctional educational programming is desperately needed. College programs should give educators the opportunity to help students who are in the most need not only to change themselves, but also change their communities, and ultimately society as a whole.

References

Davis, L. M. *et al.* (2014). How effective is correctional education and where do we go from here? The results of a comprehensive evaluation. RAND Corporation. Retrieved at https://www.rand.org/pubs/research_reports/RR564.html.

Erisman, W. and Contardo, J. B. (2005, November 30). Learning to reduce recidivism: A 50-state analysis of postsecondary correctional education policy. The Institute for Higher Education Policy.

Freire, P. (1970). *Pedagogy of the oppressed*. New York: Herder & Herder.

Nellis, A. (2016). The color of justice: Racial and ethnic disparity in state Prisons. The Sentencing Project. Retrieved at https://www.sentencingproject.org/publications/col or-of-justice-racial-and-ethnic-disparity-in-state-prisons/.

5

A NICE OUTFIT

Kimberly Erbe

While women account for approximately 6 percent of the incarcerated population nationwide, their rate of incarceration has increased 700 percent between
1980 and 2016, and at twice the rate of men (The Sentencing Project, 2018).
Despite the growing number of women in prison, they are the most underserved
segment of the incarcerated population, especially as relates to educational
opportunities. Prevailing excuses for why more academic programs operate in
men's prisons include that women serve shorter sentences, that there are too few
incarcerated women, or that the women's prisons are inconveniently located. In
Illinois, the number of women incarcerated increased from under 400 in 1980 to
over 2,500 in 2017, and as of last year, 44 percent of women were serving
somewhere between four and sixty years in the Illinois Department of Corrections, with over 350 serving sentences beyond twenty years (IDOC, 2017). There
are two prisons for women in Illinois, one in Lincoln and one in Decatur, which
are located within forty miles of each other. At least six universities and four
community colleges are within a sixty-mile radius of at least one, if not both, of
these facilities, yet women remain underserved with respect to academic educational opportunities beyond adult basic education and GED preparatory classes.

In addition, incarcerated women have access to fewer vocational opportunities
than incarcerated men. Existing programs are more paternalistic than vocational,
rooted in gender stereotypes, and only further disadvantage women by preparing
them for domesticity and employment in sex-segregated occupations. I argue that
the disparity of educational programming for incarcerated women in Illinois has
less to do with size of the population, the length of their sentence, or the rural
areas in which women's prisons are located, and is more about how incarcerated
women are valued within our society, including regressive beliefs about "female
criminality." According to Pat Carlen, one of the main issues surrounding

women's imprisonment is that women's prisons are not seen as "real prisons" and incarcerated women are not seen as "real women" (Carlen, 1983, p. 211).

"Proper Women"

Women are subject to two opposing views of femininity; they are expected to be independent and caring, while at the same time dependent and needing protection (Carlen, 1998). Those who transgress these gender norms risk becoming either the "fallen woman," in need of moral instruction and domestic training, or the "evil woman," who is beyond reform (Dodge, 2006). Historically, women were confined based on the category of "woman" in which they were placed. In Illinois, the "erring sheep," mostly white women, were imprisoned at the House of the Good Shepherd in Chicago (Dodge, 2006; Hoy, 1997). The House of the Good Shepherd was one of the Magdalen Asylums run by the Catholic Church, and was the first "prison" for women in Illinois (Jones and Record, 2014), although it was often denied that the women confined there were actually incarcerated (Hoy, 1997).

Women convicted of felonies, mostly black and immigrant women, were incarcerated within the men's prisons at Alton, Joliet, and Chester, but usually kept in the attic of the warden's house or in a building's cellar (Dodge, 2006). The early reformers focused their attention on the "misdemeanants" and ignored the women incarcerated in the men's prisons, as the "penitentiary was never considered an appropriate place for punishing 'proper women'" (Dodge, 2006, p. 259). As more institutions were built to house the growing number of incarcerated women, their imprisonment was only further denied, as the prisons were usually referred to as "clinics," "homes," "training schools," and "reformatories" (Lekkerkerker, 1931).

A common narrative surrounding incarcerated women is that they have fallen short of "womanly virtue" and their failure to conform to traditional gender roles somehow caused their "criminality." In 1964, a reporter went into the women's prison in Illinois, where she enjoyed a meal prepared by the women incarcerated there. After eating, the reporter said to one of the women, "You are a very good cook and apparently a neat housekeeper. How did you come here?" (Puracelli, 1964, p. H18). That women's incarceration was related to lack of domestic skills and aversion to familial living informed the programming inside the prison, as well as the construction of the building itself. The first recognized prison for women in Illinois was built in a "cottage style" plan, with the idea that communal living would foster a sense of family and restore them to "real women" (Dodge, 2006). Outsiders often viewed the institution as a "country club" and the women inside its walls as "girls" (Hutchinson, 1959).

However, as restoration to femininity was appropriate for "fallen women," the "evil women" were seen differently. In 1933, in support of the new women's prison amidst public outrage over the operational costs, the president of the Illinois Conference on Social Welfare, stated, "When we take into account the capacity of a bad woman to destroy men ... Illinois is justified" (Brandon, 1933, p. 12). Whether support of women's incarceration was due to the irrational beliefs regarding the causes of "female criminality" or the protection of the male status in a patriarchal society, the programs for incarcerated women in Illinois have primarily focused on reorienting women to traditional standards of "femininity," and in doing so, have perpetuated gender stratification.

"Unique Issues"

Women's prisons in Illinois have routinely been under management separate from the divisions that governed the "real prisons" of men. The Department of Public Safety operated the state penitentiary system in Illinois, yet they moved the women's prison to the Department of Public Welfare in 1953 (Illinois Blue Book, 1953–1954). Although that changed eventually sometime after the creation of the Illinois Department of Corrections (IDOC) in 1970 (Illinois Blue Book, 1971–1972), in 1999, the women's prison was again separated into a different unit than the men's when the Women and Family division was created within the IDOC to respond to the "unique issues" of the incarcerated woman (IDOC, 2018b). Addressing these "unique issues" has historically focused on traditional prescriptions of the "feminine" appearance, behavior within the community, and their roles as mothers.

According to a recent report from the IDOC, of the "most significant accomplishments" of one women's prison in fiscal year 2016 was the "opening of the 'Out in a Week Boutique,'" a program that ensures "the offender is able to wear a nice outfit home" (IDOC, 2016, p. 44). When placed in a larger social and historical context, the "Out in a Week Boutique" is of the same sentiment as Sydney Wetmore's portrayal of incarcerated women as "poor, forlorn creatures whose overriding concern was with the maintenance of an acceptable female appearance and whose greatest suffering was derived from the loss of quintessential feminine apparel" (Dodge, 2006, p. 46). Because there was a belief that women's incarceration was the result of their "failures" as "real women," there has been a suggested correlation between a woman's appearance and her "criminality."

According to the first warden at Dwight, Helen Hazard, "Give me a woman who knows she looks homely and unkempt and I'll have a potential troublemaker" (Fitzpatrick, 1947, p. 10). Jo Green viewed "'Femininity Liberation' as the most crucial need" of the incarcerated woman (Chicago Defender, 1973, p. 20) and started a "charm school" in an Illinois women's prison called "Self-Esteem Through Femininity" (Weaver, 1971, p. 4). While some would dismiss these statements as a reflection of the time period in which they occurred, "the management of women prisoners in the past links directly to the status of the female offender in modern society" (Butler, 1997, p. xvi). This idea that "female criminality" is directly related to the social prescriptions of appearance and femininity is a longstanding, pervasive notion that designs prison programming to reproduce the gender ideal, while dismissing the inherent racist and heterosexist underpinnings often embedded in those stereotypes.

Using incarceration to reproduce images of the "real woman" has also been addressed through programs aimed at "good citizenship," as a popular narrative has been "the ethical re-education of the inmates undoubtedly belongs to the most important tasks" of women's prisons (Lekkerkerker, 1931, p. 503). Women have always been responsible for setting an example of public service, usually through religious or civic organizations, and often because they were denied opportunities for education and employment that were reserved for men (Solomon, 1985). During the 1940s, women incarcerated in Illinois "were graded daily on their attitude, work, and 'citizenship' or cooperation" (Dodge, 2006, p. 206). This "ethical re-education" is not a relic of the past. According to the Women and Family division of the IDOC, when describing their current work, "A final initiative is to become good neighbors to the community" and "through joint participation by staff and offenders in these worthwhile projects, Women and Family Services hopes to raise the level of awareness of volunteerism and good faith to the community" (IDOC, 2018b). Being of service is an admirable enterprise. However, having programming focused on being a "good neighbor to the community" reinforces the societal expectations of women as nurturers and caregivers, responsible for community uplift, expected to perform free labor for the greater good, and represents little difference than the expectations of women that existed in the 1940s.

Women are often judged on the basis of their roles as mothers, and when they are imprisoned, these perceptions are amplified (Ross, 1998). Dodge states, "the very fact of their incarceration meant that they had failed both as real women and as good mothers" (Dodge, 2006, p. 257). Incarceration wreaks havoc on children, their incarcerated mothers, and those who provide care while their parent is in prison. Many programs exist around family reunification, increasing bonds with children, providing legal assistance regarding custody and parental matters, and teaching women better "parenting skills." According to the IDOC, they "provide a managed system of support and services for the female offender to reestablish and strengthen the relationship with their children. The facility offers programs that will enhance their skills for survival and growth within the family structure" (IDOC, 2016, p. 26).

While programs that focus on familial relationships are truly important, they are often the primary focus of programming in women's prisons, which is reflective of larger social issues relating the value of incarcerated women to their status as mothers. This sentiment is evident in State Representative Susan Cantania's statement in 1980 regarding program development in Illinois for incarcerated women, "The fact that most of these women are mothers makes this a much larger consideration. We have a responsibility to these children" (Ogintz, 1980c, p. N3). That incarcerated women are valued primarily as mothers is troubling, as it dismisses them as people, prevents non-maternalistic programs from being implemented, and reinforces the idea of "female criminality" being linked to a failure of fulfilling traditional gender roles.

The Pink Collar Ghetto

Vocational programs in women's prisons have either served the prison system itself by exploiting the skilled labor of incarcerated women to reduce institutional costs, or have perpetuated gender stratification by preparing women for employment in pink collar positions, many of which are still embedded with notions of femininity, caregiving, and motherhood. Currently in Illinois, women are offered programming in building maintenance and the culinary arts, or to become service nail technicians, pet groomers, cosmetologists, and dog trainers (IDOC, 2018a). While training dogs to be service animals is a worthy cause, it still is informed by the expectation of women as caregivers and tied to their status as mothers. Missy Stutler, "deputy director of female and children's services" at the IDOC, said in 2001, "The inmates we interviewed for [the start of] this program are not the inmates we see today. They are bonding with the dogs, and re-bonding with their families" (Whelpley, 2001, p. 8). This statement suggests an expected outcome of increased caring and intimacy in familial relationships through the training of service animals, and is likely more about creating "real women" and "proper mothers" than acquiring meaningful vocational skills.

There are also programs that prepare incarcerated women for the fields of cosmetology and dog grooming (IDOC, 2016). While women's prisons in Illinois have often offered cosmetology courses, the profession itself is focused on the beautification of the "other," and is a highly gendered occupation. There is also a program for the beautification of dogs, which teaches incarcerated women to be dog groomers, and although that is one of the fastest growing occupations, it, like cosmetology, is also sex segregated. According to the Bureau of Labor Statistics (BLS), dog groomers are classified as "non farm animal caretakers" and 78.4 percent of those surveyed are women (BLS, 2017a), earning on average $23,160 annually (BLS, 2017b). The mean annual wage for a hairdresser is $24,950 (BLS, 2017c), and 92.6 percent of those in that occupation were women, with both professions being categorized as "personal care and service occupations" (BLS, 2017a). Historically, incarcerated women have left prison as domestic servants (Butler, 1997, p. 193), and they are still being offered programming that will ensure encasement in the pink collar ghetto.

"Gender preconceptions determine the vocational programs" in prison (Rafter, 1985, p. 19), and "little is done to provide incarcerated women with the education or skills necessary for their survival once they are released" (Ross, 1998, p. 124). Because the narrative has been that incarcerated women were not "real women" and needed training in domestic skills to properly care for a home and family, most of the vocational and job training programs in women's prisons have prepared them for low paying, gendered occupations (Feinman, 1994; Ross,

1998; Ross and Fabiano, 1986). Feinman (1994, p. 69) asserts that "myths that women do not need to be self-supporting or that they are not interested in nontraditional employment" sometimes "prevents realistic and practical programs from being developed." However, that myth is likely aimed at programming for the "fallen woman," whereas the "evil woman" is subject to a different myth altogether.

"Bottom of the Barrel"

According to Butler (1997, p. 31), incarcerated men were given more educational programs because "women fell short of womanly virtue and constituted an unimportant segment of the prison population.". Incarcerated women were "described as 'a dangerous class' by Dorthea Dix, as 'a serious eugenic danger to society' by Josephine Shaw Lowell, and as 'the bottom of the barrel' by Essie O. Murph" (Feinman, 1994, p. 69). During the late nineteenth and early twentieth centuries in Illinois, "no outside women's, religious, or reform groups expressed interest in the plight of the state's female felons" (Dodge, 2006, p. 261). These assessments have likely influenced the type of programming available to incarcerated women, as they were "the women that nobody wants" (Carlen, 1983), unlikely to become wives or members of the community, and therefore, not in need of an education. The neglect of incarcerated women by early reformers was also likely tied to racial and ethnic discrimination, as women of color have always been overrepresented in Illinois prisons, and after 1890, in Illinois, "race had become central to the social definition of female criminality" (Dodge, 2006, p. 260).

In 1938, when making recommendations for educational opportunities for incarcerated women in Illinois, a university suggested that women should be given tests to "measure aptitude" and those scores should be "given preference over the inmate's statement of previous experience" (ISNU, 1938, p. 12). Incarcerated women were seen as "feeble minded" and it was suggested that programs "be developed with the intelligence as well as the socioeconomic status of the inmates definitely in mind" (ISNU, 1938, p. 11). It was suggested that "usual public school methods" were inappropriate for incarcerated women (Lekkerker-ker, 1931, p. 485). In the 1930s, it was suggested that it may "even be possible to earn a certificate equivalent to a high school diploma" for incarcerated women (Lekkerkerker, 1931, p. 491), because "it is sometimes most surprising how much can be achieved, even with such unpromising pupils as many delinquent women seem to be" (p. 490). According to Dodge, when vocational courses were offered, the warden would discourage black women from even taking the tests for admission to typing or clerical classes. When they persisted, and did well on the exam, they were still guided into "other channels" (Dodge, 2006, p. 211).

Incarcerated women were eventually given access to better programming. Yet, there were still gender disparities in Illinois prisons. In the 1970s and 1980s incarcerated women could earn an associate's degree, but the incarcerated men could earn a bachelor's (Sneed, 1980, p. 4). In 1980, Claudia McCormick, the administrator for the women's correctional facility in Cook County, said, "I call these people the forgotten population. It takes a Patty Hearst or Patty Columbo [both white women from affluent families] for people to pay attention to women in prison. But nothing really changes—the priorities are with the men" (Ogintz, 1980b, p. A1). Illinois State Senator Dawn Netsch said, "you have to respond to the areas that are most pressing, and that involves the men in the system" (Ogintz, 1980a, p. 1). Often, incarcerated women only gained access to the same educational opportunities as men after litigation, which usually resulted in their transfer to men's prisons (Feinman, 1994). Yet, these attempts by incarcerated women to increase their access to education and meaningful vocational programs often resulted in further punishment and increased restrictions (Dodge, 2006).

The movement of women to the men's prison in Lincoln, IL, was praised to "have a calming effect on" and a decrease in "infractions for homosexual behavior among" the men (Johnson, 1987, p. A12). Eventually, the women were blamed for the "headaches" that their presence caused the administration (Egler, 1989) and many lost more than a year of good time after becoming pregnant in the facility (Johnson, 1987). To prevent the problems women "caused" at one co-gender facility from happening at another, women were faced with even more restrictive conditions, being kept "separated from the general population of men, basically a prison within a prison" (Egler, 1989, p. D3). Evaluating the women according to how their presence affected the men and increasing the surveillance of their bodies in co-gender facilities only further tightened the control of incarcerated women within a paternalistic regime.

Further Considerations

Since the elimination of the Pell Grants in the mid-1990s, college in both men's and women's prisons has continued to decline. In Illinois, recent state budget crises have resulted in many community colleges withdrawing programming from prisons, as they could not afford to provide unpaid services. However, some universities offer programs inside men's facilities in Illinois without relying on state or federal funding. Although most do not offer degrees, the programming allows some incarcerated men to earn college credit, take academic courses, engage with faculty, and publish their work. Although women in Illinois are currently able to obtain their GED while incarcerated (IDOC, 2018a), studies indicate that "while the benefits to women of the GED are real, they do not bring economic independence" (Bills, 2004, p. 71). Although women have experienced an overall increase in employment nationwide, the "increase was greatest among well-educated women," and women with lower socioeconomic status have "experienced stagnant earnings, rising rates of poverty, limited occupational mobility, and falling access to marriage and its associated social supports for children" (Massey, 2007, p. 240).

While some men's prisons in Illinois offer the same services as the women's, including "nice" clothing when paroled, dog training and barbering courses, and programming designed to prepare them for sex-segregated occupations (IDOC, 2016), men, and their professions, are not subject to systemic gender bias. On average, women earn less than men, across almost all professions, and even when they have higher levels of education (Gould et al., 2016). For women who have been imprisoned, the disparity is compounded, as formerly incarcerated people face discrimination when applying for employment, college, and housing. Formerly incarcerated women face additional stigma, as their incarceration is society's evidence that they are not "real women," nor "good mothers." Women are more likely than men to be caregivers for children and family members upon release, yet prison programming does little to help them acquire the skills necessary to financially support themselves and those they care for. Instead, they are offered programs that reinforce traditional gender roles, prepare them for employment in pink collar professions, and maintain their status within a patriarchal society.

Incarcerated women have never been given the same opportunities as incarcerated men, and have largely been ignored by progressive feminists and liberal reformers, both within Illinois and across the nation.

Again, I argue that the lack of educational opportunities in women's prisons has less to do with the common excuses given (not enough women, too short of sentences, and rural location of the prisons) and more to do with the "fallen woman" in need of domestic training and reoriented to "femininity," and the "evil woman" who is beyond reform.

It is difficult to advocate for increased programming in women's prisons, as it means supporting continued incarceration. While it is important to acknowledge the harms caused to families when women are incarcerated and have programs focused on the mother–child relationship, those initiatives should be in addition to, not instead of, educational opportunities for incarcerated women. When subjecting women to draconian prison regimes that only further harm their families and hinder their economic opportunities, perhaps offering them "a nice outfit" to wear home is insufficient.

References

Bills, D. (2004). *The sociology of education and work*. Malden, MA: Blackwell Publishing.

Brandon, R. H. (1933, August 26). Voice of the People: Mr. Brandon on Dwight. *Chicago Tribune*.

Bureau of Labor Statistics (BLS) (2017a). Labor Force Statistics from the Current Population Survey. United States Department of Labor. Retrieved at https://www.bls.gov/cps/cpsaat11.htm.

Bureau of Labor Statistics (BLS) (2017b). Occupational Outlook Handbook. United States Department of Labor. Retrieved at https://www.bls.gov/ooh/personal-care-and-service/animal-care-and-service-workers.htm.

Bureau of Labor Statistics (BLS) (2017c). Occupational Outlook Handbook. United States Department of Labor. Retrieved at https://www.bls.gov/ooh/personal-care-and-service/barbers-hairstylists-and-cosmetologists.htm.

Butler, A. M. (1997). *Gendered justice in the American west: Women prisoners in men's penitentiaries.* Urbana, IL: University of Illinois Press.

Carlen, P. (1983). *Women's imprisonment: A study in social control.* London: Routledge & Kegan Paul.

Carlen, P. (1998). *Sledgehammer: Women's imprisonment in the millennium.* London: Mac-Millan Press.

Chicago Defender (1973, September 19). 'Fem lib' for women offenders her goal. *Chicago Defender.*

Dodge, L. M. (2006). *"Whores and thieves of the worst kind": A study of women, crime, and prisons, 1835–2000.* Dekalb, IL: Northern Illinois University Press.

Egler, D. (1989, October 2). Male-only prison to add women. *Chicago Tribune.*

Feinman, C. (1994). *Women in the criminal justice system.* 3rd edition. Westport, CT: Praeger Publishers.

Fitzpatrick, R. (1947, March 23). Oakdale prison for women high in penal scale: 'Dwight' blends leniency and firmness. *Chicago Tribune.*

Gould, E. *et al.* (2016, October 20). What is the gender pay gap and is it real? The complete guide to how women are paid less than men and why it can't be explained away. Economic Policy Institute. Retrieved at https://www.epi.org/publication/what-is-the-gender-pay-gap-and-is-it-real/.

Hoy, S. (1997). Caring for Chicago's women and girls: The Sisters of the Good Shepherd, 1859–1911. *Journal of Urban History*, 23(3), 260–294.

Hutchinson, L. (1959, March 26). Dwight offers women chance to reform: Program includes school, work. *Chicago Tribune.*

Illinois Blue Book (1953–1954). Office of the Secretary of State. Illinois State Library. Retrieved at http://www.idaillinois.org/cdm/compoundobject/collection/bb/id/10020/rec/36.

Illinois Blue Book (1971–1972). Office of the Secretary of State. Illinois State Library. Retrieved at http://www.idaillinois.org/cdm/compoundobject/collection/bb/id/34234/rec/8.

Illinois Department of Corrections (IDC) (2016). Fiscal Year 2016 Annual Report. Retrieved at https://www2.illinois.gov/idoc/reportsandstatistics/Documents/FY2016%20Annual%20Report.pdf.

Illinois Department of Corrections (IDC) (2017). Female Offender Population Data on June 30, 2017. Retrieved at https://www2.illinois.gov/idoc/reportsandstatistics/Documents/Final_Female_Fact_Sheet_Data_FY2017.pdf.

Illinois Department of Corrections (IDC) (2018a). Quarterly Report. January 1, 2018. Retrieved at https://www2.illinois.gov/idoc/reportsandstatistics/Documents/IDOC_Quarterly%20Report_January_%202018.pdf.

Illinois Department of Corrections (IDC) (2018b). Women and Family Services. Retrieved at https://www2.illinois.gov/idoc/programs/Pages/WomenFamilyServices.aspx.

Illinois State Normal University (ISNU) (1938). Dwight survey: Report of the Illinois State Normal University Committee for Advisement on the education program for the Oakdale Reformatory for women at Dwight, Illinois. Normal, IL: I.S.N.U. Press.

Johnson, D. (1987, June 1). Women blend in with men at Illinois prison. *New York Times.*

Jones, M. and Record, L. (2014). Magdalene laundries: The first prisons for women in the United States. *Journal of the Indiana Academy of the Social Sciences*, 17, 166–179.

Lekkerkerker, E. C. (1931). *Reformatories for women in the United States*. Batavia: J.B. Wolters.

Massey, D. S. (2007). *Categorically unequal: The American stratification system*. New York: Russell Sage Foundation.

Ogintz, E. (1980a, August 3). Women in prison: You learn 'how to really hate'. *Chicago Tribune*.

Ogintz, E. (1980b, August 5). Rehabilitation? Women's skills training falls short. *Chicago Tribune*.

Ogintz, E. (1980c, August 9). Legislators to aid women prisoners. *Chicago Tribune*.

Puracelli, M. (1964, March 15). Women in prison. *Chicago Tribune*.

Rafter, N. (1985, October 8). Perspective: Women: Second class inmates. *Chicago Tribune*.

Ross, L. (1998). *Inventing the savage: The social construction of Native American criminality*. Austin, TX: University of Texas Press.

Ross, R. R. and Fabiano, E. A. (1986). *Female offenders: Correctional afterthoughts*. Jefferson, NC: McFarland & Company, Inc.

Solomon, B. (1985). *In the company of educated women: A history of women and higher education in America*. New Haven, CT: Yale University Press.

Sneed, M. (1980, September 7). Patty Columbo's prison life: College courses and growing. *Chicago Tribune*.

The Sentencing Project (2018). Incarcerated women and girls, 1980–2016. Retrieved at https://www.sentencingproject.org/publications/incarcerated-women-and-girls/.

Weaver, A. (1971, January 19). Expand charm prison project. *Chicago Daily Defender*.

Whelpley, R. (2001, March). Prison program saves dogs, trains cons and serves the disabled. *Illinois Issues*. Retrieved at http://www.lib.niu.edu/2001/ii010308.html.

6

FROM AFRICA TO HIGH DESERT STATE PRISON: JOURNEYS OF AN INVISIBLE TEACHER

James Kilgore

This essay describes my evolution as an educator. At first glance, it may not seem like this should be included in a book on prison higher education. After all, though I have taught in many places and institutions, I have never taught higher education in prison. I would argue that my story fits in here for three reasons. First, in describing my experience as an educator in a number of contexts, I am inserting the dynamics of race, class, gender, place, space, and methodology of prison education into a broader educational framework where it is too often omitted. Second, since much of my experience as an educator on the streets addresses the issue of education for liberation, especially in an African context, I am adding some new dimensions to how we look at critical pedagogy in a carceral setting. Lastly, I am making the case for what I call "invisible educators"—those incarcerated educators in prison, like myself, who don't teach college classes, who may not teach formal classes at all but are the driving force behind educational inspiration.

While I respect the traditional notions of university faculty going into prisons to teach fully accredited courses to incarcerated individuals, most prisons have no such programs. I spent six and a half years in four different prisons and never saw a single college faculty person in our education space. Even in the prisons where formal higher education exists, only a small sliver of the population accesses those courses. Educators who come from outside to teach college courses don't meet characters like Jose, Ernie, or John or the men in the GED class at Lompoc whom you will encounter in this essay. But more importantly, those students who end up in higher ed classes in prison have to come from somewhere, have to get the basics, the language skills, the mathematics expertise, and, most importantly, the motivation from somewhere.

Just about every higher education student in prison can name another incarcerated person, maybe several, who convinced them of the value of education, who supported them emotionally and by sharing books and ideas—their mentor, the educator who liberated them from ignorance.

So while I never formally taught higher ed in prison, like so many other men and women, most more anonymous than me, I fed incarcerated people to higher education. I helped build their wisdom, their ability to make sense of their lives. For many I lit the first sparks of an intellectual fire that made them want to ask bigger questions, to solve bigger problems, and to figure out ways to do that which didn't involve either going back to the streets or becoming a soulless bureaucrat or business owner.

Ultimately, higher education in prison is a bigger project than the colleges, universities, and departments of corrections would have us believe. Academics and university administrators may readily step forward to claim the awards and the funding in response to the individual success stories, but in the background we invisible teachers have run our own courses, built out our own curriculum, and watched with pride as our students put on that prison-designed graduation gown to take a picture to send back home to mom. Though I am no longer in their ranks, today I know thousands of those invisible teachers are still imparting wisdom as they do their daily rounds of burpees, are still fighting with libraries and mail rooms to get precious learning materials to share with their comrades in arms. As we say in southern Africa—a luta continua. The struggle continues.

Prologue

In June of 1982 I was fresh off the plane from Minnesota. I had been assigned to teach at Mabvuku High School, in one of the black high-density areas of Harare, the capital of Zimbabwe. The school secretary directed me to the Deputy Headmaster's office. Mr. Samuriwo, as the wooden name tag on his desk labelled him, wore a brown suit and brown tie. We exchanged handshakes and he asked me how my day was going.

"So far, so good," I said. He smiled.

"Can you teach geography?" he asked.

"Actually, we don't do geography as a school subject in America," I told him, "I'd rather teach maths." He looked puzzled. He shuffled a couple papers on his desk.

"All right," he said, "find Mr. Nyamadzawo and tell him you're going to be taking his maths classes. You can give him this timetable for geography." He handed me a sheet of newsprint that said "Geography Timetable" at the top.

"Where is his class?" I asked.

"Room 33," Samuriwo said without looking up from a stack of papers that had captured his attention. I had no idea where room 33 was but I didn't feel like I could ask. I walked down the hallway and out into the large paved space between the two brick classroom blocks. A few voices drifted out from the classes. Someone was talking about simultaneous linear equations.

"Can I help you, sir?" came the voice of a young girl from behind. I turned around. She averted my gaze.

"I'm looking for the staff room," I told her.

"It's through there," she said pointing towards a red metal door. She curtsied, then ran away.

A middle-aged black woman wearing a bright red dress and high-heeled shoes was the only person in the staff room. She was sitting at a table with a pile of notebooks next to her, eating some salt and vinegar potato chips.

"Do you know where I can find Mr. Nyamadzawo?" I asked, struggling to pronounce his name.

"He should be here shortly," she said, looking at her watch, "It's almost break time."

Suddenly a cow bell clanged in the distance. The school's silence converted instantly to a quiet roar. The staff room quickly filled with new fresh black faces chattering in Shona. A young man tapped me on the shoulder.

"I'm Nyamadzawo," he said and shook my hand.

"Nice to meet you," I said handing him the piece of paper from Samuriwo. "I think you are supposed to teach geography now. I am going to be taking over your maths classes."

He looked at the paper.

"Geography?" he said, then repeated it again in disbelief. He said something in Shona which I hoped wasn't about me. "I'll get you the plan book," he said and walked away.

Fifteen minutes later, I was standing in front of a class of forty-four black ninth graders in their school uniforms. They were ready for maths class. They were deathly quiet as they stared at their new teacher. My mouth was as dry as a saltine cracker. I felt as white as a saltine as well. Before I could say anything a girl in the school uniform came in and knelt at my feet looking down. Not sure of the custom, I knelt and looked at her face to face. The silence turned to giggles then unbridled laughter. My first day of teaching was under way.

★★★

It was June of 2002. Like everyone else around me I was wearing the khaki pants and shirt of a federal prisoner. I was new to this penitentiary game. I'd been assigned to my prison job—high school teacher's aide. I had found my way to the library where the school was located. It was a large open space full of men seated at tables reading newspapers and talking. I went to the office. Mr. Claridy was in charge.

"Can you teach GED math?" he asked me. He stood up from his desk and looked around, then grabbed a book off the shelf. He was quite tall.

"Definitely," I said, "I was a teacher for almost twenty years on the streets."

He handed me a GED math book, three pieces of chalk and an eraser.

"Your classroom is at the back," he said, "be sure to record the names of everyone in the class. If you need anything, just ask."

"How many students are in the class?" I asked.

"Go and count them," he said and sat back down at his desk.

Five minutes later, I was standing in front of a class of four, three black men and one white guy. The black men looked like body builders. The white guy had long hair and lots of missing teeth. My mouth was as dry as a saltine cracker. Even though one of the students was white, I still felt white as a saltine. Class and education also have a color.

★★★

These scenarios frame the two major journeys of my career as a teacher. They happened two decades and nearly 9,000 miles apart but they are deeply intertwined in my pedagogy and, dare I say, my educational soul. Education has been my life, though in a wide variety of contexts. In southern Africa I painted on a canvas of hope and liberation. My teaching sat in the midst of an historical period of oppressed people bursting forth from the shackles of colonialism and white supremacy. Though my environment was steeped in the history of racism and minority rule, the people around me accepted my educational efforts once I showed that I supported their struggles. And my students had boundless hopes. They were studying in newly liberated societies, Zimbabwe in the early 1980s right after independence, then South Africa during the transition from apartheid to democracy. By contrast as a prison educator in the US in the 2000s, shackles were part of our landscape. And razor wire. Instead of boundless hope, my students wallowed in despair and racial hatred. White students sported swastika tattoos or old English letters that read "Thank God I'm white." Some Latinos would rather stand in my classes than take a seat next to a black man. There was no talk of liberation here and only a few dared to speak of hopes. Many were serving life sentences or even longer. A judge had given one of my friends in the federal system a sentence of 552 years. How was GED math going to help him through decades under the thumb of the carceral state? I had no answer.

Southern Africa

I came to southern Africa as a solidarity activist but also a fugitive. I came to support a cause I held dear but also to run away from the "problems" I left behind—a series of criminal charges which would have left me behind bars for decades. So while southern Africa was finding its way to liberation, I was also buying my freedom with distance and new identities. Like every teacher I brought my personal baggage into the classroom every day, only my baggage was perhaps a little heavier and more complex than average. But my baggage, even though I was a college-educated white man, brought me closer to understanding what it meant to struggle for liberation.

My work as a teacher in southern Africa took place in three phases. The first phase began at Mabvuku. I was a teacher, but I was an impostor. In Zimbabwe a person could teach without any training. During the colonial period up to 1980, there were no public high schools for black students in the rural parts of the country where 70 percent of the population lived. In 1980, the new government promised to expand education. In the first two years after independence the Ministry of Education built 613 new rural schools (Pape, 1998). Moving this quickly dictated the need to use every available resource to provide education. On the ground, this meant people who had finished high school often became high school teachers. Any university graduate, from virtually anywhere, could teach. So though I was new to education, technically I was qualified. I had a university degree.

For youth in Zimbabwe in the 1980s, education was gold. At the end of the first class that I described above, I assigned homework. I gave them five math problems to do. "We want more," came the demand. "Give us ten." "Fifteen." They were like bidders in an auction trying to show who really wanted the item in question—most homework.

I taught in Zimbabwean high schools and colleges for seven years. "Give us more," could have been the title of a theme song for my classes. My high school students constantly pleaded with me to come to school on Saturdays to teach extra lessons. They wanted me to come during Christmas break as well. I had one student who begged me for extra reading, novels so he could improve his English. (None of the students was a first language English speaker.) Over the course of the school year he borrowed twenty-seven novels from my personal collection and read them. He also used to hand me extra essays and extra math problems to read and correct. His name was Tafirenyika Sevenzai. His last name means "work."

Tafirenyika was not alone. The historically oppressed black population viewed education as the vehicle to the success that colonialism and white supremacy had blocked from them during the days of colonial rule under what was then called Rhodesia. Colonial rule meant the segregation of everything—land, neighborhoods, schools, sidewalks, and toilets. The doors were opened after 1980 but only a certain amount of people could rush through the openings. Zimbabweans believed the most educated would be the ones through the doors.

While the motivation level in these schools was high, the curriculum and governance were backward. The history books still informed the students that blacks were taken to be enslaved in the cotton fields of the U.S. because they were better able to withstand the heat and the bending than white people. In geography class they studied maps of North America and Europe, nothing about Africa. We teachers, both black and white, tried to compensate for this with our own interventions but it was often difficult.

In terms of governance, the headmaster (principal) was the absolute ruler of the school. When there was discussion of an issue, he would conclude the discussion by saying, "thank you for your contributions, but we will do it my way."

Teachers practiced old school discipline. Some carried switches into the classrooms and swatted the students if they gave a wrong answer or engaged in illicit talking.

Furthermore, the curriculum was totally focused on external exams. The fabled Cambridge "O" levels were the gold standard. A student's grades on those O levels would determine their future—job opportunities, openings for higher education. This meant that any time a teacher began to talk about something that was not on the O level syllabus the students would suddenly become animated. They were quiet when asked a content issue, but very vocal about any deviations from O level curriculum.

As a white foreign male, I had to navigate this terrain in at least three ways. First, and foremost, I had to demonstrate to the staff and students that I was an anti-racist, that I didn't share the colonial values they associated with most white people. Since I had been an anti-racist most of my life and had lots of experiences interacting with black Zimbabweans before I came to Zimbabwe, this was not so difficult. I avoided sitting in clumps with white teachers in the staff room, called them out on their racist behavior, and learned to speak a fair amount of Shona. All of that gave me a lot of credibility. Second, I had to navigate the educational terrain—balancing the tightrope of not teaching colonial content but also not ignoring the students' demands and need to pass their exams. I set my own rules in terms of discipline. I wasn't going to carry a switch but I also didn't think it was my place to attack Zimbabwean teachers and headmasters who did (at least not openly). That was often a hard pill to swallow.

Over the years, I developed my own style. Though all classes were supposed to be taught in English, like nearly all the other teachers, I sometimes lapsed into Shona. I gradually learned how to generate activities, to develop group work-sheets and role plays, always keeping within the bounds of the curriculum. I also developed very systematic strategies for preparing students for exams and gave them lots of practice tests, to satisfy their need and quest to pass. I thought I had found my m.o. as a teacher in southern Africa. I was competent, well organized, an effective functionary in a reforming African education system. And my students were passing their exams. Then in 1991 I moved to South Africa.

South Africa

I taught in a small college on the fifth floor of an office building in downtown Johannesburg, Khanya (Light) College. This was the period of transition. Nelson Mandela was out of prison but the political settlement was still under negotiation. Black students were preparing to assume positions of power. Khanya was a one-year bridging program for politicized black students—those who had fought against apartheid in student organizations, trade unions, as guerrilla fighters and in other capacities. They had graduated from high school but their grades in the horribly racialized apartheid education system were not good enough to get them into the historically white universities where they wanted to go. Khanya gave them the credentials to gain admission.

But Khanya was more than an academic training ground. The college's slogan was "Education for Liberation." Contrary to the Zimbabwean model, Khanya students were educated in revolution. Their curriculum was explicitly anti-racist, anti-sexist, and in many instances anti-capitalist. In this curriculum slavery was not something for which Africans were especially suited but an oppressive mode of produce essential to the process of capital accumulation and industrialization.

Khanya had two ironies in its ethos of liberation. The first was that all of the teaching staff and administration, except for one person, were white, a fact I didn't know until I got there. At the assembly during my first week, the College Co-ordinator (Khanya didn't believe in headmasters, principals, CEOs, or directors) introduced all the faculty. All the students were black and once again I felt as white as a saltine. Education for Liberation or not, this was upside down.

Second, and more troubling, the students at Khanya were ill-prepared and not accustomed to studying. Their schooling years had often been interrupted by strikes and stayaways. Their curriculum was dumbed down by the apartheid system and teachers ultimately had never held them accountable, never expected much from them. Their motivation was low and they couldn't perform what should have been simple tasks for college freshmen—calculating percentage or writing a short essay. There were no Tafirenyika Sevenzais.

I recast myself as taskmaster, driving the students to do more work than they had ever done. I forced them to go through the humiliating process of learning what should have been seventh grade math by convincing them that their ignorance was not due to their own inadequacies but was part of the equation of political power of the apartheid regime.

My Khanya experience went well beyond the classroom. Education for Liberation also included informal education for resistance organizations—education that would empower them to advance their interests once the apartheid government had been voted out. (We were all confident that was imminent—and we were right). Our collective goal was abolition—abolition not just of the racial segregation of apartheid but of the system of apartheid capitalism.

To accomplish this, we studied Paolo Freire. Gradually, I became what Freire might call a "critical pedagogue" or a "popular educator." The resistance organizations brought us what Gramsci called "organic intellectuals" (Gramsci, 1971), people who gained their understanding of theory through drawing conclusions and studying based on their own practice. I met union shop stewards and community activists who had not graduated from high school, for whom English was a fourth or fifth language, who could articulate the political program of austerity advanced by the World Bank and explain why it was antagonistic to the interests of the South African working class. As a student radical in the U.S. I had read and sometimes preached about the revolutionary potential of the working class but in the U.S. I never witnessed it in action. Here I confronted it up close—in the streets when I joined them in their stayaways and marches which often shut down the city of Johannesburg (population three million). These workers demanded participation in their education. They didn't tolerate academic lectures. It was learning by doing— group work, role plays, and simulation exercises. We used activities to review complex policy documents, knowing that our education had only one purpose—to contribute to the creation of a liberated South Africa. For a popular educator, this was nirvana.

But I was more than an educator. After three years, I became the overall Coordinator of the college, a decision maker. I met with union leaders and international donors to strategize on how we could use our educational programs to advance the interests of the working class in post-apartheid South Africa. Once I even had the honor of speaking on the same platform as Nelson Mandela in Soweto.

After six years at Khanya, I left and moved to Cape Town to continue my work, becoming the Co-Director of the International Labour Resource and Information Group (ILRIG) at the University of Cape Town. Not only did I direct these organizations and plan worker education, I also travelled as a spokesperson. I visited the United Kingdom, Ethiopia, Germany to attend conferences and meet with donors. In my pseudonym, John Pape, I gained a small international profile as a worker educator, a practitioner of Freirian pedagogy, even writing a number of pieces on worker education (Pape, 1997, 1998, and 2001). Though South Africa had not turned into the worker-controlled republic we had hoped for, there was space to fight for the working class. I was in the thick of that fight. I met with the education departments of the largest unions of the Congress of South African Trade Unions—worker organizations that believed in the gospel according to Freire. We were all on the same wave length. We agreed that education for liberation meant building people's understanding of the world from their own experience and shaping that understanding to become effective in movements for social change. Education for liberation was ultimately not about the individual but about transforming society through collective, focused, "educated" action, in this instance fighting against the efforts by the global forces of neoliberalism to crush the South African working-class movement.

My working life went hand in hand with my family. I was married with young soccer- and cricket-playing sons who loved South Africa. Then on November 8, 2002, on my way home from my work, having picked up my eight-year-old son from cricket practice, I was greeted by the united forces of the South African police, Interpol, and the FBI. I was on my way to prison in the U.S. I would be leaving my family and everything I had known for the previous twenty years. What in the hell would a popular educator do in a U.S. prison?

Prison Educator

Once I landed in a cage in the U.S., I had no formula to follow. No one who came before me spoke of critical pedagogy. I didn't bother even dropping the term "education for liberation." Liberation for who? From what? The only liberation people in prison wanted to hear about was the liberation that would get them out of cages. I didn't have the key to the cages. There was no immediate hope for a change of residence.

Despite these troubling questions, I looked for blank spaces and inserted education to see what would happen. In the federal pre-trial lockup in Dublin I organized Spanish as a second language class. The Spanish classes became a social venue, breaking down racial barriers. In the Spanish class, Latinos became the experts and black and white men who didn't normally congregate with "Mexicans" rolled out of bed at 9 a.m. to learn the next round of vocabulary. I watched as they repeated after José, the man I had convinced to run these classes. "A dónde vas?" he asks the class (where are you going?) There is silence, then someone stammers out "a la tienda." Of course we were going nowhere but it doesn't matter. We were travelling into new intellectual territory. Not quite liberation but a few sparks of light beyond the domino board.

At the U.S. Penitentiary in Lompoc I taught GED math and basic computer skills in the library I described above. Educators in prison, I find out, are a combination of useful and nerdy. We are useful because we know stuff, we can write letters and writs. Often through our job we have access to markers, pens, and paper that we can steal from the education department. For a small fee, we can photocopy someone's appeal, or, if we are willing, their pornographic photos or football betting cards.

I learned to adapt education to different times and spaces, doing tutorials from the day room floor, consultations about grammar at the pullup bars in the yard, historical discussions in line at the chow hall. We are locked up but our classrooms have no walls. In fact real classrooms are not safe spaces for everyone. Some people feel safer in a cell or in an isolated corner of the yard where no one can hear their query, in case it might fall into the category of "stupid question."

Keeping face is nearly everything in prison for most men.

I find that there are kindred souls here, men who have felt the spark and power of intellectual query and want to share it, want to offer it as an alternative to becoming a fallen soldier on the losing side in the War on Drugs. They are seeking pathways to liberation as well.

We are curriculum developers and counselors. We develop courses that take people beyond high school and GED but don't give them credit. Our courses hang on the thinnest of threads. For some of us that might be a worn-out photocopy of an article about the Black Panther Party or an equation drawn in the dust of the yard. During lockdowns we pass notes that we call kites to our learners and our intellectual peers, giving them comments on their essays, asking them questions about a book. That is who we are and what we do. There are many ideas of liberation here. Some of these educators have found Jesus, some have found Allah, some have found their supposed Nordic ancestors. Some find liberation in the sweat lodge. Not my ideas of liberation but I have to reserve judgement. Judgement can be lethal here. Follow your own path and try to make it welcoming to others. Who am I to judge?

Education for Liberation in the Prison Yard

After five years I have tried lots of educational experiments behind the walls. I have left the federal system to inhabit California State Prison at High Desert in Susanville, California. Susanville has been the subject of a PBS documentary entitled "Prison Town USA." This town of 13,000 holds three prisons.

In my last year at High Desert I land a job as teacher's aide for Ms. Glenn. As far as prison teachers go, she is acceptable. She calls the men by the title Mr. and I think she would genuinely like them to learn something. When one of them passes the GED she posts a piece of paper congratulating them on the bulletin board in the hallway. She tells me how much she likes James Loewen's book *Lies My Teacher Told Me: Everything Your American History Textbook Got Wrong* (Loewen, 1996), which clearly places her ideologically miles outside the normal FOX News channel listener pedagogy I have encountered thus far.

The 2008 financial crisis is in full swing. As I read more about it, I think more about South Africa. If I were still there I'd be running workshops for shop stewards on this topic, explaining the housing bubble, identifying the bad guys, bemoaning the contradictions of capitalism. People in U.S. prisons don't have a vocabulary or a context for that. But I decide to try. I ask Ms. Glenn if I can do something different—run a workshop style class with flip charts, worksheets, and small group discussions. When I say small group discussions, she balks.

"I tried that once about four years ago and it didn't work," she said, "the men said I was trying to get them killed. But if you keep them in their groups."

Groups is code for race in this yard. As in all California prisons, apartheid has been resurrected. Unlike federal facilities, state penitentiaries in California are totally segregated. People of different "races" don't share cells, don't play sports together. The space in the building is racialized. There are black phones and white phones, black showers and white showers. The Latinos fall on either side depending on whether they identify as Northerns or Southerns. Native Americans for some reason, only explicable by the horrific racial hatred and history of California prisons, share space with the whites rather than with black men.

By the time I reach Ms. Glenn's class I have lived for nearly two years in this segregated world. Pushing back is a death or near-death sentence. I have been warned for talking too much to black men, for sitting at a table with a black man at breakfast, been cautioned that even if I don't eat all the food on my tray at dinner, I can't give the extra to a black or brown person. That is "bringing down the race," being a "race traitor" and will get you a stabbing.

"I won't do that, Ms. Glenn. I am not going to teach a workshop that is segregated."

She grows very uncomfortable.

"I don't want violence in my class."

I tell her I will go and speak to everyone in the class individually and get them to agree.

"If you can do that, then we can go ahead."

There are twenty-five men in the class. I talk to them all one by one. The persons I am most worried about are John and Ernie. John is a white guy from some rural town who has a huge tumor in his stomach. He is supposed to be going for surgery soon. When I ask him he quickly agrees, like he couldn't care at all. Ernie is equally nonchalant. I guess he has forgotten those SS tattoos that he has on his leg mean that he has carried out a mission against a member of another race.

I get the materials ready. Ms. Glenn has found me some flip charts and marking pens for group work. I have been cutting articles out of the *USA Today* which we usually get about three days late. That's right on time for our work.

The workshop begins with me making a brief presentation on the crisis. I outline how the banks have set up this system of predatory loans, putting people in credit over their ears. I talk about the role of Fannie Mae and the finance houses, the way in which the impact of this rolls downhill, hitting farmers, working people, the inner city, and the Global South. The guys are riveted. This is much more gripping than Pythagorean theorems.

I have structured this as a global role play, with each group representing a different constituency in the U.S. or global economy. I am setting this up as a session at the United Nations where each of them is called upon to deliver a short speech that expresses the sentiments of their constituency. Then we will open it up to the floor. One group is the World Bank, another the mortgage lenders, another U.S. farmers, and the final group African farmers. I group them and they get busy. Each group has a scenario and a set of questions. They write the answers on the flip charts. They have never done this before. One group tapes their flip chart onto the window that exposes the classroom to the eye of guards. Ms. Glenn quickly tells them to take it down. She definitely doesn't want to incur the wrath of the officers for this crazy workshop.

Ernie, as it turns out, is the spokesperson for African farmers. He notes how the crisis is pushing "his people" to the brink of survival, that the big banks are winning at the expense of the poor people of the world. Cleon, a young black man, speaks up on behalf of the World Bank, emphasizing that these African countries need to increase their export crops so they can survive in the world.

"If you all keep producing food crops," he says, pointing a finger at Ernie, "You Africans are going to lose out." Ernie looks outraged. The other guys in his group mumble something about rich bankers.

After twenty minutes, we stop the role play and move back to our reality.

"So what did you learn from this?" I asked.

"The global economy is rigged," says Cleon, "that's why we end up here."

I laugh. Ms. Glenn is fidgeting but she lets the conversation go.

"Africa never had a chance," says Ernie. "They got no money, no clout."
At this point, Ms. Glenn drives her bus into the middle of our park.

"Thank you, Mr. Kilgore," she says. "It has been very enlightening."

I gather up the flip charts and marking pens and we prepare to exit. That Sunday, Ernie tells me that he had a visit from his family and he explained the whole financial crisis to them. He says they couldn't figure out how he knew more about what was happening on the streets even though he was in prison. I told him that is what we call education for liberation. He didn't know quite what I meant but it felt good to say it.

Bibliography

Gramsci, A. (1971). *Selections from the prison notebooks*. New York: International.

Kilgore, J. (2013). Is another pedagogical world possible? Teaching globalization to my fellow prisoners. *The Radical Teacher*, 95, 40–51.

Loewen, J. (1996). *Lies my teacher told me: Everything your American history textbook got wrong*. New York: Touchstone.

Pape, J. (1997). Khanya College Johannesburg: Ten years of "education for liberation": An assessment. *International Journal of Lifelong Education*, 16(4), 290–297.

Pape, J. (1998). Changing education for majority rule in Zimbabwe and South Africa. *Comparative Education Review*, 42(3), 253–266.

Pape, J. (2001). A public sector alternative: SAMWU's efforts. *South African Labour Bulletin*, 25(4), 45–50.

7

THE PERILS OF TRANSFORMATION TALK IN HIGHER EDUCATION IN PRISON

Raphael Ginsberg

Higher education in prison is rife with celebrations of its transformative power, how it deepens, expands, and liberates prisoners' views of themselves and the world. These celebrations assume education shapes and nourishes students and that the values and priorities of the college classroom stand in absolute difference from those in prison generally, providing the conditions for fundamental change for students. Built into these triumphant narratives are assertions of who people in prison are and their experience of being in prison, and the notion that pedagogues have both the ability and right to make such determinations. Further, it assumes that students are in need of transformation and want higher education to transform them.

While transformation talk is deployed by programs with a range of pedagogical philosophies, this chapter focuses on these claims in critical pedagogy. Critical pedagogy was conceived as a method of addressing oppression, and the fundamental oppression of incarceration makes critical pedagogy a natural framework for higher education in prison. However, central elements of the critical pedagogical project are not possible in the prison classroom. Critical pedagogy analyzes students' social and cultural identities and the mechanisms that form them, seeking to reframe and disrupt such identities. However, the identity "prisoner" ultimately cannot be either liberated or reframed through pedagogical strategies. Also, the incarcerated student's identity as "prisoner" is unintelligible to the non-incarcerated instructor, making critical pedagogy's insistence on student transformation epistemologically baseless.

The concept of experience is central to this chapter, as it evaluates prison pedagogy's engagement with the experience of being a person in prison. However, I make no claims about students in prison as "they really are" qua people in prison or the experience of incarceration itself, as both are impossible to capture. I do, however, examine the discourses of the prisoner in the United States, including the boundaries within which it exists and the terms available with which to construct it. This emphasis on discourse rather than lived experience follows the work of Joan Scott (1991), who argues that analysts must try to "understand the operations of the complex and changing discursive processes by which identities are ascribed" (p. 792). Identities—such as the "prisoner" identity—are discursive events, and commentators must approach the experience of anyone in that identity category as such, without making experiential claims grounded in the first-hand observation to which instructors have access.

Existing Prison Pedagogical Literature

A central question in prison pedagogy is how, among all of the characteristics of prison students, should the pedagogue address the fact that students are prisoners? However, prison pedagogy scholarship does not address students in prison as *prison* students. Gaskew's (2015) and Colson's (2013) discussion of race in the prison classroom and Trounstine's (2008) of gender do not address students in their specificity as prison students, instead as African Americans, men, or women respectively. The themes engaged by the prison reading group Sweeney (2008) describes—power, revenge, gender—are not unique to the prison context, and their engagement is not framed by being in prison.

Thus far, prison pedagogy identifying as critical pedagogy has not addressed teaching students in prison as prison students. In a 2017 article addressing the forces shaping pedagogical practices in prison, Brawn, in conversation with Castro, argues that constraints on the availability of information in prison reduce the dialogical capacities necessary for critical pedagogy. Further, both discuss how the violence of incarceration harms students' ability to complete schoolwork. They observe that critical pedagogy cannot work towards dismantling oppression in prison, as "non-incarcerated instructors with the privilege to go into prisons and teach about a system of oppression from which they (we) benefit" (Castro and Brawn, 2017, p. 117). While the essay seeks to explore the consequences of the students being prisoners, ultimately its analysis concerns the facility and not the students, focusing on where the teaching takes place rather than who is being taught.

Leading higher education in prison practitioners endorse critical pedagogy in the prison classroom, but have not articulated critical pedagogy strategies specific to students in prison. Erzen (2016) describes a critical inquiry group made up of both professors and students in prison that examines "ideas that animate higher education in the prison: critical pedagogy, authority in the classroom, and how gender and race underpin educational justice and community" (p. 355). Her discussion of this group is general, and does not describe how or whether the group's inquiries were shaped by taking place in a prison with a mix of incarcerated and non-incarcerated members. Scott (2012) advocates creating a classroom space specific to the prison context and recognizing students in their identity as prisoners. He writes, "Teachers are in a position to invite connections between the classroom discussion and the networks of meanings circulating in a prison" (p. 26). According to Scott, creating a critical pedagogical space requires that participants interrogate their own incarcerated/non-incarcerated positionality. His analysis ends without exploring the methods and benefits of that interrogation or the strategies that follow.

Freire and Giroux

Critical pedagogy brings issues of power into the center of pedagogical analysis, treating education as a key site of political, cultural, and economic struggle. Accordingly, education is not the simple transmission of neutral skills and knowledge, but it is a space where multiple forms of capital are inequitably distributed and power relations are reproduced and legitimated. Critical pedagogy seeks strategies to disrupt this reproduction and legitimation. Its pursuit of egalitarian transformation of power relations focuses on changing curricula, instituting democratic processes into and reformulating hierarchical student/teacher relations, and incorporating student knowledges and experience into pedagogical activities, making schools places of liberations rather than guarantors of oppression.

Paulo Freire and Henry Giroux are two of critical pedagogy's foundational figures. Freire's (1970) pedagogy seeks to reach students where they are, in order to activate a critical sensibility towards their oppression, catalyzing a political awakening. Without this awakening, oppressed students exist in a state of blindness, as "oppressive reality absorbs those within it and thereby acts to submerge human beings' consciousness" (p. 33). After seeing themselves outside of the conditions of their oppression, students engage "in the ontological and historical vocation of becoming more human" (p. 48). Liberating this critical consciousness through pedagogical practice humanizes students, who no longer internalize and see their oppression as natural but as a "limiting situation which they can transform" (p. 31) through struggle.

Giroux (1986) followed Freire by envisioning a classroom space which "makes problematic how teachers and students sustain, or resist, or accommodate those languages, ideologies, social processes, and myths that position them within existing relations of power and dependency" (p. 60). Students recognize power hierarchies for what they are, rejecting the naturalness of their location within them. This process demands attention to "the histories, dreams, and experiences that such students bring to schools" in order to determine how "they can be translated into a language of possibility" (p. 64). Teachers utilize students' sensibilities and how they live their lives to "understand, affirm, and analyze such experience," making it both critical and liberatory (Giroux and McLaren, 1986, p. 234). Further, for Giroux (1997) students personalize abstract concepts by examining their lived experience through them. For example, educators must ask "[white] students to address ... how their Whiteness functions in society as a marker of privilege and power" (p. 297). Without such engagement, whiteness—and race generally—remains a foreign concept to white students.

For both Giroux and Freire, teachers facilitate recognition and then disruption: first students recognize the socioeconomic conditions in which they live—conditions of either oppression or privilege—before dismantling the identity formed by these conditions to form a new, liberated identity. An accurate account of students' conditions renders inaccurate the identity formed in such conditions. Implementing this pedagogical project in the prison classroom requires students to define themselves as prisoners in order to change their conceptions of both themselves and the conditions of their oppression while incarcerated. They must go to class not just to be students but to also *be* prisoners.

However, this self-definition demands that students engage with prison's abjectness and their own loss of agency.[1] Everyone occupies multiple identities, with some providing agency, joy, and affirmation, and others denying them. Like everyone else, people in prison occupy multiple roles, identifying as—among others—friend, family member, worker, spiritual practitioner, and, in circumstances all too rare, college student. By occupying non-abject, empowered roles, people in prison ultimately create non-abject existences.

But, the prisoner on its own is an abject category in the United States, making it impossible to deconstruct the prisoner identity and reconstitute it in liberated form. It is wholly constituted by oppression—incarceration's rigid routines, constraints on movement, constant threat of violence, and separation from friends and family—lacking any non-abject space for people in prison qua prisoners to occupy. In other words, there isn't anything to work with. The possibility of agency and liberation demands departing from the "prisoner" identity altogether, and demanding that students "be" prisoners traps them in their abjectness with no liberatory possibilities.

Ellsworth's Intervention

Elizabeth Ellsworth (1989) also argues that engaging personal experience and identity is integral to radical pedagogy. But she takes a different view of accessing and communicating experience and sensibility across identity categories. Cross-identity communication is fraught, as intersectionality fragments sensibilities, and personal access to experience is forever partial, contextual, and temporary. Further, privilege—racial, sexuality, class, linguistic, and gender (among others)—guarantees the marginalization and silencing of subordinate voices. However, for Ellsworth, Giroux's pedagogy deploys "ahistorical and depoliticized abstractions" (p. 307) that conceal every classroom's inequitable, inherently antagonistic power relations. Critical pedagogy's faith in cross-identity intelligibility—which grounds notions of dialogical learning and student empowerment—maintains instructors' omniscience and classroom authority. Acknowledging epistemological barriers troubles the authority that grounds instructor/student hierarchies.

Nevertheless, a thread of communicability survives Ellsworth's critique. While Ellsworth finds difference in its totality forever unknowable and uncommunicable, it is intelligible in partial, contradictory, and temporary ways. Accordingly, to foster cross-identity understanding and solidarity Ellsworth advocates (pp. 317–318) creating student affinity groups—organized according to sexuality, race, and so on—that would present their course analysis to other student affinity groups. These presentations would provide views of that group's experience and sensibilities, a strategy that assumes that some part of what one affinity group presents can be made meaningful for and understood by others.

The prison classroom is similarly vulnerable to hierarchical power relations and the silencing of marginal and subordinate voices, which requires strategies to democratize student-to-student and instructor-to-student relations and provide space for all experiences. However, students in prison cannot communicate the experience of being a prisoner to its corresponding affinity group, the non-incarcerated instructors, tutors, and program administrators, even in partial, contradictory, and temporary ways. The mechanics of identity are fundamentally different in the prison classroom than they are on campus. All outside students belong to different identity categories, even if identifications with any one category differ from student to student. Understanding the process of any one identification provides a framework for analyzing the process of identification generally. For example, each student—white, black, and so on—identifies in some way as "raced," and a student's examination of the mechanisms that "race" himself/herself/themselves enables that student's examination of the mechanisms that "race" students across racial identities. The white student may not understand what it means to be black, but gains some view of what it means to be white and to "be" a race.

Instructors and students in prison identify as either non-incarcerated or incarcerated. However, being non-incarcerated is an amorphous identity, and examining the process of identifying as non-incarcerated provides no clarity on the process of identifying as incarcerated. The pervasiveness of one's non-incarceration prevents it from taking form and becoming recognizable. There are no processes of identification compelling the non-incarcerated to identify as such. By contrast, incarceration compels people in prison to identify as incarcerated on a minute-by-minute basis, by controlling how they eat, sleep, communicate, and so on. The totalization of incarceration makes its experience unintelligible to the non-incarcerated, making it impossible to communicate across the incarcerated/non-incarcerated divide to pursue "commonality in the experience of difference" (p. 324). Of course, many other affinity groups exist in the prison classroom, but the incarcerated and the non-incarcerated (with the important exception of the formerly incarcerated) cannot recognize each other as such, and Ellsworth's methods cannot function in the *prison* classroom.

Discussion

The above seems contradictory. On one hand, students in prison are unintelligible as *prison* students by non-incarcerated instructors, even in fragmented and incomplete form, intelligibility crucial to the critical pedagogy project. Those limits apply to me, denying me the ability to make claims as to who *prison* students are. However, my claim that the *prisoner* identity is necessarily abject and without liberatory potential demands that I have exactly this authority. The contradiction seems clear.

However, I claim no access to the experience of living people in prison, but instead to the discourses of people in prison in the United States. These discourses provide a point of entry for analyzing the contexts in which identities are formed and experience constructed, to determine the terms available for and the constraints imposed upon the prisoner. These discourses are dismal: in the rare circumstances that people in prison are represented, they are monsters with no value to society, reduced to mug shots on the screen or in the newspaper, who are excluded from the basic categories of what it is to be human—self-determination, familial love, learning, and self-realization. People in prison are both grave threats and objects of no concern, whose existence the public has only a vague (but visceral) idea about, because, once incapacitated, few care about them. These ideas take material form in the design and operation of prison facilities themselves, its rigid routines, spatial constraints, and constant threat of violence. Critiques of mass incarceration too often treat people in prison as statistics: either threats to recidivate or wastes of money. Even those whose opposition to mass incarceration is grounded in assertions of the humanity of people in prison, it is incarceration's dehumanization that is objectionable.

The challenge for higher education in prison is to counter this construction to show that students are more than prisoners as constructed in the United States, to move them out of the category "prisoner."

A primary tactic has been deploying the concept of transformation. In diverse ways, higher education in prison programs pursue three forms of student transformation. First, higher education in prison programs transform the living conditions of students while incarcerated, including how, where, and with whom time is spent. Second, higher education in prison programs transform the post-incarceration possibilities available to students—economic, professional, and academic—as skills and credentials change such possibilities for everyone, justice involved or not.

Third, higher education in prison seeks to transform students in prisons themselves: to reconfigure how they see themselves and their relationships with other people and the world at large. Among other things, education will deepen students' critical capacities, cultivate ways of contributing to society upon their release, and provide tools to understand their own pasts. This third form of transformation requires concrete knowledge of exactly who students in prison are before, during, and after their education, that is, what they were and what they were transformed into. Without this concreteness, there is no way to know how students in prison should change or whether they have changed through higher education. But, the unbridgeable intelligibility gap between instructor and student makes finding a concrete, forever-identical prisoner identity impossible, making a transformation-driven pedagogical project impossible as well.[2] In the absence of certainty about the prisoner, there can be no certainty about the student in prison's transformation.

A tension in prison education exists between seeing incarcerated and non-incarcerated students as fundamentally different and insisting on their equivalence. The former risks exoticizing students in prison, treating them as "less than" non-incarcerated students or as representing pure difference, with wisdom grounded in life experience, making them, among the many other categories of student, uniquely beneficial classmates for non-prison students.

Despite these dangers, pedagogues must account for differences between incarcerated and non-incarcerated students. Incarceration's degradation increases instructor–student power disparities, as non-incarcerated instructors gain power when students lack it, especially when instructors are valorized for teaching degraded students. In prison, instructors have the authority both of their credentials and expertise but of their imputed virtue as well. But, instructors should not address this uniqueness through critical pedagogy's transformational strategies, which demands hailing students in prison as prisoners in order to reach them where they are and utilize their expertise, a strategy that traps them in their identity and cements the power disparities unique to prison.

Transformation discourses assume that pedagogues have the authority to determine who prisoners are, but that authority is baseless and illusory. Pedagogues can only make guesses, and these guesses are exercises in privilege, acts of psychic invasion inflicted on acutely vulnerable students who lack the ability to represent themselves and higher education in prison in the media, academic articles, and development materials.

This chapter does not offer any solutions to the darkness inherent in the prison classroom's power dynamics, but instead stands as a modest corrective to higher education in prison's triumphant transformational narratives. Prison pedagogy should question any claims about prisoner identity. As far as the pedagogue is concerned, the prison student should only be a student. Pedagogues should be similarly suspicious of any transformational demands placed upon students, as students may have no need to transform or interest in transforming. Treating the prison classroom as a space of transformation reduces and ultimately exploits the students on whose behalf the pedagogue works.

Notes

1 I agree with Dylan Rodriguez's (2006) notion of the ontological deformity of prisoners, but he sees this deformity as what enables the political radicalism of people in prison, i. e. their abjectness makes them non-abject, contrary to my position. However, his criticism of higher education in prison consists of the obvious point that higher education in prison programs must accommodate the demands of the prisons in which they

operate, but he fails to provide any examples of how that accommodation is fundamentally fatal to the project overall.

2 Given the countless contingencies of incarceration in the United States, I would go further and argue that not even people in prison themselves can find a concrete identity all people in prison have.

References

Castro, E. L. and Brawn, M. (2017). Critiquing critical pedagogies inside the prison classroom: A dialogue between student and teacher. *Harvard Educational Review*, 87(1), 99–121.

Colson, D. (2013). Geographies of prejudice: Self-narration and radical teaching in prison. *Radical Teacher*, 95, 51–56.

Ellsworth, E. (1989). Why doesn't this feel empowering? Working through the repressive myths of critical pedagogy. *Harvard Educational Review*, 59(3), 297–324.

Erzen, T. (2016). The broom closet: Pedagogy in and of the prison. *American Quarterly*, 68(2), 355–359.

Freire, P. (1970). *The pedagogy of the oppressed*, trans. M. B. Ramos. New York: Penguin Books.

Gaskew, T. (2015). Developing a prison education pedagogy. *New Directions for Community Colleges*, 170, 67–78.

Giroux, H. A. (1986). Radical pedagogy and the politics of student voice. *Interchange*, 17(1), 48–69.

Giroux, H. A. (1997). Rewriting the discourse of racial identity: Towards a pedagogy and politics of whiteness. *Harvard Educational Review*, 67(2), 285–320.

Giroux, H. A. and McLaren, P. (1986). Teacher education and the politics of engagement: The case for democratic schools. *Harvard Educational Review*, 56(3), 213–238.

Rodriguez, D. (2006). *Forced passages: Imprisoned radical intellectuals and the U.S. prison regime*. Minneapolis: University of Minnesota Press.

Scott, J. W. (1991). The evidence of experience. *Critical Inquiry*, 17(4), 773–797.

Scott, R. (2012). Distinguishing radical teaching from merely having intense experiences while teaching in prison. *Radical Teacher*, 95, 22–32.

Sweeney, M. (2008). Books as bombs: Incendiary reading practices in women's prisons. *PMLA*, 123(3), 666–673.

Trounstine, J. (2008). Beyond prison education. *PMLA*, 123(3), 674–677.

8

ON THE PRACTICE AND ETHOS OF SELF-COMPASSION FOR HIGHER EDUCATORS IN PRISONS

Thomas Fabisiak

People who are drawn to teaching college in prisons often see their work as a moral calling. They may be dedicated to promoting the right to education, to challenging systemic inequality, or to disrupting white supremacy. These commitments are valuable, and they come with certain risks. Idealistic celebrations of this work as liberative or transformative can contribute to a savior complex; they can exacerbate troubling power dynamics between free teachers and incarcerated students. They can lead teachers to overlook the ways that higher education in prisons depends on and reproduces aspects of carceral institutions that they oppose in principle. Other contributors to this volume have highlighted these risks. I believe we should be equally wary of the related tendency, common among academics committed to social justice, towards ascetic self-criticism. Teachers in prisons are likely to witness and, perhaps, participate in, events that challenge them morally. In this context, relentlessly self-critical attitudes can increase the risk of burnout and compassion fatigue. Even more, they can distract us from the day-to-day experience of our work and lead to harm to students and other people in prison with whom teachers interact.

I argue in this chapter for the value of self-compassion for teachers in prisons as a means of threading a path between excessive self-praise and self-criticism. "Self-compassion" refers to a mindful, compassionate awareness of the difficult realities of one's experience. It comprises self-kindness and nonjudgmental confrontation with our suffering and shortcomings, the capacity to acknowledge our limitations honestly while seeing them as part of shared human existence (Neff, 2003). Practices of self-compassion have been shown to have significant psychological benefits (Alkema et al., 2008; Barnard and Curry, 2012; Denckla et al., 2016; Figley, 2002; Leary et al., 2007; Marshall et al., 2015; Neely et al., 2009; Raes, 2010), many of which are relevant for mitigating harms that people who work in environments of pervasive trauma may experience—harms such as burnout, compassion fatigue, and moral injury. Self-compassion also has an ethical dimension. One might assume that being compassionate to yourself would lead to making excuses or ignoring ethical challenges—including, in this case, the challenges of our positionality as free teachers working with incarcerated students. In fact, the opposite has been shown to be the case. Practices of self-compassion support an other-focused disposition, a sense of connection with other human beings, and the capacity to recognize boundaries and limits while improving on inadequacies (Breines and Chen, 2012; Neff and Pommier, 2013; Wang et al., 2016). Self-compassion can therefore provide an essential counterpart to practices of social critique and engagement, in which each sustains and deepens the other.

I highlight these psychological and ethical benefits of self-compassion in order to recommend it as a practice for people who provide higher education in prisons. But I also wish to suggest that it can serve as part of an ethos of this work. By "ethos" I mean both the dispositions we strive to adopt and the culture we strive to create. Cultivating an ethos of self-compassion would mean acknowledging the difficult realities involved in prison education, recognizing that we are limited human beings operating in complex, ethically irrational environments. Such an attitude helps to sustain this work while keeping open the futures to which it may lead. At the same time, it constitutes a humanizing disposition. Self-compassion opposes abstract, morally rigid conceptions of ourselves and others—conceptions in which prisons are rooted and to which progressive educators may be prone. If the harms associated with prisons are defined in part by trauma and systemic violence, they are also defined by the ways that abstract generalizations are imposed on the people who are confined in them. Embodied dispositions may therefore contribute as much in daily practice as cognitive assent to the most critical, radical principles to resisting dehumanizing aspects of the institutions in which we teach.

Self-Compassion as a Practice

Compassion refers to the capacity to encounter other people's pain without disconnecting, so that we are moved to wish to alleviate their suffering. Where suffering is isolating, compassion keeps us open to the vulnerability of others and draws us closer to them. It is "nonjudgmental" in the sense that even if we disagree with or disapprove of a person's actions, we hope for their suffering to end and avoid deprecating them personally. "Self-compassion" directs this honest encounter with painful experiences and limitations inward. Kristin Neff, who introduced the concept into the field of psychology, defines it in terms of three interrelated components:

> (a) self-kindness—being kind and understanding toward oneself in instances of pain or failure rather than being harshly self-critical, (b) common humanity— perceiving one's experiences as part of the larger human experience rather than

seeing them as separating and isolating, and (c) mindfulness—holding painful thoughts and feelings in balanced awareness rather than over-identifying with them (Neff, 2003).

Taken together, these components counter a number of adverse tendencies in people's experience of suffering. It counters avoidance and denial by fostering honest engagement with our wounds. But it also counters the tendency to ruminate on pain or to see it as in terms of isolating, personal failures. It thereby encourages growth and resilience, the ability to learn from our failings and cultivate our strengths.

Practices of self-compassion often involve reflecting on painful experiences while adopting a kind and soothing attitude, avoiding critical self-talk. For example, you might take a troubling challenge that you are facing and imagine a close friend in the same situation. You would consider what you might say to your friend, and then practice saying it to yourself. The practice might involve a guided meditation or a writing exercise. Other practices build on compassion and mindfulness; some include somatic components (for examples, see www.selfcompassion.org/category/exercises and www.compassionateintegrity.org/downloads/).

Self-compassion has a number of psychological and emotional benefits, including reduced depression (Raes, 2010), less negative self-feelings resulting from faults (Leary et al., 2007), increased self-esteem (Marshall et al., 2015), and a number of other positive psychological traits (Neff et al., 2007). Other benefits are particularly relevant for people who spend time in correctional institutions, that is, in spaces defined by trauma.

Rates of exposure to trauma and PTSD are extraordinarily high among incarcerated people (Baranyi et al., 2018). Systemic inequalities in distributions of vulnerability and exposure to violence affect communities, poor communities of color in particular, who are disproportionately imprisoned, and people in prisons experience higher rates of child abuse and interpersonal violence (Richie, 2012; Wolff and Shi, 2012). These inequalities intertwine with legacies of historical and generational trauma, from slavery and racial terror to disenfranchisement and colonialism. At the same time, imprisonment is itself a traumatic experience. People who live in prisons experience extremes of vulnerability and disempowerment. Violence is common, and daily routines are subject to frequent and sudden disruptions. PTSD and other psychological wounds affect people who have been in prison long after they have been released (Liem and Kunst, 2013).

People who work or teach in prisons will do well to adopt trauma-informed approaches. Such an approach should include serious consideration of what these conditions mean for one's own well-being. Correctional staff frequently encounter traumatic events, and they have been shown to experience high rates of PTSD (Spinaris et al., 2012). They can experience empathic distress, the adverse suffering that comes from empathizing with another person's pain, and counselors who work with traumatized people may suffer secondary trauma.

They are also prone to moral harm, namely the psychological and emotional damage that comes from witnessing or participating in acts that violate their core values or moral expectations.

In extreme cases, such harms constitute full-fledged "moral injury," a condition that was originally documented in veterans of wars (Litz et al., 2009; Shay, 2014). Exposure to trauma, secondary trauma, and moral harm can have severe consequences, especially when the associated experiences are severe or repeated. Staff may experience burnout, for example, which is often accompanied by compassion fatigue (see Craig and Sprang, 2010; Keidel, 2002; and Killian, 2008). Moral injury includes symptoms that resemble those of PTSD: constrictive and intrusive thoughts, numbing, and avoidance (Shay, 2014). These symptoms are personally debilitating and they compromise our ability to be present with others. Compassion fatigue, a reduced ability to feel concern or care, can have troubling repercussions in a total institution where staff are tasked with caring for or managing substantial aspects of people's lives.

Few teachers in college programs will spend as much time in correctional institutions as full-time staff. Nevertheless, there are reasons for them to take these risks seriously. Some are especially relevant. For example, people who feel called to teach in prison are likely to be passionately critical of aspects of the prison environment, an attitude that naturally raises the risk of moral injury. The stakes are also high. If teachers experience burnout or compassion fatigue, this can limit the effectiveness of their pedagogy and the sustainability of their work. It can also harm students. Burnout and compassion fatigue reduce our ability to hear and acknowledge others, and to interact with them in ways that honor their personhood.

Practices of self-compassion can reduce these risks. Studies have shown associations between self-compassion and reduced compassion fatigue (Alkema et al., 2008; Figley, 2002), while lower self-compassion has been associated with burnout (Alkema et al., 2008; Barnard and Curry, 2012). Self-compassion also raises self-awareness, enabling people to grapple with how burnout is affecting them (Dev et al., 2018). Nor should we understand these benefits only in a negative way, in terms of how self-compassion prevents harms. Practices of self-compassion have been shown to contribute positively to an other-directed focus and concern for the well-being of others (Neff and Pommier, 2013). The benefits of self-compassion are not merely therapeutic in a narrow sense, then. They are also ethical, and can contribute to sustaining the dimensions of our work that relate to social justice.

The Ethical Dimension of Self-Compassion

Audre Lorde famously stated that self-care is a radical act. But in what does this radicalism consist? The statement has the clearest relevance for those who face oppression as a result of their social location or identity. In a culture that refuses to care for the most vulnerable, self-care is a means of resisting internalized oppression—resisting the oppressor in each of us. This resistance would oppose the internal workings of cultural violence: patriarchy, white supremacy, and trans- and homophobia, among others. Self-care counters negative self-images as well as a cultural ethos according to which the least cared for are expected to be the most self-sacrificing, with gendered and racial ideologies sustaining these expectations.

Self-compassion has demonstrable positive effects in this regard. In promoting self-kindness and connection to others, it combats internalized stigma. In a 2017 study with LGBTQ youth in a midwestern high school, Vigna et al. (2017) found that self-compassion may interrupt the process by which stigma is internalized. Self-compassion was associated with better mental health among participants who faced stigma, namely, and higher resistance to the effects of bullying behavior. It can provide a counterpart, in that sense, to approaches that promote awareness of systems of oppression; critical social analysis and self-compassion can support and deepen one another (cf. Crowder, 2016).

Still, one may wonder what ethical or political value self-compassion would have for those who do not suffer from stigma or oppression. I, for one, benefit from multiple, overlapping forms of privilege. Why should I practice self-compassion? The question is more relevant than ever in contemporary American culture, where "self-care" often signals a display of privileged self-indulgence and consumerism (see Kisner, 2017). Mantras of self-care may serve as excuses to avoid self-scrutiny or social responsibility. Inversely, they may shift responsibility from institutions to individuals in ways that legitimize exploitation. Consider how corporate offices now encourage self-care—an only apparent concession to the needs of stressed, overworked employees, and one that enables business to continue as usual: If I burn out at work, this is not because I am required to work sixty hours a week, be available to answer emails or texts at all hours of the day, put my work before my family, see my benefits chipped away, or live with the knowledge that I may be fired and replaced at any time; it is because I do not spend enough time cultivating mindfulness!

How much more pernicious is it, then, to promote self-kindness and a nonjudgmental awareness of our limitations in a total institution structured by radical inequalities? It seems appropriate and fitting that teachers exercise vigilant self-criticism and remain focused on wrongs under such conditions. Does the suffering involved in mass incarceration not demand that we "fixate on" it until we have created the idioms and modes of living adequate to transforming it from the inside out? All free people are in positions of relative privilege when they enter a space of confinement. If we take time for self-compassion, are we suppressing critical self-analysis? Or are we quieting stirrings of resistance, learning to endure what should not be endured?

There are good reasons to believe that self-compassion has precisely the opposite effect—that it contributes to promoting critical analysis, beginning with self-analysis, and sustaining resistance. Studies of self-compassion have provided evidence that it supports moral insight and action. Exercising self-compassion has been shown to make people more likely to admit and take responsibility for their own failures, for example (Leary et al., 2007). Nor does this mean, contrary to what you might expect, that people take these failings as inevitable. High self-compassion is associated with lower acceptance of one's own moral failings (Wang et al., 2016), and people who engage their mistakes with self-compassion have been shown to be more likely to strive to improve on past behavior (Breines and Chen, 2012).

The key in each of these cases is that self-compassion leads people to face limitations and acknowledge difficult realities without fixating on them. In the context of teaching in prison, such limitations would include the institutional conditions under which we work, but also the radical differentials of power and divides of experience between teachers and students; difficult realities include ideologies of white supremacy, the daily traumas of people's lives before and in prisons, economic exploitation, patriarchy, and the enduring legacies of enslavement and racial terror, among others. These are painful, challenging subjects. Any consideration of them will involve troubling encounters with our privilege and positionality. Attempts to engage them may provoke denial, avoidance, or other forms of resistance, as in the well-documented phenomenon of white fragility (see DiAngelo, 2011). By promoting ethical self-awareness and engagement, practices of self-compassion provide an essential counter-measure, one that can be learned and sustained over time.

An Ethos of Self-Compassion

I have highlighted these benefits of self-compassion in part to recommend it as a practice. But I also want to suggest, ultimately, that we can learn from this concept in thinking about the ethos of teaching college in prison. By "ethos" I mean both the moral disposition we adopt as teachers and the culture we strive to create in the field of higher education in prison. The value of self-compassion in these areas would lie in the path it threads between an effusively optimistic attitude, on the one hand, and an ascetically self-critical one, on the other.

People involved in higher education in prison have already identified significant problems with the former, that is, with overly celebratory attitudes towards this work (see e.g., Scott, 2013). To recapitulate, there is a common tendency for teachers to focus on "transformative" or "liberative" dimensions of the work. It is natural that teachers should want to do so. Education aims to empower and liberate. The prison context raises the stakes and potential of these aims. In a place that strips people of agency, empowerment seems crucial, humanizing; in spaces of confinement, liberation can appear excitingly subversive; in institutions that define people by a single act, "transformation" can seem radical. Most people who teach in prisons have positive experiences that reinforce their commitment to these aims—for example, students who are in prison tend to be vocally appreciative of rare opportunities for empowerment and intellectual growth that students on the outside may take for granted.

But celebratory attitudes may lead to blind spots. These include the ways that educational programs can be complicit in oppressive dimensions of the prison system—how, for instance, it is possible to affirm ideas about rehabilitation that define people in problematic ways or reinforce separations between those who supposedly can or cannot be rehabilitated. Indeed, we only teach on the condition of accepting certain aspects of the prison, and it is always possible that our work will serve as a justification for allowing flawed institutions and practices to persist ("look at all the good this prison does; we are even giving people college degrees!"). We may also end up overlooking—and perpetuating—colonizing dynamics or developing a savior complex. We may obscure the ways that "transformative" experiences are enabled by troubling and extreme differentials of power and privilege.

At the same time, the space of the prison reconfigures any aims we might have for our work. Self-compassion involves mindful acknowledgement of our limits and inadequacies. In the prison, these limits are often structural. An ethos that encourages this kind of acknowledgement would converge, in that sense, with what Erin Castro and Michael Brawn have recently described as an "emplaced pedagogy" (Castro and Brawn, 2017). Castro and Brawn follow others (Kilgore, 2011; Thomas, 1995) who have examined the constraints that prisons place upon critical pedagogy. They point out that prisons are infused with authoritarian principles that contradict the democratic ethos of those who see education as part of a liberative or humanizing project. If critical pedagogies support freedom and dignity, the space of prisons undermines these relentlessly. The very structure of the prison classroom may subvert them. No measure of critical self-reflexivity will be sufficient to overcome these obstacles. The authors therefore highlight the irony of promoting agency and critical engagement in a space that limits opportunities to exercise either one. They suggest that teachers in prisons should embrace critical pedagogy, but with the essential recognition that "our endeavors will always be tragic (Thomas, 1995), incomplete, and messy (Lather, 1998)" (Castro and Brawn, 2017, p. 118).

To say that our efforts are messy and incomplete leads to a second dimension of self-compassion, one which may be less familiar, and perhaps comfortable, to people in our field: if self-compassion resists blind self-esteem, it equally calls into question ruthless self-criticism. Self-criticism can be understood in contrast to any of the levels of self-compassion. It occurs when I engage in self-abuse after I fail to meet my expectations; when, instead of recognizing what I have in common with others, I treat my responsibilities as unique and my experience as isolated; or when, instead of nonjudgmentally acknowledging the conditions of my work, I fixate obsessively on them. Self-criticism is, as such, more closely related to blinkered self-esteem than it might initially appear: it nourishes and is nourished by an idealized sense of self. Self-criticism is a risk when we presume that we can identify every possible wrong or assume full responsibility for them. This can exacerbate anxieties that we foist onto students; at the extreme it can foster an aggrandized self-conception. In the place of a savior complex in which people see themselves as liberators, there is a self-critical savior complex in which people see themselves as martyrs: ascetic figures striving in isolation against impossible conditions.

The potential for extremes of self-criticism is high in work motivated by idealism. If I hold a principled belief in the humanity of all people at the same time that I am required to witness and participate in dehumanizing acts in order to do my work, then I will experience this as a moral harm. Does this mean that I should give up my principles? I suspect it means, rather, that I should not hold myself to an inhuman standard of ethical consistency in practice, especially in the context of large and complex institutions. It means that I should admit that I am not perfect, that I will at times do and see things that I find ethically troubling.

Consider the following example. In the compound on which I teach, staff and volunteers are required to carry keys. The compound is impossible to navigate without a means of opening locks on gates. As you might expect, non-security staff and volunteers are not permitted, according to policy, to open gates for incarcerated people. In principle, this is a straightforward rule. Nevertheless, it happens regularly that a security staff member will ask or allow me to let someone through a gate. They may do so when they are preoccupied in a different part of the building, for example. The compound is sprawling, officers are stretched thin, and it is rare that one will be able to be present at all gates for which they are responsible at all times. As a result, I have been in the position of opening a door for one person for whom I have permission and then closing it on the person directly behind them—perhaps someone whom I know, perhaps a student in one of the programs in which I have taught, perhaps someone for whom I have opened a door in the past. This person may have had a real, pressing need to get through the door: to get to a class, the store, a medical or chaplaincy appointment, a parole hearing, or a visit with a family member, for example, in an allotted window of time that was rapidly closing.

In the grand scheme of the kinds of trauma and violence that we associate with prisons, this small act of obligatory inconsideration seems pretty harmless. But more severe examples can overshadow the small, commonplace ways in which institutions can erode our moral well-being, day by day. When you are expected to keep people from going through locked doors on a frequent enough basis, it begins to weigh on you. There is something viscerally unsettling about closing a door in the face of someone who has sat in a classroom with you, who has been kind to you, whose work you have admired and who has said things that changed your mind—in sum, in the face of someone whose humanity you recognize not only in principle but as a given fact, inscribed in your muscle memory.

There are of course more dramatic examples one could call to mind. Teachers in prisons may discover disturbing facts about their students' lives in prison; they may witness overtly violent acts; they may have to deal with the aftermath of having classrooms shaken down and students sent to lockdown; they may arrive at their institutions to find a student has been kicked out of a program. In each of these instances, teachers may perceive themselves to be powerless to affect the outcome, they may feel complicit, or they may believe that their response was inadequate. But all of these cases are symptomatic of the same essential condition of moral and emotional risk, one that the example of the locked door speaks to in its mundaneness. No matter the institution in which you work, and in spite of any principles you adopt in your pedagogy, it is likely you will experience or feel required at some point to do something that is inconsistent with your values.

No honest evaluation of ethics is possible without an equally honest evaluation of the conditions under which ethical action might be possible. And this consideration points to a deeper concern: the conditions in which incarcerated students live are exponentially more stringent and coercive than our own; if we risk routine moral harm when we teach in prisons, the people who live there are highly likely to have experienced moral injury. After all, when they witness something that violates their principles, the consequences they face for responding are significantly more severe than they would be for someone on the outside.

To model ideological purity or ethical consistency can therefore serve as a subtle assertion of power. I may be able to speak and act in a relatively consistent ethical way when all I risk losing is my position as a teacher. We, unlike incarcerated students, get to leave the prison, a space in which the associated problems are inescapable. After a student develops a clear-sighted analysis of structural violence, for example, power dynamics, or racial injustice in their context, their means for effectively addressing those issues are profoundly limited. Nor do they always have the luxury of stepping back from those conditions to process them. There is little space or time to reflect, and there may not be anyone with whom to discuss them without taking a serious risk. Topics that are taboo in mainstream society often fall under stronger prohibitions in prisons. Of course, students and teachers outside the prison may face similar problems, but they are inevitable in an environment where people have to live together in small communities in close, closed quarters—an environment, moreover, of which cultural and structural violence are defining conditions. I by no means wish to suggest that teachers should avoid difficult critical topics. Rather, an ethos of self-compassion would reaffirm Castro and Brawn's point that effective engagement with these topics starts with frank acknowledgement of the conditions under which we engage them.

But this ethos would include an additional consideration as well, one that does not concern the limits of the prison per se. When we fail, under such conditions, to live up to our ideals, we should not see this only as a function of contextual restraints, but as a function of our common humanity. Self-compassion involves recognizing the fact that, as human beings, we are likely to err in thought, speech, and action. My commitments may need revising; I may fail to live up to them. Such an attitude tempers our ethical commitments with humility and openness. It enables a certain comfort with moral ambiguity, in that sense, not only as a condition of being in ethically irrational spaces like prisons, but as a condition of being honest and present with others. Moral clarity, even in a critical stance, can close us off to what connects us: our vulnerability, our suffering, our common experiences of uncertainty and fear. Self-compassion consequently represents a humanizing disposition in dehumanizing spaces.

It bears recalling that prisons are physical manifestations of ideological abstractions about human beings. Attitudes of moral judgement and self-righteousness are etched into their architecture. They isolate and alienate. Nonjudgmental mindfulness of wrongs and awareness of the human limitations that we share may therefore do more in practice than assent to the most consistent, radical positions to resist ideologies of judgement and punishment within them. Ideology is not only what we think. It lives in our bodies. It shapes the spaces through which we move. To orient oneself in the space of the prison with self-compassion is to embody a disposition that rejects its core presuppositions.

Conclusion

Practices of self-compassion provide important resources for teachers in prisons to resist harms and sustain ethical engagement. An ethos of self-compassion provides a humanizing, realistic way to approach our work. In each of these respects, the concept of self-compassion offers means of living into challenging realities of teaching in prisons, that is, in spaces of profound moral ambiguity, pervasive trauma, and structural violence. To "live into" these realities is to acknowledge them honestly and recognize their intractability, but also to stay present in spite of them, and to be open, in doing so, to unknown possibilities to which our work might lead.

No universally accepted program exists to end the harms of mass incarceration. Even if we agree that the very idea of prisons is horrific, for example, and that they should be abolished, it is unlikely that we will agree on how to reach that end. It is equally unlikely that any particular approach will be effective in isolation. Teaching in prisons is a means of abiding in this complexity, creating new networks and local solidarities, sharing assets and resources, and building community in spaces that fracture, exclude, alienate, and render invisible. I do not believe anyone can know what the long-term outcomes of this work will be. But I also believe there is value in a stance that resists claiming to know, in building community, and being present before we have a clear concept of what it will mean or a detailed vision of the future to which it will lead.

Bibliography

Alkema, K. *et al.* (2008). A study of the relationship between self-care, compassion satisfaction, compassion fatigue, and burnout among hospice professionals. *Journal of Social Work in End of Life & Palliative Care*, 4(2), 101–119.

Baranyi, G. *et al.* (2018). Prevalence of Posttraumatic Stress Disorder in prisoners. *Epidemiologic Reviews*, 40(1), 134–145.

Barnard, L. and Curry, J. (2012). The relationship of clergy burnout to self-compassion and other personality dimensions. *Pastoral Psychology*, 61, 149–163.

Breines, J. G. and Chen, S. (2012). Self-compassion increases self-improvement motivation. *Personality and Social Psychology Bulletin*, 38, 1133–1143.

Castro, E. L. and Brawn, M. (2017). Critiquing critical pedagogies inside the prison classroom: A dialogue between student and teacher. *Harvard Educational Review*, 87(1), 99–121.

Cole, T. (2012, March 21). The white savior industrial complex. *Atlantic Monthly*. Retrieved at www.theatlantic.com/international/archive/2012/03/the-white-savior-industrial-complex/254843/. Accessed June 12, 2018.

Compassionateintegrity.org. Center for Compassion, Integrity, and Secular Ethics; Life University. Retrieved at www.compassionateintegrity.org. Accessed June 19, 2018.

Corbett, E. (2017, Oct 13). Teaching inside: On the dangers of the savior complex (in prison education but also generally). *Medium*. Retrieved at https://medium.com/@Dr_ESC/on-the-dangers-of-the-savior-complex-in-prison-education-but-also-genera lly-b22b48fc72b0. Accessed June 19, 2018.

Craig, C. D. and Sprang, G. (2010). Compassion satisfaction, compassion fatigue, and burnout in a national sample of trauma treatment therapists. *Anxiety, Stress, & Coping*, 23(3), 319–339.

Crowder, R. (2016). Mindfulness based feminist therapy: The intermingling edges of self-compassion and social justice. *Journal of Religion & Spirituality in Social Work: Social Thought*, 35(1–2), 24–40.

Denckla, C. A. *et al.* (2017). Self-compassion mediates the link between dependency and depressive symptomatology in college students. *Self and Identity: The Journal of the International Society for Self and Identity*, 16(4), 373–383.

Dev, V. *et al.* (2018). Does self-compassion mitigate the relationship between burnout and barriers to compassion? A cross-sectional quantitative study of 799 nurses. *International Journal of Nursing Studies*, 81, 81–88.

DeVeaux, M. (2013). The trauma of the incarceration experience. *Harvard Civil Rights-Civil Liberties Law Review*, 48(2), 257–277.

DiAngelo, R. (2011). White fragility. *The International Journal of Critical Pedagogy*, 3(3), 54–70.

Erlbaum, J. (2015, August 24). Confessions of a (former) white savior. *Thought Catalogue*. Retrieved at https://thoughtcatalog.com/janice-erlbaum/2015/08/confessions-of-a-white-savior/. Accessed June 14, 2018.

Figley, C. R. (2002). Compassion fatigue: Psychotherapists' chronic lack of self care. *Journal of Clinical Psychology*, 58(11), 1433–1441.

Keidel, G. C. (2002). Burnout and compassion fatigue among hospice caregivers. *American Journal of Hospice and Palliative Medicine*, 19(3), 200–205.

Kilgore, J. (2011). Bringing Freire behind the walls: The perils and pluses of critical pedagogy in prison education. *Radical Teacher*, 90(1), 57–66.

Kilgore, J. (2014, June 6). Repackaging mass incarceration. *CounterPunch*. Retrieved at www.counterpunch.org/2014/06/06/repackaging-mass-incarceration. Accessed June 19, 2018.

Killian, K. D. (2008). Helping till it hurts? A multimethod study of compassion fatigue, burnout, and self-care in clinicians working with trauma survivors. *Traumatology*, 14(2), 32–44.

Kisner, J. (2017, March 14). The politics of conspicuous displays of self-care. *New Yorker*. Retrieved at www.newyorker.com/culture/culture-desk/the-politics-of-selfcare. Accessed June 19, 2018.

Leary, M. R. *et al.* (2007). Self-Compassion and reactions to unpleasant self-relevant events: The implications of treating oneself kindly. *Journal of Personality and Social Psychology*, 92(5), 887–904.

Liem, M. and Kunst, M. (2013). Is there a recognizable post-incarceration syndrome among released 'lifers'? *International Journal of Law and Psychiatry*, 36(3–4), 333–337.

Litz, B. T. *et al.* (2009). Moral injury and moral repair in war veterans: A preliminary model and intervention strategy. *Clinical Psychology Review*, 29(8), 695–706.

Marshall, S. L. *et al.* (2015). Self-compassion protects against the negative effects of low self-esteem: A longitudinal study in a large adolescent sample. *Personality and Individual Differences*, 74, 116–121.

Neely, M. E. *et al.* (2009). Self-kindness when facing stress: The role of self-compassion, goal regulation, and support in college students' well-being. *Motivation and Emotion*, 33(1), 88–97.

Neff, K. (2003). Self-Compassion: An alternative conception of a healthy attitude toward oneself. *Self and Identity*, 2(2), 85–101.

Neff, K. (2018). Self-Compassion. Retrieved at www.self-compassion.org. Accessed June 19, 2018.

Neff, K., and Pommier, E. (2013). The relationship between self-compassion and other-focused concern among college undergraduates, community adults, and practicing meditators. *Self and Identity*, 12(2), 160–176.

Neff, K. *et al.* (2007). An examination of self-compassion in relation to positive psychological functioning and personality traits. *Journal of Research in Personality*, 41(4), 908–916.

Raes, F. (2010). Rumination and worry as mediators of the relationship between self-compassion and depression and anxiety. *Personality and Individual Differences*, 48(6), 757–761.

Richie, B. (2012). *Arrested justice: Black women, violence, and America's prison nation*. New York: NYU Press.

Scott, R. (2013). Distinguishing radical teaching from merely having intense experiences while teaching in prison. *Radical Teacher*, 95(1), 22–32.

Shay, J. (2014). Moral injury. *Psychoanalytic Psychology*, 31(2), 182–191.

Spinaris, C. G. *et al.* (2012). Posttraumatic stress disorder in United States corrections professionals: Prevalence and impact on health and functioning. *Desert Waters Correctional Outreach*, 1–32.

Thomas, Jim. (1995). The ironies of prison education. In H. S. Davidson (ed.), *Schooling in a "total institution": Critical perspectives on prison education*, pp. 25–41. Westport, CT: Bergin & Garvey.

Vigna, A. J. *et al.* (2017). Does self-compassion facilitate resilience to stigma? A school-based study of sexual and gender minority youth. *Mindfulness*, 9(3), 914–924.

Wang, X. *et al.* (2016). Self-Compassion decreases acceptance of own immoral behaviors. *Personality and Individual Differences*, 106, 329–333.

Wolff, N. and Shi, J. (2012). Childhood and adult trauma experiences of incarcerated persons and their relationship to adult behavioral health problems and treatment. *International Journal of Environmental Research and Public Health*, 9(5), 1908–1926.

9

BEYOND PROGRESS: INDIGENOUS SCHOLARS, RELATIONAL METHODOLOGIES, AND DECOLONIAL OPTIONS FOR THE PRISON CLASSROOM

Anna Plemons

> Research is about unanswered questions, but it also reveals our unquestioned answers.
>
> *Shawn Wilson,* Research Is Ceremony

Lori Maracle (1990) suggests that theory and story are dialectical parts of a whole which should not be separated, so I begin with my own story. I started teaching in the Arts in Corrections (AIC) Program at New Folsom Prison in 2009, a year before I returned to the university to work on a doctorate. Every story from that early experience had a relational root—there were relational threads that authorized AIC's existence inside a near-totalizing institution, relational threads that explained why Spoon Jackson decided to stay and be an incarcerated teaching artist at New Folsom despite opportunities to transfer to lower-level prisons, and there were also my own personal ties. I had agreed to start teaching at New Folsom after the Artist Facilitator positions, one of which was held by my dad, Jim Carlson, were cut from the state budget. The final fiscal death of AIC in 2009 coincided with his sixtieth birthday and I thought he should write a book about his twenty-five-year tenure teaching art inside. He had no intention of doing so but suggested instead that I come teach as a volunteer in the shell of what had once been a thriving prison arts program.[1]

Even without a theoretical frame through which to understand my early experiences, I understood that there was a relational reality to AIC that, in every way, explained how it came to be and why it survived as long as it did. But when I returned to the university I found myself at odds with the methodological options sanctioned by my institution, the models of research on prison education available in both scholarly and popular discourse, and the stories of actual incarcerated students I knew at New Folsom, many of whom were serving Life

Without the Possibility of Parole (LWOP) sentences. At that point, Kristin Arola introduced me to Shawn Wilson's (2008) Indigenous methodology for research and I began to see, through Wilson's framework, a model expansive and sensitive enough to account for something other than an immediate, economic value such as recidivism.

Before I progress further, I want to be clear that I come to Indigenous scholarship as an outsider and worry about the dangers of appropriation and misuse. I take seriously Arola and Arola's (2017) warning that

> even if our objective is to create in such a way as to open up new worlds of possibility in response to a confrontation with problems that we presently lack the resources to resolve, we still must be cautious that our employment of and engagement with the world do not unconsciously repeat and reinforce the world from which we are attempting to find lines of flight (p. 219).

I understand that Indigenous ways of knowing and ways of being have often been romanticized, tokenized, and/or stripped of the context of struggle against settler colonialism[2] to which many of the authors cited here speak. With that said, I also find myself among the "many non-Indigenous" scholars "seeking ways to understand the world without harming it" and find that there is a relational reality inherent in the prison classroom to which even non-Indigenous teacher-scholars must respond (Kovach, 2009, p. 11).

My intention in sharing how these scholars and texts have influenced my teaching and research is to suggest that theoretically grounded ways of valuing and evaluating prison education already exist that do not consider the individual as the primary unit of analysis and that such ways of knowing hold important possibilities for scholars interested in constructing decolonial paradigms for the prison classroom. Furthermore, I also see historical and material connections between histories of settler colonialism and the history of mass incarceration in the U.S., and those connections suggest some overlap in how both realities can be engaged. Beyond wanting to be clear about my positionality, I also want to acknowledge that an Indigenous methodology is not a general panacea for ending mass incarceration. That "deadly phenomenon," as Danial Karpowitz (2017) has pointed out, "can only be addressed by putting fewer people in prison and for less time; by making our economy less punitive; and by eliminating the stark racial disparities that mar all aspects of American inequality and especially criminal justice" (p. 25).

This chapter comes in four parts. First, I quickly argue that the conversation about prison teaching and research has, for the most part, made use of the individualistic, economic ideology of education-as-progress. Second, I point to a few Indigenous scholars whose work disrupts such an ideology. Third, I offer a methodological framework for prison teachers and scholars informed by the work of Margaret Kovach and Shawn Wilson. And lastly, I use a current AIC project as context for describing that methodology in action.

Something Other Than Progress

Writing in 1920, J. B. Bury (1920) claims that "the doctrine of Progress" is "the animating and controlling idea of western civilization" (p. vii). To the claim that the ideology of progress is central to Western ways of knowing and being, Walter Mignolo (2011) adds that the project of modernity has shape-shifted. Terms like *salvation* have been replaced with words like *development*, but the underlying ideology—that such processes are individualistic and teleological—remains. The broad strokes of Bury and Mignolo respectively find evidence in the specific history of prison education. From its inception at Cherry Hill, prison education has been rooted in narratives of salvation. Erica Meiners (2007) identifies the problematic ubiquity of such narratives and outlines their structural pattern: "I was born; I had problems; I made the wrong choices; I was apprehended by the police; I was incarcerated; I found God [or writing] and He [it] helped me. And … my life is now on a better track" (p. 139).

To be fair, many incarcerated students *do* find that the educational processes to which they commit themselves help them develop as people and/or prepare them for life after prison. What is problematic, however, is the way that trans-formational narratives are commodified and used as a primary tool for assessing the value and efficacy of prison education programs. This commodification of personal narrative fits within the neoliberal logic[3] that Wendy Brown (2015) suggests extends "a specific formulation of economic values, practices, and metrics to every dimension of human life" (p. 30). In her book, Brown lays out the collateral consequences of such a logic, including the "replacing of measures of educational quality with metrics oriented entirely to return on investment (ROI) and centered on what kind of job placement and income enhancement student investors may expect from any given institution" (p. 23). In the context of prison education, the persistent application of "economic values, practices and metrics" is troublesome in the ways that it often further commodifies and dehumanizes incarcerated people and works against the liberatory intentions of many educa-tional justice programs.

For example, citing reduced recidivism as a primary goal and/or evaluative tool of a program forecloses, among other things, the inclusion of students who will not parole. It also circumvents a critical conversation about the systemic factors that coalesce to create the revolving prison door through which many people repeatedly pass. Furthermore, as a measure of assessment, in the end, demonstra-tions of transformation are not as effective as those who traffic in them want to believe. If they were, Michelle Jones's invitation to study at Harvard would not have been overturned (Hager, 2017).

Considering the troubling connection between narratives of individual trans-formation and histories of systemic injustice, scholars and teachers working in the prison benefit from a wider menu of options for theoretically framing prison education research and pedagogy. Specifically, there is a need for methodological options that bring intention and practice into closer alignment. Ellen Cushman (2016) suggests that the disconnection between intention and practice hobbles the work of "emancipatory projects" which "fall short of their social justice goals because they critique a content or place of practice without revealing and altering their own structuring tenets" (p. 239). Not only do scholars often fail to identify a sedimented coloniality in the structures of study to which they consent, they can also be tone deaf to the ways that neoliberalism is naturalized in academic discourse. "Scholars who feel like victims of neoliberal hegemony may actually be working as its co-creators through the form and content of their academic arguments, their teaching, and their pursuit of recognition and reward" (Tomlinson and Lipsitz, 2013, p. 7). In sum, a failure to question the relationship between modernistic academic ideologies and educator complicity in their perpetuation significantly contributes to a chronic disconnection between decolonial intent and actual practice.

Specific to this chapter, a critique of the ideological primacy of the individual and the idea of progress in prison education opens up some space in which to consider other possible structural tenets or other ways of knowing and making meaning of what happens in the prison classroom. Mignolo (2011) suggests that engaging in processes of "decolonizing knowledge" is not a full-stop rejection of "Western epistemic contributions to the world" (p. 82) but rather a purposeful legitimization of "ways of knowing and sensing (feeling) that do not conform to the epistemology and aesthesis of the zero point"—ways of knowing that have otherwise been re-inscribed as "myth, legend, folklore, local knowledge, and the like" (p. 80). The work of Indigenous scholars, as described in the next section, offers a few such options.

Indigenous Scholars and Relational Methodologies

A host of Indigenous scholars discuss the principle of relationality,[4] being clear that the claim that all things are related is not a suggestion for how to create relationships but rather an ontological explanation of "how it is" (Cordova, 2007).[5] More specifically, Wilson (2008) suggests that "relationships do not merely shape reality, they are reality" (p. 7). Here he describes a world in which even non-Indigenous teachers and students exist, whether or not they understand or acknowledge it. Reasserting the claim that all things are related is particularly important in prison where relationality is abstracted both by physical separation (from family, from communities, from the land, from each other, etc.) and the myriad dehumanizing protocols that structure life inside for incarcerated people and prison staff alike. Wilson suggests that an attention to relationality ought to deeply inform choices about "research topic, methods of data collection, form of analysis and presentation of information" (p. 7). When research projects recognize their inherent relationality and are constructed in ways that are relationally accountable, then "research is a ceremony" whose purpose is the strengthening of relationships and/or the bridging of distance (p. 11). This idea—that the purpose of research is making relationships stronger and spanning distances—speaks directly to many of the motivations for education that students at New Folsom have articulated.

Many students at New Folsom pursue higher education, even in spite of life without parole (LWOP) status. They have a wide range of reasons for doing so, many of them relational. I am thinking here of one gentleman who completed his college degree as an example for his grandchildren. This student might never make it on to the tally sheets of college grads who successfully parole and work their way off the carcereal merry-go-round. Nevertheless, a multigenerational assessment of his educational experience could attend to the effects that his role as an educational patriarch played in the educational attainment in his grandchildren and/or the disruption of the cycle of justice involvement in his family. Such an assessment stretches the boundaries of time and broadens the definition of what counts as progress, challenging the value of short-term, individualistic assessments. It also highlights the relational threads that already exist between incarcerated students and the communities inside and outside the prison that see them as cultural assets. This type of complicated qualitative and quantitative undertaking would be cumbersome, but it would also provide a much richer understanding of the impact of higher education in prison (here I am thinking of the distinction between *big* and *thick* data in the work of Tricia Wang, 2013).

In her monograph *Indigenous Methodologies*, Margaret Kovach (2009) describes how she "utilized a methodology based upon an Indigenous research framework centered on Plains Cree knowledge" (p. 44). As a non-Indigenous scholar, my understanding of Indigenous ontology and epistemology is limited, and I cannot and would not claim that my own teaching and research practices are rooted in tribal epistemology. Nonetheless, the characteristics of Kovach's model resonate with what I know to be real in my experience teaching at New Folsom and how I know it to be such. For that reason, an interpretive methodology, aligned as closely as possible with Kovach's model, has helped make some space for the design of projects at New Folsom that pay attention to relationality. And such projects have allowed us to broaden both the calculus of what counts as progress and expands the roles available to incarcerated students beyond that of the individual recipient of knowledge or behavioral intervention.

I understand that historically "within an Indigenous research context, the result has been an attempt to weld Indigenous methods to existing bodies of Western knowledge, resulting in confused efforts and methodological floundering" (Kovach, 2009, p. 36). Indigenous philosophy has also been misrepresented through the idea that a "common set of beliefs" exists which "leads the philosopher astray in picking and choosing bits and pieces from the alien culture to satisfy the longing for a common theme" (Cordova, 2007, p. 59). When scholar-practitioners hailing from Western theoretical genealogies (like me) endeavor to see the possibilities for using Indigenous theory as an interpretive framework in the prison classroom, it is important to listening with and through the epistemologies that frame ways of knowing outside of Western schools of thought (Kovach, 2009; Powell, 2012). Attempting to understand foundational ideas on their own terms (I hope) disrupts the historical welding or ornamentation that Kovach warns against.

In Search of Decolonial Options: A Five-Part Relational Methodology for the Prison Classroom

In the call for decolonial methodologies, Mignolo and Cushman suggest that scholars move beyond simple inversions in the nexus of power and instead construct a range of options for doing decolonial work. What follows is one such option. It is not intended to be prescriptive nor does it claim to singularly disrupt the persistent and pervasive grip of neoliberalism on prison education. Rather, it suggests that theoretical and practical means for aligning decolonial intention and practice already exists. The framework is oriented to an audience of prison educators, administrators, and scholars. Taken together, the five areas (adapted from Kovach's model) ask prison teacher-scholars designing curriculum and assessments to deeply consider the interconnected relationships between: their teaching and/or research; the colonial legacies that inspired and sustain prison education; their personal motivations; the cultural assets and articulated needs of incarcerated students; and the connections incarcerated students have to communities outside the prison.

A Relational Methodological Framework for the Prison Classroom

Decolonial Intention and Ethic: the researcher is committed to examining how both individuals and groups have been affected by and complicit in colonial legacies. Furthermore, the researcher is committed to asking questions that challenge the Western knowledge systems that define what is real and how we know it to be such (Haas, 2012).

a   Researcher Preparation: the researcher is committed to exploring their own relationship to the research or project, finding and making sense of the memories and stories that inform their motivation for the work (Hampton, 1995).
b   Community Accountability: the research project responds to the articulated needs and/or desires of the community, evolves in response to community feedback, and is terminated when or if the community decides that the project is at odds with its health and sovereignty (Wilson, 2008).
c   Reciprocity/Community Benefit: the research project is designed in such a way that it respects participants as already valuable members of their respective communities and directly works to support community members in

those existing roles. Benefits to the community, made primarily by the community members themselves, are part of the clearly articulated outcomes of the research project (Wilson, 2008).

d   Knowledge Gathering/Meaning Making: the types of knowledge gathered through the project and the meanings that are constructed about that knowledge privilege the community as the unit of analysis (versus the individual), balances a need for data with a respect for participants' desire to protect sacred and/or private knowledge, and directly includes the community in the process of meaning making and subsequent distribution of knowledge (Kovach, 2009).

"Together We Can": Applying the Model

A second story: I first met Aaché when she enrolled in a rhetoric class I was teaching at the university. For her course project, she set out to create better tools for adults to talk with children who have an incarcerated parent. The first thing she found was *The Prison Alphabet* (Muhammad and Muntaquim, 2013), a coloring book for children that, in the authors' own words, was "created to serve as a conversation starter between adults who plan to talk about parental incarceration with affected children." But, despite what appeared to be good intentions, the book recirculates damaging stereotypes about who is in prison and presents an infantilizing picture of people who are incarcerated. I took the coloring book to Arts in Corrections (AIC) visual arts and creative writing classes at New Folsom. Some men thought it was sad, some were angered. I noticed that a child coloring in this book would only need four crayons: grey, brown, blue, and orange.

A month later, Aaché attended these same AIC classes and we worked together with AIC students to create an alternative to this coloring book— something less mired in negative, overdetermined messages about people of color, something more humanizing and connective. The AIC students involved in this project see the book they created, titled "Together We Can," as a tool for connecting with children who are important to them and as a chance to speak back to pervasive and damaging messages about who is in prison and how the public should understand the day-to-day experience of incarceration. They see that the book works to support them as they support the children in their respective families and appreciate that it gives them agency and due credit by citing them as authors on the front cover. Furthermore, the experience of coming inside and working with these students has led to additional opportunities for Aaché in her field of study.

Beyond happy anecdotes and photo ops, my experience participating in this project raises important questions about the often-fraught relationship between data-driven, evidence-based program models and dialectical, responsive classroom pedagogy. Since the framework outlined above was used in the development of the interactive drawing and writing journal, "Together We Can," a more in-depth discussion of the project provides as useful example in context. The story of how this project came to be reinforces the need for a wider range of available methodological options. For example, the ability to imagine "Together We Can" was predicated on understanding incarcerated students as already related to communities outside the prison where they are seen as cultural assets. And that idea—that incarcerated students have a direct contribution to make to communities outside the prison—is the foundation on which the project was constructed.

Decolonial Intention and Ethic

Angela Haas (2012) asks scholars to consider how the "effects and complicities of historical and contemporary colonialism influence research and educational institutions, theories, methodologies, methods, and scholarship" and play out in our "everyday embodied practices" (p. 191). Claiming that representations matter, this project set out to explicitly challenge negative commonplaces about incarcerated people that are readily available in popular discourse. Furthermore, the genesis of the project was Aaché's interest in critiquing and reconceptualizing what messages children receive about incarceration. In this way, the project addresses the community and individual effects of particular colonial legacies. By situating relationality as its epistemic foundation, the project also challenges Western knowledge systems for which the individual is the primary unit of analysis.

Researcher Preparation

Eber Hampton (1995) suggests that "memory comes before knowledge" and that researchers need to examine and make sense of the memories and stories that animate their interest in and motivation for their work (p. 48). When Aaché approached me about her course project, she already had a clear idea of why it was that she was personally interested in this project at this moment. I was also able to recall the story that was motivating my interest. As I have relayed elsewhere, my dad once told me about a student in a juggling class at San Quentin who said that learning to juggle had given him something he could teach his children in the Visiting Room. He said that crumpling up paper and teaching his sons to juggle had helped him feel like a father for the first time during his incarceration. That story, of the juggler I never met, deeply informs my interest in prison projects that pay attention to relationality.

As the project developed to include students in visual arts and creative writing groups at New Folsom, we also had to make space in the process for those participants to explore, through writing and group discussion, the stories that informed their desire to participate. Many were heart-wrenching. But there were also stories of fathers who could describe for the group the myriad strategies they were using to stay connected with their kids in a system that makes almost no provision for that connection.

Community Accountability

Shawn Wilson (2008) argues that "relational accountability requires me to form reciprocal and respectful relationships within the communities where I am conducting research" (p. 40). In order to make sure that the project responded to the articulated needs and desires of the community and evolved in response to community feedback, a multistage process was set up. First, we developed a lesson plan that would allow the visual arts and writing classes to interact with *The Prison Alphabet* and explore the specific ways that it reified negative messages about incarcerated people. Next, we generated some desired outcomes for our project and brainstormed possible themes. One month later, Aaché came to the prison to share the results of a focus group she had conducted with adults that discussed their feelings about growing up with an incarcerated parent.

Once enough time had passed and there were a variety of voices, we reopened the conversation about theme. The group decided on "Together We Can" because of its generative possibilities to help kids imagine ways, through writing and drawing, that they were still connected to their incarcerated adult (parent, grandparent, uncle/aunt, friend, etc.). After much negotiation, ten drawing/writing topics were chosen that support the theme, "Together We Can":

1. Teach Each Other
2. Build
3. Aspire
4. Figure It Out
5. Overcome
6. Play and Have Fun
7. Dream
8. Fly
9. Cry When We're Sad
10. Talk and Listen

In choosing the topics, the group worked to find a balance between explicit and implicit messages about family connection, self-esteem, educational attainment, modeling emotional openness, and other values they wanted to impart such as perseverance and resilience.

Reciprocity/Community Benefit

Wilson clearly articulates that respect and reciprocity ought to be foundational in the design of a project. As has already been discussed, the "Together We Can" project presumes that incarcerated people are already cultural assets in communities outside the prison and works to support and amplify them in that role by co-creating a tool they can use to strengthen their relationships with children through drawing and writing, either together in the Visiting Room or through correspondence. Because the project is co-authored with incarcerated writers and artists at New Folsom, and because participants choose to whom their copies of the book are distributed, the project structure also recognizes their vital role in making the book a reality and works to allow them as much autonomy as possible in how the book is circulated and used.

Knowledge Gathering/Meaning Making

After enough time has passed, we plan to collect quantitative and qualitative data about this project. We will work with the incarcerated participants to decide what data should be collected (e.g., rate of circulation, quality of engagement, family response, etc.). But what will not be required will be examples of the children's writings and drawings. That knowledge belongs to the families and since the project does not require individual narratives of transformation, there are no implicit pressures for participants to parade their children's work before granters or administrators with whom participants have no relationship or reason to expect that those representations would be handled with care. This may seem like a small point, but it is important for two reasons. First, it protects what little privacy incarcerated students are able to construct for themselves. Second, it offers a model for assessment that responds respectfully—but still with data—to the tension between a critical, responsive pedagogy and the neoliberal calculus which still, at least in part, sanctions educational justice programs in prisons.

Circling Back

I hope that this chapter is read by people teaching in prisons and that it gives them permission to interrogate the "structural tenets" (to use Cushman's words) that undergird the enterprise of prison education and to carefully find ways of knowing and ways of being that are more respectful, reciprocal, and relational. Instead of accepting a Western methodology of reductionism and its "tendency to divide, subdivide, and subdivide again in order to find the constituents of an entity or event" (Deloria, 1999, p. 129), I hope that prison educators can find ways to broaden and increase their understanding of and support for the relationships that are already part of the prison classroom and invite all of those relations to the table. If I am being honest, what I really hope is that in my lifetime we will see a seismic shift away from the neoliberal ideology that has authorized the unprecedented expansion of the carceral state. That project requires a wider web of relations than has been discussed here. But while we wait and work towards those loftier goals, I hope that we can unapologetically develop methodologies for the prison classroom that measure something other than individual progress.

Notes

1 Since then I have also taught credit-bearing college-level writing courses to incarcerated students and see that the model outlined in this chapter is applicable to credit-bearing contexts.
2 For the purposes of this chapter, *settler colonialism* is understood as a form of colonialism marked by the replacement of indigenous populations with a new society made up of settlers (Tuck and Yang, 2012).
3 For the purposes of this chapter, the term *neoliberal* refers to economic and social policies, including privatization, deregulation, etc., that generally encourage an increase in the role of the private sector in the economy and economically driven decision-making processes in society (Brown, 2015).
4 Arola, 2017; Cordova, 2007; Deloria, 1999; Haas, 2012; Hampton, 1995; King et al., 2015; Maracle, 1990; Mihesuah and Wilson, 2004; Smith, 2012; Wilson, 2008.
5 Margaret Kovach (2009) is clear to point out that "Indigenous methodologies are not solely relational, but involve other characteristics that create a distinctive methodological approach. These traits include the tribal epistemology at the heart of this approach and a decolonizing aim, both of which are born of a unique relationship with Indigenous lands" (p. 35).

References

Arola, K. and Arola, A. (2017). An ethics of assemblage: Creative repetition and the "Electric Pow Wow." In K. Yancey and S. McElroy (eds.), *Assembling composition*, pp. 204–221. Logan, UT: Studies in Writing and Rhetoric.

Brown, W. (2015). *Undoing the demos: Neoliberalism's stealth revolution*. Brooklyn, NY: Zone Books.

Bury, J. B. (1920). *The idea of progress: An inquiry into its origin and growth*. London: Dover Publications.

Cordova, V. F. (2007). *How it is: The Native American philosophy of V. F. Cordova*. Edited by K. D. Moore *et al.* Tuscon, AZ: University of Arizona Press.

Cushman, E. (2016). Translingual and decolonial approaches to meaning making. *College English*, 78(3), 234–242.

Deloria, Jr., V. (1999). *The Vine Deloria, Jr., reader*. Edited by B. Deloria *et al.* Golden, CO: Fulcrum Publishing.

Haas, A. (2012). Race, rhetoric, and technology: A case study of decolonial technical communication theory, methodology, and pedagogy. *Journal of Business and Technical Communication*, 26, 277–310.

Hager, E. (2017, September 13). From prison to Ph.D.: The redemption and rejection of Michelle Jones. *New York Times*.

Hampton, E. (1995). Memory comes before knowledge: Research may improve if researchers remember their motives. *Canadian Journal of Native Education*, 21, 46–54.

Karpowitz, D. (2017). *College in prison: Reading in an age of mass incarceration*. New Brunswick, NJ: Rutgers University Press.

King, L. *et al.* (eds.) (2015). *Survivance, sovereignty, and story: Teaching American Indian rhetorics*. Logan, UT: Utah State University Press.

Kovach, M. (2009). *Indigenous methodologies: Characteristics, conversations, and contexts*. Toronto, Canada: University of Toronto Press.

Maracle, L. (1990). *Oratory: Coming to theory*. North Vancouver, BC: Gallerie Publications.

Meiners, E. (2007). *Right to be hostile: Schools, prisons, and the making of public enemies*. New York, NY: Routledge.

Mignolo, W. (2011). *The darker side of western modernity: Global futures, decolonial options.* Durham, NC: Duke University Press.

Mihesuah, D. and Wilson, A. (eds.) (2004). *Indigenizing the academy: Transforming scholarship and empowering communities.* Lincoln, NE: University of Nebraska Press.

Muhammad, B. and Muntaquim, M. (2013). *The prison alphabet: An educational coloring book for children of incarcerated parents.* Atlanta, GA: Goldest Karat Publishing.

Powell, M. (2012). 2012 CCCC Chair's address: Stories take place: A performance in one act. *College Composition and Communication,* 64(2), 383–406.

Smith, L. T. (2012). *Decolonizing methodologies.* 2nd ed. New York: Zed Books.

Tomlinson, B. and Lipsitz, G. (2013). American studies as accompaniment. *American Quarterly,* 65(1), 1–30.

Tuck, E. and Yang, K. (2012). Decolonization is not a metaphor. *Decolonization: Indigeneity, Education & Society,* 1(1), 1–40.

Wang, T. (2013, May 13). Big data needs thick data. *Ethnography Matters.*

Wilson, S. (2008). *Research is ceremony.* Halifax, Canada: Fernwood Publishing.

10

NO ONE EVER ASKED ME: EMBRACING EMBODIED PEDAGOGY IN THE CREATIVE WRITING CLASSROOM

Sarah Shotland

The first creative writing course I taught at the Allegheny County Jail was with a group of fifteen women. My fellow teacher Adrienne and I were new to teaching, and often we would rely on very simple fill-in-the-blank prompts that involved students completing a sentence. Three weeks into the course, we asked students to complete the sentence "No one ever asked me ..." and then continue writing for fifteen minutes.

Every person in the room, including Adrienne and myself, completed the sentence with some version of:

> No one ever asked me if I wanted to have sex.
> No one ever asked me if I liked sex.
> No one ever asked me if I was interested in sex with men.
> No one ever asked me if I was a virgin.
> No one ever asked me if I was ready for sex.
> No one ever asked me if I was tired of sex.
> No one ever asked me if sex hurt.

When I began teaching creative writing in jails and prisons, I hadn't planned on writing about and responding to writing about sexual assault and rape. I had anticipated a dozen different disasters, none of which had to do with the body.

★★★

That class was almost ten years ago, and since then, I've taught hundreds of incarcerated and formerly incarcerated writers in jails, prisons, and rehab centers in Pittsburgh through a program I co-founded with Dr. Sheryl St. Germain called

Words Without Walls. Our creative writing courses are taught by university professors and graduate students, but they aren't credit-bearing, and they usually aren't part of a comprehensive curriculum. One of the places we work is in a county jail, and our students there are much more transient than the writers we work with in prison classrooms.

At the Allegheny County Jail, we have students who take a single class, and we also have students who take courses each semester that they're able, sometimes for years-long stretches. We've had to find ways to build a curriculum that's always doing double-duty: If a student comes once, they leave with something meaningful and complete; if they come back year after year, the material hasn't become redundant. This is one of the most crucial differences in designing curriculum in the field of corrections: It's always having to do more than you think it will be able to. It has to meet the needs of a variety of students, who have a variety of motivations and ambitions for their writings, and it has to deliver writing instruction that constantly balances compassion with critique; rigor with encouragement; and craft with content. And unlike university campus classrooms, it relies solely on the internal motivations and intrinsic value of the writing itself. There are no grades in our program. There are no degrees. There are no fellowships or faculty advisors, and yet, what I've learned teaching without those things has dramatically impacted the way I teach when I do have them. My creative writing pedagogy in spaces on and off campus has been profoundly impacted by my work in jails and prisons.

From that very first class, I quickly realized that the way we'd been teaching creative writing in the academy was missing something: it was missing a body. In the subsequent years, I've been searching for and developing an embodied pedagogy for creative writing classrooms. By embodied pedagogy, I mean acknowledging that writing is a physical practice; that the craft of creative writing can be improved by a writer's development of that physical practice; and that classroom critiques should embrace a compassionate, nonviolent strategy that does not attempt to erase the writer's body.

★★★

I shouldn't have been surprised by the results of the *no one-ever-asked-me* writing exercise, since almost 90 percent of women who are incarcerated have experienced sexual violence in their lives (Swavola et al., 2016) Many women avoid processing the trauma of their lives by keeping busy. The kids, the carpool, punching in and out, the laundry, the groceries, the bills are due, the cat is sick, the roof is leaking, punching in and out again. It is not until there are no tasks or crises or blaring TVs or crying babies that women begin to confront the trauma that has stowed itself away in the knees and knuckles, hip bones and elbows. A social worker told me that trauma often surfaces for women in things like a yoga class or when they're trying to take a nap or a bath—places that are still and quiet. In places where people start to take deeper breaths.

Places like creative writing classrooms.

And yet. Even with my training and understanding of statistics, I hadn't explicitly considered that the women I'd be writing with were likely to have experienced profound trauma, much of it inflicted on their bodies.

★★★

The kinds of creative writing workshops I participated in as both an undergraduate and graduate student are incredibly common. The dominant model to "teach" creative writing comes from the University of Iowa's storied Iowa Writers Workshop, a process where a writer submits a story or poem to the class in advance, giving everyone time to read the work before returning to class the following week. During class, the writer sits on one side of the room, usually separated from the rest of the students. For the duration of class time, the writer remains silent, listening in on a conversation about the text. To minimize the possibility that someone might take a criticism personally, no one uses the writer's name, instead simply referring to "the writer" as though this person is a stranger rather than a dear friend who is sitting in plain sight.

These conversations attempt to centralize craft concerns. Is the narrative voice carrying the precise amount of authority required? Is the setting vivid and evocative without devolving into needless description? Is the plot sufficiently engaging without being gimmicky, or worse, fun? My favorite: Are the characters consistent? Do I believe the choices they're making? What the story is about (or About) is irrelevant, because the notion is that no matter what you write about, if you write about it well, it is a success. *How* the story is written is privileged above all else; to waste time talking about the *what* of the story, or even worse the *who* of the writer, is generally dismissed as insignificant. There is a privilege given to an imagined objectivity of critique if these things aren't foregrounded in the discussion of the work.

Of course, as this model rose to prominence, the number of readers interested in literary fiction has plummeted and the vast majority of Americans cannot name a living poet. Success! We've created a model so dysfunctional that we've rendered ourselves almost entirely obsolete and irrelevant.

When I was participating in these workshops as a student, they seemed awkward and occasionally silly, but I was eager to be part of the creative writing tribe. I wanted acceptance into these rituals, and slowly I became accustomed to them, not noticing how disembodied and bizarre they could be, holding my breath as I took my turn to listen in on the discussion of my work.

★★★

The way people notice one another in a jail is different than the way we notice one another on the street. Most of the people in a jail or prison are wearing a uniform—some version of a bland set of scrubs or utility clothing. Whether watcher or watched, there is a set of visual cues alerting everyone to the position of power that a body occupies. But teachers from the outside do not wear uniforms, and so I was, even in the most superficial sense, noticeable as free. One of the first lessons I learned teaching in a jail was that my body was a blinking neon sign: *open, open.*

There are also strict boundaries drawn in this physical space. At Allegheny County Jail, there are thick pieces of red tape running through all the corridors to signify where employees walk versus where the incarcerated walk. In my classroom, the same tape marks a space surrounding the desk and printer: Teachers Only.

I began to think about my body more once I taught inside a jail, how it functioned as a disguise and an invitation. In class, I was constantly aware of each twitch of my leg, each flick of a finger; how everyone could smell that my shampoo was scented with gardenia, that I had a slight sunburn, shiny with aloe; that my polish was chipped. Somehow, these details began to matter more, to signify some meaning that in the outside world I could forget about. I became hyper-aware of my own body and its positionality in the jail, along with the bodies of all the men and women who I wrote with in these spaces.

Being aware of these bodies and their relationship to one another made using the workshop model in jail problematic and absurd. My goal in facilitating a writing practice was not, after all, to turn people away from writing, or to turn them away from one another. In this community, meaning is discovered through making. Clarity and specificity require naming things; the events of the narrative, the specific contradictions of the characters involved matters. The *what happened* and *to whom* are more central questions than the *how it was written*. Most important is the underlying *why* of a story or poem—why was it breathed into the world? Why does it need to be read? Why should I care to pick it up and rip it out of its neat binding, so that it can hang above my desk or bed or bathroom mirror? The *why* of the piece is almost always inextricably linked to the *who* of the writer.

Even if I had wanted to try workshops with my students at the jail, it would have been impossible. A workshop requires a stable and consistent group of writers who work on a very tight and regimented schedule. People must submit work to the group ahead of time, and they must know who should receive copies. In my courses, these seemingly simple constraints were huge challenges to overcome, and based on the success rate of the Workshop model, I was unwilling to spend my time and energy trying to recreate the dysfunctional method in a new class, already engorged with its own specific dysfunctional systems.

In my classes at the jail, I began to experiment with ways of centering the writer so that they might clarify their work (rather than justify or defend), and so that they might have the opportunity to "write out loud," finding meaning in the process of discussing stories and poems. After all, for most of my students there, class time was the *only* time each week that there was an opportunity to do the intellectual work of unpacking an idea or complicating a question. Dialogue became critical to improving the creative work that students determined was ready to be revised and turned from private writing into public writing. In these first courses, I began to question my lesson plans and formal training, choosing instead to search for an embodied pedagogy that would respect the body of the writer so that the writer could create a body of work.

Dance theorist Liz Lerman's book *Critical Response Process* has been immensely helpful in shaping my practice, which made perfect sense when I began understanding writing as a physical practice closer to dance than an intellectual practice like philosophy. Lerman's approach to critical feedback involves a four-step process: statements of meaning; artist as questioner; neutral questions from audience; and opinions (Lerman and Borstel, 2003). Each of these steps is facilitated by a moderator, and the artist can opt out of opinions, based on their intentions for the work. While I haven't used Lerman's methods precisely, they serve as a template that I can add to or revise based on the time constraints, space constraints, and students in any given course.

Instead of the readers asking questions of the text to each other while the muted writer listens, in our workshops readers ask the writer questions. I grant myself the right to reject any question, and the writer, too, gets the authority to refuse answering any question they do not want to talk through publicly. This process of formulating questions requires a deep engagement with the text, a critical response from readers, and intent listening from the writer. It requires the writer to reengage with their own text and allows them to hear and see it with new perspective. If the goal of the traditional workshop is to make the work self-evident to the writer, I would argue this model achieves the same ends more efficiently and compassionately, without reinforcing the erasure of the writer; an erasure that in a prison system would be an inexcusable redundancy.

It's important to note that the craft of writing isn't ignored when the writer is centralized. Quite the opposite. Craft and content are intertwined, and it is a disservice to students in the academy that we so often divorce them from one another. Without a rigorous examination of the content of the piece, it is almost impossible to know what craft choices will best illuminate meaning and sharpen the story. Without acknowledging the writer and their specific concerns, intentions, and limitations, suggesting craft-based "fixes" are clumsy and often random. I realized how important this was for my students on campus, too, and I've fully incorporated an embodied workshop method in all my classrooms.

One of the most important advantages of an embodied workshop is its efficiency. Just like class is the only time for discussing creative work, it was often the only time for writing as well. This varies from group to group, but I've found the most important part of the creative writing class is the *writing*. This is different from most university classrooms, where I can safely assign writing outside class time, using in-class time for discussion and critique. This makes the efficiency of the workshop doubly important. If there is a detail in the work that needs clarification, it doesn't make any sense to waste precious minutes puzzling toge-ther textual details or guessing at answers that can't be known. We need to ask the writer simply and directly what they want. We need to get to the point so that we can get to the writing. We need to acknowledge that the writer is in the room, give the writer agency to direct the conversation, and allow them to respond to our questions rather than simply listen to them. This opens new pos-sibilities for creative work while allowing more time for that work to be written.

***

Prison is punctuated by buzzers sounding and doors slamming and keys jan-gling and TVs blaring. Bodies are constantly being miscounted and made to shuffle somewhere different. It is difficult to concentrate. People are uncomfor-table in shoes that have been handed down in imprecise sizes, in underwear that is government issued. It is too cold and it is too hot, the water doesn't always work, it smells. People don't have their medications, or they're now, suddenly on medication; nicotine is scarce and precious. I remember leaving the jail in my first several weeks realizing how thirsty I was from just a few hours inside because of the lack of water fountains. There aren't real mirrors in jail and prison, and the women in my courses often told me that they were also preoccupied with how bad they imagined they looked and the inability to confirm their own suspicions with precision. Incarcerated life is full of distraction and interruption, a toxic combination for writers, even the ones who gathered each week in my class-room, so accustomed to dealing with it.

I quickly realized that these obstacles made it difficult to foster the stillness and quiet that most people need to create and sustain a meaningful writing practice. I began to see our circle of desks as a shield to neutralize the noise pollution we were always experiencing. I also began to see the need for an extended dedica-tion to what many educators refer to as the anticipatory set in a lesson plan. I needed the first part of class to drastically change the tone and tenor of the environment, even though I understood I could never fully divorce our class-room from the building it was situated within. And yet most art requires a sus-pension of disbelief. So, too, would our classroom.

I did things like fold individualized writing prompts into sealed envelopes so that people had to do something physical to discover the prompt. Even a small act like that required the writer to consider the prompt as a physical invitation for a few seconds. Anything to slow down and create a space that separated this classroom from the corridor right outside. I would leave instructions on desks that included things like: *I'm requesting that you remain as quiet as possible for the first ten minutes of class today so that we can write undistracted before we begin our discussion.* It was unnatural for me at first, because I was accustomed to starting my classes on a high note—previously, I'd always thought of the first moments of class as the time that I would be harnessing the energy of the students in a classroom, making a big splash, proving that my enthusiasm was enough to propel us forward. But teaching at a jail required me to find the power in silence, and it required me to find the ways that I could lead with a whisper. As Anne Dalke, a contributor to this volume, explores extensively in her essay, time became so much more apparent to me as a teacher in a jail. There was too much time in all the wrong places, and I had to be greedy with each minute in the classroom in order to press all the components of a writing practice into a single block of class time. Those first few minutes couldn't be wasted.

In jails and prisons, I find ways to make my writing classes more like a visual arts studio than the traditional collegiate writing workshop. I have taken that technique back with me to campus, giving my students more time in-class, or in-studio writing, an approach I have found to produce some of the most stimulating and productive uses of our time together.

★★★

Though it was important to get quiet in the classroom, once it was accomplished, things like the *no one-ever-asked-me* prompt started happening. For the women who were so accustomed to the chaos of noise and distraction and drama and crisis, entering a quiet space resulted in tears and revelations that they often said they'd never shared before.

This is different than any creative writing classroom I've experienced at a university. It would be dishonest to say that the classroom in the jail can exactly replicate the creative writing classes I teach on campus for all sorts of reasons, but one that I've realized is the trauma that so often surfaces through the physical practice of writing. University students have generally been cultured to resist emotional displays. They are familiar with the boundaries that we adhere to in professional and academic life. English professors are fond of quoting Hemingway's famous "writing is easy, just sit in front of the typewriter and bleed," or Robert Frost's "no tears for the writer, no tears for the reader," but all that work is to be done in private. By the time we get to the classroom and the public critique, we expect our writers to emotionally detach.

This detachment isn't necessarily cruel in an on-campus setting—there are plenty of good reasons for it—but it's a privilege that is impossible to re-create in a prison classroom. If my goal is to facilitate a meaningful writing practice for my students, they must be able to reflect on their pasts and confront complicated truths about themselves, their loved ones, and the society we share. They must do a lot of personal writing before they're able to move towards a public writing practice, and because I've established the classroom as a writing *studio*, both private and public writing will happen in the space. In a jail or prison, I must do many things at once: create a space "private" enough to write personal work that doesn't need to be made public, and to write it in the presence of other people; cultivate a community which can responsibly hold the weight of hearing and sharing that private work; and foster an environment where people can also take the necessary steps to transform that private writing into public work. We're moving through the entire creative process in a single space, which requires risks, mistakes, failure, encouragement, self-doubt, discovery, and, yes, tears.

I'm fascinated by writing with other people because our bodies twist and contort when we write. Some people like to lay their heads down near their paper; others curl in on themselves becoming beetles with pencils; some people like to write on the floor, or to stretch their legs onto a second chair. Some people stare into space for long periods of times. We shake our hands out as they cramp. We sigh. We tap our pencils and our toes. We close our eyes, hum, nod our heads. I love the deep sigh of satisfaction that comes when a poem finds its final image. So often, writers do this physical work alone, as I am while writing this essay; but there is an added dimension of physicality that comes when a piece is created in a shared writing space. We not only confront our own physical practice, but we have to navigate the group's physical presence. Writing in groups has transformed my artistic practice. For ten years, I have been writing in circles with people who are crying as they scratch out the first draft. There is snot in the notebooks we write in. People sometimes need to pace, or even leave the room for short breaks. Sometimes I see someone reach out and grab the hand of the woman beside them as she writes. This physical demonstration of emotional investment from my students has demanded that I put in the same effort, that I mine the same depths to prove I am fit to teach them.

These factors complicate my classroom considerations in ways I never have to navigate at the university, where I can assume that all writing brought to the classroom is public. While there are many strategies I've brought back to the university from the prison, the invitation to share private writing isn't one of them. I make clear in my on-campus classrooms that students are expected to have made a choice *before* coming to class about the public nature of a creative piece. It's one of the few things that's drastically different between my inside and outside classrooms.

This has meant that I have become more explicit about my expectations for students in both settings. I discuss the creative process and the difference between public and private writing early and often. Before I taught in jails, I took for granted that students understood their own artistic practices and that they could identify which of their works were ready for an audience. I've realized that most students don't, no matter where I encounter them. Because of this, I've added instructional input about the creative process, borrowing heavily from the visual and performing arts, whose disciplines are much more transparent about the process by which work is created. Sadly, many writers, even in the academy, still perpetuate the myth that good writing happens through a mystical summoning of genius. It's much closer to the way a play is created: tedious, nightly rehearsals that slowly stagger towards an inevitable opening night. Dress rehearsal, like a rough draft, might be a disaster, but that does not give anyone permission to quit.

The first time a composer sits at the piano, she does not produce a polished hit single. Using these interdisciplinary metaphors (and strategies) helps students to see themselves as artists moving through a process rather than thinkers whose ideas tumble onto blank pages, fully formed and brilliant.

The arts are often relegated to a second-class status in academia, perhaps in part because of the disembodied intellect that's celebrated there. In an effort to be seen as legitimate within the academy, creative writers have embraced strategies that take us farther away from an artistic practice and more towards an artistic theory. There is no crying in academia.

We should embrace the emotional response of writers in the process of creative writing because it creates better art. Emotionally constipated poems are not generally published. And when they are, they are quickly forgotten. Stories that avoid the true heart of the matter are overlooked by editors and publishers because they lack resonance. Writers must accept we are working through an emotional, untidy process that might result in unpretty, unpublishable writing. Honoring those ugly, unsharable drafts is an important part of teaching *process* rather than product, and we have the opportunity to do it in classrooms, in jail or on campus. A draft can be perfect even if it is unpublishable, simply for its having been made, and when a student has the agency to keep a draft private, they're able to exercise some personal power over their creative practice. That's an important part of building an artistic identity and claiming artistic agency. For some professors, it's going to be uncomfortable to make that transition from a classroom where the public nature of the work is taken for granted, but the rewards for sitting in that discomfort and remembering we, too, have tear ducts are powerful and profound.

★★★

When I listen to educators and activists talk about building community, I almost always think about that first group of women, that simple writing exercise that immediately bonded us as sisters. It's not the sort of thing you can build into an icebreaker. No one's going to play get-to-know-you rape bingo, or introduce themselves with their first name and an adjective that describes their first sexual assault. And it may be the kind of experience that creative writing is uniquely situated to facilitate as long as people understand that their hands are doing the writing, not their heads. Because trauma lives in the body, it must come out through the body. Our hands holding a pen are as good a tool as any to press out and massage those traumas from our muscles and blood and teeth.

When we shared our *no one-ever-asked-me*'s with each other, we not only made ourselves vulnerable, but we also saw our own experiences mirrored back at us through someone else's voice and body. There wasn't just a support system in that moment, there was also the realization of a *pattern*. Perhaps it wasn't a coincidence that we had all had the same experience and all wound up in the same place, at the same time, even if contextually different. Writing provides a way to identify patterns between people and in our own lives. It also creates a physical archive of a life. Ink is evidence.

The value of evidence, of accountability, of patterns, was something that I had given lip service to in university classrooms, but that first class at the Allegheny County Jail taught me just how central those functions are for writers. If writers want to remain relevant inside the academy and out, we have to acknowledge the many purposes of sharing stories. One of those is the ability for language to communicate the experience of having a body. We don't diminish ourselves as scholars or artists when we acknowledge that in *all* of our classrooms through an embodied pedagogy; in fact, when we ignore it, we do a disservice to all our students, no matter where they write.

References

Lerman, L. and Borstel, J. (2003). *Liz Lerman's critical response process*. Minneapolis, MN: Dance Exchange.

Swavola, E. *et al.* (2016). *Overlooked: Women and jails in an era of reform*. New York: Vera Institute of Justice.

11

"GO HARD": BRINGING PRIVILEGE-INDUSTRY PEDAGOGIES INTO A COLLEGE WRITING CLASSROOM IN PRISON

Stacy Bell McQuaide

The Privilege Industry versus the Punishment Industry

I am a permanent faculty member in a selective liberal arts college with a side hustle in a post-secondary degree program in prison. Moving back and forth between the *privilege industry* and the *punishment industry* fills me with dis-ease, and compels me to articulate the salient differences between teaching writing in these two contexts. I have written this chapter as a process of identifying the first-year writing "best practices" that are specific to the prison classroom.

When I refer to the *privilege-industry* classroom, I imagine a four-year liberal arts or pre-professional program, public or private, where the majority of students have matriculated within a year or two after high school. I do not suggest that all students enrolled in such programs are equally *privileged*. Rather, I argue that the goals of the curriculum and the instruction that takes place are designed to propel students *towards privilege*. Writing courses in these programs are designed to help students develop "academic" reading, writing, and researching skills, preparing them for professional careers in entrepreneurship, leadership, management, and development. The prison classroom is situated within the *punishment industry*, which discourages agency and critical reflection. Prisoners are not expected to lead; they are expected to obey. Introducing the post-secondary privilege-industry goals and values into the prison has risks. Those of us acculturated to the norms of the privilege industry must not only bring careful scrutiny to bear on *why* we teach, but especially on *what* and *how* we teach in prison.

The Privilege Industry

Higher education is a privilege industry. Colleges and universities are status factories, where privilege and opportunity are reproduced. They select up. If we do not start from this premise then nothing else we say about pedagogy matters, because once we leave our free-world campuses and enter prison, no matter what we do, we can reproduce very little privilege. A common ethos, particularly in traditional institutions, is to argue for "inclusivity" while celebrating exclusivity—or selectivity—in admissions. Selective admissions make an institution special. There is a problematic irony to these conflicting goals. Power is camouflaged. Traditional college students, treated as paying customers, have access to multiple resources for academic success and emotional and physical well-being.

Privilege-industry educational programs endow students with the credentials they need to enter the professions, or to seek forms of employment allowing upward mobility. The "liberal arts" promises to teach an individual to lead an examined life. Current writing pedagogy complements these goals by inviting "novice" writers to decode the "rhetorical situation" with awareness of how these skills "transfer" across academic contexts (see Nowacek, 2011, and Yancey et al., 2014). First-year writing students acquire skills and "content knowledge" that enable them to "enter the conversation" with experts (see Graff et al., 2016) in the "Burkean parlor" (see Lunsford, 1991). Assignments are tailored to students' expectations and aspirations: emails, cover letters, critical and literary analysis, personal narrative, research writing within a discipline, grant writing, blogging, project design. Students' writing reflects their careerist inclinations and their professors' commitment to the intrinsic value of a broad education across the disciplines.

The Punishment Industry

Those of us who teach in the privilege industry bring our privilege with us into prison: we wear our privilege in our good shoes and serviceable coats, we speak it in our disciplinary jargon, we carry it in our clear plastic bags filled with expensive pens. I sometimes show my privilege in a slight scowl when an officer yells at my students.[1] Each of us makes a choice about how we present ourselves inside. We may try to "soften" the distinction between ourselves and our students, but they want us to be professionals, so we act the part. They deserve nothing less. Pretending to be anything else seems disingenuous, so we walk a fine line between being our authentic outside selves and living, breathing reminders of what our students cannot have.

Like an elite college, prison is a status factory, but rather than selecting upward it selects downward. Incarceration reflects, in many cases, limited life chances, and it confers another layer of stigma onto the already stigmatized. The incarcerated have experienced trauma and poverty disproportionately to those in the free world; 86 percent of women in prison have experienced some form of abuse prior to incarceration (see www.sentencingproject.org). Prisoners can seek little to no relief for their personal troubles. Power is explicit in prison's primary functions of incapacitation, deterrence, and retribution. Panoptic discourse prevails. Prisoners have made "bad choices" and have "failed" to exercise control; prison with its various privations purports to teach the incarcerated "pro-social" exercise of agency and self-control. Conflicting ideologies and goals are apparent: How can an individual inside a total institution, from whom all apparent forms of agency have been removed, exercise agency in "pro-social" ways? Can a space that punishes also educate? Self-awareness of our roles within this system, as well as pedagogical awareness, are equally important. Can we adapt writing assignments and practices to the prison classroom in a way that both recognizes the empowering function of writing and meets curricular goals?

It could be argued that writing teachers do reproduce privilege for the incarcerated students by guiding them through the process of developing important communication skills. My students report that they are seen by other prisoners as leaders and role models; several of them are teachers' aides in the GED program. Some even have co-teacher roles, an increase in status which can be seen as a form of privilege. I remain concerned about this form of cost-shifting inside prison, and the ways in which education and status can make these individuals targets for exploitation. At the end of the day, Foucault was right: the state controls the bodies and has little concern for the minds. A well-behaved body that can perform an essential role is a resource. Students in college-in-prison may occupy a liminal space where they embrace the "liberating" elements of education while at the same time struggling to protect themselves from the resentment of their peers and exploitation by the administration. They navigate structural obstacles in the form of scarce material resources, limited movement to and from the classroom, theft of unsecured personal belongings, and confiscation of coursework through random "shakedowns." Their lived experiences are in stark contrast to those of most of our free-world students.

Privilege is reproduced when any student acquires skills to achieve upward mobility. In theory, incarcerated students may use their writing skills to achieve upward mobility, if they are released from prison and obtain jobs where writing skills are a resource. What about students who, having entered the justice system at a young age and bypassed conventional education, struggle to acquire the performative literacy required in the workplace? What about students at the end of long sentences, autodidacts with considerable wisdom and knowledge but little or no formal acculturation to the post-secondary classroom? What about older students who may encounter, upon release, workforce age discrimination? What about students serving life without parole? In the punishment industry, where inequality is reproduced, students may pursue education simply for education's sake. They may or may not anticipate a release date; they may or may not have a supportive community to return to in the "free" world; they may or may not anticipate "doing" anything with their college education beyond appreciating it.

All of these students are equally entitled to higher education, and they bring an array of competencies and aspirations to the classroom. Traditional *privilege-industry* educational paradigms cannot anticipate every need in the carceral writing classroom. I suggest, therefore, that writing teachers in college-in-prison programs incorporate these strategies into their course planning: *negotiation* of text selection and assignment design with attention to process, allotted time for *one-on-one consultation* and *multiple opportunities for revision*, and *flexibility* in classroom structure and participation.

Negotiation

During a one-on-one conversation, J. explains how she was brainstorming a letter to the warden.

"My thesis needs to be clear and brief," she says, "and I made sure it appears at the beginning."

"That's a great observation," I reply, "because it's hard to predict how much he'll read, so you need to make your point up front." She nods. We roll our eyes at the irony of "letter to warden" as genre.

Another student, J. C., observes, "Prison is no place to be an activist, but that doesn't mean our education doesn't give us confidence and earn us respect." Effective writing skills bestow incarcerated students with important forms of agency, perhaps the most relevant of which is social capital. Developing critical reading and writing skills enables an individual to critique, argue, and advocate more effectively, often on behalf of others. Even in knowing the limits of the rhetorical situation—subverting it—there is agency. There is power. J. C. reminds us how agency and power can be dangerous for prisoners.

Novice writers learn to ask, *What kind of writing is this? Who is it for? What should it do?* A genre is a category governed by conventions that tell the writer how to write and the reader how to read. The rhetorical situation is the context in which any writing act takes place. A prison writing course should investigate the *rhetorical situation* and employ "academic genres" and "prison genres." J. demonstrated understanding of how and why genre matters when she drafted her letter to the warden. She considered how a person with significantly higher status and power, whose time is limited, would read her letter. She anticipated that having read many "inmate complaints," he would read hers if she could make it stand out.

Her classmate J. C. sees the value in learning to write like a "disciplinary expert," even if her current audience is limited to instructor and classmates. Other students will design "inmate to inmate" mentoring programs, and, like J., they will draft a proposal for the administration. K. is concerned about the "juvenile offenders" housed in the prison, and will appeal to an elected state representative through a carefully researched letter.

Some of the students write "correct" Standard English prose and demonstrate mastery of the conventions of "formal" writing at the college level, for example correct punctuation, citations, and document formatting. Others produce written texts rich in content but marked by surface errors characteristic of basic writers. How does one writing class meet the needs of such a diverse cohort of writers? Berry (2018) describes the way reading and writing "construct a *cultural now*" (p. 14) in the classroom, a space in which writing creates meaning and meaningful engagement. However, students must also learn to identify and revise for error in the production of "polished" writing. We disserve them if our pedagogy does not help them accomplish both goals.

Negotiation is not so much about contracting with students about type and length of assignments as about learning who they are, the prior experience they bring to the classroom, and their future goals. A rhetorical approach to writing introduces them to the many ways they will use writing across disciplines. Allowing them to adapt course objectives to their personal goals increases their agency.

One-on-One Consultation and Multiple Opportunities for Revision

Building in time for one-on-one consultations with students in a writing course is as important as allowing multiple opportunities for revision. In the traditional college classroom, writing faculty typically allow opportunities for revision, but they are constrained by time. First-year writing class caps vary institutionally, from twelve to twenty-five or more. Feedback to writing should be prompt, and the quality of feedback should enable students to build on skills throughout the term.

"They Say/I Say": The Moves That Matter in Academic Writing (Graff et al., 2006) is popular as a first-year writing text because its praxis invites novice writers into scholarly discourse, gradually acquiring the skills of listening, summarizing, and evaluating and citing evidence. My incarcerated students like "*They Say/I Say*" because it allows them to position themselves on the novice–expert continuum, while acknowledging their wide range of experiences with education, their complex and multidimensional literacies, and their often-frustrating struggles with error.

I caution against labeling incarcerated writers as "basic writers," those identified by Shaughnessy (1977) as "beginners" for whom college writing is a "trap." Far from "beginners," incarcerated student writers are pursuing multiple writing goals. Prior to entering the classroom, many have developed a sophisticated writing identity. Writing remains the primary means of communication in prison. The students may edit newsletters; they may be fiction writers, memoirists, and poets. In my experience, students will revise their essays multiple times before final grades are submitted. Their previous experience with formal education may have been punitive, but they embrace writing instruction with determination; writing is a necessity. Responding to error by offering opportunities for revision should be part of a recursive process that emphasizes genre and audience awareness, a process undergirded by trust in students' desire to learn.

Warner (2017) writes insightfully about the "why can't students write" genre—now a trope among college professors lamenting the poor writing of *traditional* college students. Warner argues that such laments are not only unproductive but inaccurate. He reminds us that writing is hard. We meet students in specific contexts, often with no knowledge of how they perform in other areas of their lives. Writing is a skill developed over time, with much practice, requiring supportive feedback. It takes years to develop an expert disciplinary voice, and we meet undergraduates at the beginning of the process. Every writing teacher has felt frustration when the same errors appear over and over in a student's written work. We can tell when students have not put the maximum effort into an essay. We may laugh at their failed efforts to use words they do not understand. Prison is by definition a punitive space, and condescension is a punitive response when, by every indication, a student is trying to improve their writing skills. Offering incarcerated students the opportunity to extend the feedback loop throughout the term is both humanizing and pedagogically sound.

Communicating with incarcerated students beyond the classroom is challenging. Access to online platforms like Blackboard, as my students have, is the exception. Even when incarcerated students can send a Blackboard message or email, their reliance on these digital technologies is inconsistent. Students who are many years into very long sentences, who had no prior experience with digital technologies, may not acculturate to screen media the way traditional college students usually do. As well, the communication that takes place through these platforms may be monitored, and incarcerated students have reason to use them cautiously. No matter the freedom these communication privileges seem to confer, the total institution prevails and communication is never completely safe or reliable. If the technology fails, or a student is sick or otherwise loses access to the classroom, they cannot communicate with their faculty on the outside. Those with no access to an online platform may have no means of communication in the days or weeks between classes.

On the other hand, communication in the traditional classroom is relatively fluid. Teachers and students can communicate through text, email, online classrooms, and real-time meetings. Schedules are flexible. My traditional liberal arts campus has a well-staffed writing center. Students have multiple opportunities—in addition to consultation with professors—to seek help with their writing before submitting an assignment. The prison program I teach in has little academic support: the students act as each other's mentors, tutors, motivators, and therapists. Peer mentoring becomes burdensome when one or two "strong" writers are responsible for their entire cohort. My program has tried to create a writing consultation partnership with free-world students, but the institutional barriers to access are hard to overcome.

Those who teach inside learn quickly to adjust expectations and be flexible. But curriculum and objectives cannot be watered down. Accreditation prescribes "student hour" contact. Given the many ways that contact hours can be disrupted throughout the term, time for one-on-one consultation may seem impossible to allocate. Nonetheless, in a writing course, time for one-on-one consultation—for brainstorming, crafting a thesis, planning an outline, and interpreting feedback—is indispensable to effective instruction. Writing instructors must develop creative strategies for building it in. Arriving to the prison well before class begins, setting aside some portion of each class session, or designating one class period every few weeks for one-on-one meetings are reasonable strategies.

Flexibility

One of the perversities of the *prison as punishment industry* in juxtaposition to the *traditional college classroom as privilege industry* is the inverse attitude that the students in each context bring to bear on the learning experience. Traditional college students may view education as a form of "punishment," as we see when they "blow off" class and turn in work late, or when they contest unsatisfactory grades. Students in prison, on the other hand, may view education as a privilege. They are well aware of the obstacles to achieving a college degree in a punitive environment. They may argue that they need greater motivation relative to free-world students in order to maintain stamina against so many structural impediments.

In the traditional college classroom, faculty must consider how well prepared their students will be when they proceed to the next level. Prescribed content must be covered before the end of term. Barring illness or legitimate emergencies, students face relatively few barriers to showing up and doing their work. Even as depression and anxiety are endemic on college and university campuses, students have access to resources that might alleviate their suffering. Faculty on the traditional campus can be flexible—to a point. Students who cannot meet course objectives may receive an incomplete grade, or they may withdraw from a class and enroll again later, or they may take a medical leave. The prison classroom may require more, or different forms of, flexibility. Those of us teaching in the carceral classroom must (re)imagine our solidarity with those oppressed by the system, and respond to students as trustworthy individuals capable of making responsible decisions. We should avoid a "pedagogy of whiteness" and pay "attention to our biases, expectations, and traditions" (Mitchell et al., 2012, p. 613). We should avoid applying privilege-industry expectations in a punitive setting, without critically examining the context.

Teaching first-year writing in the prison classroom has brought into focus my implicit biases about what college students in a first-year writing course "should" do. I began my first class with a syllabus, a set of proposed readings and assignments, determined *not* to reveal my biases or naiveté. Incarcerated student and writer Andra Slater identifies the "Wow! factor" (Castro et. al., 2015) as the surprised response of prison educators at the breadth and depth of learning and engagement that takes place in multiple spaces inside prisons. I want to be "woke," but my learning curve is steep. Even as I write for others about how to teach writing in prison, I own that doing this work well is an ongoing developmental process.

What role should incarcerated students play in determining curricula and representation? *Educentricity* is a term coined by prison ethnographer Anita Wilson (2007) to describe the ways in which groups or individuals use a lens limited to their specific context and experiences to view the educational experiences of others. Educentricity poses a problem when the curriculum is viewed through a narrow, self-imposed and traditionally Euro-centric lens. Decisions about curriculum are made mostly by faculty, often without input from students, perhaps without attention to the ways in which student populations are changing due to generational shifts, an increase in international students in the U.S., the rising cost of higher education, and more. *Inclusivity* as a pedagogical goal implies that we can teach more effectively by considering the changing needs of diverse student populations.

Every prison is different, but one characteristic every prison has in common is organized chaos. The only thing predictable is unpredictability. Because my incarcerated students have been accepted into a competitive college program, I have made assumptions about their motivation, their past educational experiences, their skill sets, and their personal goals. Many of them had completed rigorous certificate programs prior to enrolling in the college program. In my classroom, nonetheless, they represent a range of educational backgrounds and experiences. Some anticipate that a college degree will help them pursue a career after release, while others are serving life without parole. Each has access to a personal laptop, so I require them to type their essays and apply MLA format. Why did it not occur to me that not every student would be comfortable with word processing and academic style conventions?

Having taught non-native-English speakers for many years, I have learned to create a "low-context" classroom (see Hall, 1989), where expectations—and the skills needed to meet them—are made explicit. Warner's reminder to meet our student writers *where they are* within specific contexts comes to mind again. One strategy for determining the critical needs of the cohort is to develop a pre-course skills and knowledge assessment instrument which matches necessary skills to learning outcomes. Because the program in which I teach is a cohort model, students do not choose their courses, nor do they complete a writing placement assessment. It is essential, especially given our limited time with and access to most incarcerated students, to gather information before the term begins about individual students' prior experiences with writing, their facility with the required modes of production, and their goals for writing within and beyond prison. The more information we gather, the more flexible we can be in designing and implementing an effective course.

Conclusion

"Go hard on me," my students insist. "Don't give me a 'lite' version of college writing." We absolutely should strive to reproduce the quality of education that is often taken for granted in the privilege industry. After examining the differences between students inside and outside prison, I want to also reflect on the similarities between them. A colleague of mine on the traditional campus—an economics professor—observed, "Our students are economists, just like us, just like everybody. We are all busy people with competing demands, and we're always calculating where to invest our resources for the largest return." Her observation has softened my response to students when they procrastinate or prioritize other tasks over my assignments. The "Wow! factor" cuts both ways. If you (naively) assume that intelligence, motivation, and academic aptitude are rare traits in prison, you will be "wowed" by the breadth of talent you encounter in the classroom. At the same time, if you try to over-correct against "naïve" assumptions, you may be surprised when incarcerated students act like … students. Even highly motivated students sometimes do mediocre work, or feign interest in texts and topics, or prioritize projects for other courses. Many years of teaching have made me not only humble, but realistic. I love the work I do, and I know it is important, but that does not mean it is students' most important work, or that it is the only important work they do in college.

We treat incarcerated students as human beings, knowing that the system for the most part does not. Our privilege makes the work we do in prison possible, but it also makes it precarious. The last thing we want to do is reproduce systemic biases against incarcerated students. We must not fetishize them by making assumptions, positive or negative, about their agency. Instead, we should embrace our privilege and reproduce our faith in higher education as a right. Negotiation, opportunity, and flexibility are rare in prison, but they can be abundant in our classrooms.

Note

1   I teach in a maximum-security prison for women but make every effort not to ascribe to the gender binary language imposed by the institution on the prisoners, not all of whom identify as women.

References

Berry, P. (2018). *Doing time, writing lives: Reconfiguring literacy and higher education in prison.* Carbondale: Southern Illinois University Press.

Castro, E. L. *et al.* (2015). Higher education in an era of mass incarceration: Possibility under constraint. *Journal of Critical Scholarship on Higher Education and Student Affairs,* 1(1), 13–31.

Graff, G. *et al.* (2006). *"They say/I say": The moves that matter in academic writing.* New York: W. W. Norton.

Hall, E. T. (1989). *Beyond culture.* New York: Anchor.

Lunsford, A. (1991). Collaboration, control, and the idea of a writing center. *The Writing Center Journal,* 12(1), 3–10.

Mitchell, T. D. *et al.* (2012). Service learning as a pedagogy of whiteness. *Equity & Excellence in Education,* 45(4), 612–629.

Nowacek, R. S. (2011). *Agents of integration: Understanding transfer as a rhetorical act.* Carbondale: Southern Illinois University Press.

Shaughnessy, M. P. (1977). *A guide for the teacher of basic writing*. New York: Oxford University Press.

Warner, J. (2017, August 20). We know how to teach writing. *Inside Higher Ed*. Retrieved at https://www.insidehighered.com/blogs/just-visiting/we-know-how-teach-writing.

Wilson, A. (2007). "I go to get away from the cockroaches:" Educentricity and the politics of education in prisons. *Journal of Correctional Education*, 58(2), 185–203.

Yancey, K. *et al.* (2014). *Writing across contexts: Transfer, composition, and sites of writing*. Logan: Utah State University Press.

12

WOMEN'S WRITING GROUPS INSIDE: HEALING, RESISTANCE, AND CHANGE

Susan Castagnetto and Mary L. (Molly) Shanley

This paper arises from conversations over several years about why we so value our experiences leading women's writing groups in prisons and jails. We have a lot riding on this: we want to contribute to social and political change, and we want to continue this work because it gives us great personal satisfaction and pleasure. There is considerable literature questioning whether teaching inside does anything to oppose the prison industrial complex, or simply supports the status quo—making the institution "look good" or performing a "credentialing" for our students (Drabinski and Harkins, 2013; Foucault, 1979; Rafay, 2011; Rodriguez, 2010; Sudbury, 2009). We agree with Julia Sudbury (2009) that "there is no pure activist scholarship [or teaching] that is untainted by our social location within a global political economy that so deeply depends on policing, surveillance, and punishment" (p. 32). Yet, we believe our groups counter harmful aspects of carceral institutions. They reflect values based on care, empathy and non-domination, found also in feminist work and in indigenous and restorative justice healing practices that support relationships. They embody Susan Sherwin's (1992) hope that "Through working and talking together, we can discover and pursue other models of relationships" built on connection rather than domination (p. 27). And because they focus on writing, they remind us of Ursula Le Guin's (2014) insistence that "Any human power can be resisted and changed by human beings. Resistance and change often begin in art. Very often in our art, the art of words."

We begin with a brief discussion of incarceration's harms, then describe how our projects counter those harms: they encourage participants to develop their creative potential and gain insight through writing about their lives; build positive connections with others through sharing writing; and contribute to creating consciousness and solidarity that can lead to social change. Each serves to disrupt our present carceral system.

Incarceration, Individualism, and Harm

Theoretically and in implementation, Western punishment focuses on the individual, either as *deserving* punishment or as needing *rehabilitation* to fix her "defects." The *individual* is held accountable for her crime; incarceration punishes by taking away the individual's rights and liberties.[1] Ann Stanford (2004) captures this focus in describing her group at Chicago's Cook County Jail: "although the women are encouraged to get along with each other, there is a great deal of public rhetoric that emphasizes individualism, the redemption of an individual life, and the return to one's 'own' family (read husband and children)" (p. 29).

The focus on individual culpability reinforces the idea that those inside *are* their crimes, hence are failures. The retributive reminder that one must pay for one's crimes makes it difficult to see oneself as more than a "criminal." Psychologist Craig Haney (2002) observes, "Prisoners may come to think of themselves as 'the kind of person' who deserves only the degradation and stigma to which they have been subjected while incarcerated" (p. 11). This degradation is a harm that goes beyond deprivation of rights, and indeed runs counter to rehabilitation, which entails acknowledging one's past decisions and actions while *not* succumbing to the pitfall of assuming those actions define who one is. Further degradation includes denial of personhood and agency—for example, being assigned numbers and subjected to a regimen that controls almost every aspect of life inside.

The trope of individual culpability is exemplified in a piece by Carley, from Molly's group. "Mommy" reflects Carley's internalization of the shameful identity of drug addict and self-recrimination over relapse:

> I lied never realizing you were the one who was really by my side, instead I was just too damn hooked to take two minutes to stop and look so I kept doing drugs. [T]hought I was right until I got high and had sex and became pregnant that night, then gave birth to a beautiful baby girl ... I'm the cause of her being taken away, I'm sorry I couldn't stop using on my own them days, I'm sorry it took your granddaughter and son away ... (as cited in Achorn-Rubenstein, 2013, p. 87).[2]

Carley blames herself for her inability to stop using, losing her daughter, and depriving her mother of her granddaughter. She frames her addiction and sexual activity as personal failings, weakness of character, and bad choices, omitting any mention of services that might have helped her.

Incarceration also harms through deprivation of relationships, a harm obscured by the individualistic focus we've described.[3] This is not just collateral damage of incarceration, but a central, if unacknowledged, feature. Prisons and jails separate those inside from their families and communities. Visiting can be difficult and expensive, and phone calls costly. Separation is painful for those inside and those left behind, particularly children, with harmful consequences for all. The ACLU report "Caught in the Net" notes:

> Incarcerated mothers experience significant emotional trauma when separated from their children, contributing to depression, loneliness, and despair. For some women, separation from their children is worse than serving time in a prison (ACLU, 2005, p. 49).

Prisons also minimize connection to the civic community. They are largely invisible to the "outside" and are hard to get into. This barrier perpetuates stereotypes of those inside and encourages those outside to "take prisons for granted" and to "think of [them] as disconnected from our own lives" (Davis, 2003, p. 15).

Carceral institutions thwart positive relationships among those inside as well. Jane Dorotik (2011), a member of Sue's group, describes how prison culture accomplishes this:[4]

> [The] culture of domination is all encompassing, not just specific to the guards or the managerial staff; it seems to infect and become a way of being and thinking for all prisoners ... Even individuals who try to care for each other ... end up tacitly agreeing to the hierarchy of domination just to survive ... It all boils down to trust and our perception of our world. If we see the world as distrustful, unbearable, and hostile, we will enter into all relationships with this overarching belief system, which will then become a self-fulfilling prophecy (pp. 109–114).

Urging alternatives to incarceration, Dorotik states, "We must believe, and *show* through our actions, that we acknowledge that all people can make valuable contributions to mutual growth and development" (p. 113), emphasizing the role of relationships in doing so.

Restorative justice theorist J. Braithwaite (2010) notes, "[B]ecause crime hurts, justice should heal. And punishments that obstruct healing by insisting on adding more hurt to the world are not justice" (p. 33). We believe that the writing groups push back against the harms of punishment we've described, the degradation, isolation, distrust, and invisibility experienced by incarcerated women, and that they contribute to healing, helping participants achieve new understandings of themselves, their crimes, their relationships to one another, and their roles as citizens.

The Writing Groups: Challenging Harm

Through writing about and sharing their experiences, our writers are indeed "reinvented" by telling their stories. Part of that reinvention stems from the self-understanding gained by introspection. As Rebecca Solnit (2006) has noted,

"Stories matter. People die of pernicious stories, are reinvented by new stories, and make stories to shelter themselves" (para. 12). Another part stems from the women's sharing their writings in the group. Through reading, listening, and responding, the women forge relationships that challenge the isolation and lack of trust that incarceration fosters. Finally, through their sense of relationship and community, they move beyond seeing themselves as "criminals" and begin to regard themselves as citizens with experiences and stories to contribute to public discussions.

Molly leads a weekly writing group with about twelve members at a county jail in New York's Mid-Hudson Valley. The jail has an ever-changing population of about fifty women—some of them pretrial and presentencing; some serving sentences; others awaiting transfer to state prison or a place in a rehab center. Sue organizes a semester-long series of writing workshops with a group of twenty to thirty women, serving both short and long sentences, at a state prison in Southern California, and about twenty students from the Claremont Colleges. Sue's group does writing exercises during sessions, sometimes facilitated by guest writers, with writing shared aloud. Molly's group members read aloud journal entries or poems written outside the session.

As facilitators, we aim to create an egalitarian, supportive space. Inside participants comment that the groups provide a sense of "normalcy," as if they were not in prison. More than simply escaping the prison regimen, this is about being in a space where the domination and hierarchy described by Dorotik are absent, and in which mutual respect and relationships are forged through writing, reading aloud, and listening to others. Outside students have remarked that they get to know their classmates better in the writing group than on campus: "It was amazing to see everyone participating with one another unabashedly in ways that often don't happen in a classroom. The writing workshop became an equalizer for the diverse group of people involved." Writing and reading together disrupts the implicit hierarchies in the typical college classroom as well as prison.

Personal Narratives: A Path to "Restorying"

The groups enable women inside to construct new narratives about themselves to move beyond the "criminal" label. Tobi Jacobi (2011) writes that one goal of her workshops is "the production of work that seeks to counter media-driven identity narratives for incarcerated women" (p. 42). They also see themselves—and each other—*as writers*. Kathy Boudin (2011) reflects on the power of societal labels when incarcerated:

> In prison you crave space, space to be someone other than a label of "murderer," "bad mother," "drug addict," "baby killer," "terrorist," "victim of abuse," "abuser," "AIDS-ridden," "bitch"—labels from society, labels from one another ... [T]hose labels often connect to a vulnerable pocket inside

the woman. Women are craving space to forge identities that are truer, more complex, and that enable them to move forward instead of being cemented into a hole (p. xix).

Practitioners of restorative justice describe how "restorative storytelling" provides a starting point for those who've committed crimes to become more empathetic and willing to take responsibility for their acts (Gill, 2014, p. 196). Braithwaite (2010) describes Shadd Maruna's findings about the importance of creating new identities:

> [Maruna showed] that serious Liverpool offenders who went straight had to find a new way of making sense of their lives. They had to restory their life histories. They defined a new ethical identity for themselves, that meant that they were able to say, looking back at their former criminal selves, that they were "not like that any more." [Persistent reoffenders], in contrast, were locked into "condemnation scripts," whereby they saw themselves as irrevocably condemned to their criminal self story (p. 342).

This "restorying" describes how our writers come to see their own histories more clearly, including how they have been shaped by abuse. Delaney, in Molly's group, recounts her abuse as a child and freeing herself from its effects:

> Dear little girl why did the people
>
> you love just sit and watch
>
> other people hurt you?
>
> Don't they realize that what happens
>
> when you're a little girl
>
> shapes your future?
>
> Dear little girl you're all grown up
>
> how are you doing now?
>
> I was blind but now I see, I was
>
> lost but now I'm found, I'm ready

to let go of that little girl (as cited in Achorn-Rubenstein, 2013, p. 104). Similarly, Alicia L. (2017) constructs a dialogue with part of herself she wishes to reject, affirming her determination to understand, forgive, and transcend past trauma and its damage to others and herself:

> No, I don't need you. You are the side of me still holding onto the pain and heartache of being a little girl trying to fill the shoes of an adult, a parent to

all those around her ... I didn't ask for all the endless nights watching the fights, watching a woman called Mother fight harder for her drugs and money than she did for her own children, for me. Stop telling me her addiction was my fault ...

Let me believe I did my best. Stop holding me back from forgiving and believing in myself ... You're the side of me who's sick and suffering. Let go of me and I'll let go of you. Without you I am free (p. 5).

Similarly, a member of Sue's group commented on how the exercises enabled her to recover her sense of being a whole person, not just a "criminal":

I value the fact that I am 40 years old and this class ... has brought my childhood back to me. I have been able to reconnect with the little girl Julie, the teenager Julie and the Julie of my twenties. I am remembering what a good family I had and am coming to value the way I was raised. I appreciate this class and all the insight it continues to bring my way.[5]

These passages suggest that writing and reading together invites women who have internalized dominant social narratives about themselves as morally flawed to find new ways of making sense of their lives, with new ethical identities.

Sharing One's Story: Doorway to Relationship

The environment of the writing groups engenders a willingness to share, to be vulnerable. Lysette Navarro observed, "You contribute something and speak out yourself, and then all of a sudden, everyone wants to give something, throw something in, you can feel the room shift, the automatic clicking as connections are made ..." (as cited in Davis, 2013, p. 173). Empathy, care, and a sense of connection emerge, similar to what Simone Weil Davis (2013) experienced as "the force of generosity" in a prison creative writing class she taught (p. 171).

A woman from the community in Sue's group captures these elements in describing sharing a piece she wrote, inspired by George Ella Lyon's poem "Where I'm From," about her family's history of slave-owning and taking indigenous land:

Several [women] came up afterwards to thank me for my candor and courage for writing and reading my piece. [One] simply said, "No judgment." I blinked, disbelieving. She repeated, "No judgment," with an expression of compassion. I felt warmth surge through my body. Something like guilt dropped away.

All the following week ... I felt something shift in me, my mind letting go of what imprisons me—guilt and shame and unnecessary complaining about not enough time, not enough ...[6]

This also exemplifies how others' acceptance can lead to self-forgiveness, critical to "restorying."

Having outside students participate in Sue's group also creates relationships that undermine the inside–outside barrier that sustains the carceral system. Meeting women inside shatters stereotypes of prisoners. One commented that she

> felt a strong connection with all those who were able to participate. There were moments just before the ... workshop began where we just conversed with the women ... It was all about giving and sharing pieces of ourselves.[7]

For women inside, having "outsiders" in the group challenges their self-perception of criminality: "[The students] make me feel like a real person, like they really want to hear anything I have to say. They make me feel ... like I matter ... like I'm ... free." They are also disabused of stereotypes of college students as living privileged, problem-free lives: "We ... realize as people we share some of the same pain as well as victories." Simone Davis (2013) notes of her mixed population class, "Students ... never dismissed one another for a failure to understand, and looked beyond and beneath classed and raced stereotypes about 'college girls' and 'convicts' to address the intellect and personality beyond" (p. 171).

As participants listen and engage in conversation about one another's works, they begin to see themselves as "part of something larger than their own individual life stories" (Stanford, 2004, p. 291). They recognize similar experiences of abuse, neglect, romantic and sexual relationships that subverted their interests, untreated mental illness, and lack of resources to help break their addictions. These patterns complicate the narrative of individual culpability as the cause of their crime and incarceration and prompt discussions of social and economic structures that influenced their behaviors.

Civic Engagement and Social Change

Although it is not our immediate goal to engage in political or systemic change-making, the groups illustrate Le Guin's (2014) observation that "resistance and change often begin in ... the art of words." For women inside, the affirmation of the value of their distinct voice and insight can generate solidarity, "a mutual sense of connection, respect, affection and gratitude" that Jody Lewen (2014) identifies as essential for collective action (p. 361). Stories and dialogue elucidate how personal difficulties (often attributed to individual defects) are shared by others and shaped by social and institutional forces, challenging in another way the notion that people are in prison because they are inherently criminal. The personal is, in fact, political.[8]

Describing writing groups she has facilitated, Jacobi (2011) observes how "the penning of counternarratives" effectively "pave[s] the way for more ardent activism" (p. 41). In a yearly anthology, *SpeakOut!*, the women's writings give voice to their experience and counter media stereotypes of incarcerated women. Lewen (2014) points out that "being able to find the words to say what you want to say ... is a vital part of the advocacy and social transformation" necessary for both personal growth and cultural change (p. 359). Braithwaite (2010) notes the deep sense of responsibility that can emerge when those who've committed crimes, their victims, and community members share their stories in restorative justice circles; the emphasis on "passive responsibility"—holding people accountable for past acts—is replaced by "active responsibility"—"taking responsibility for repairing the harm that has been done, the relationships that have been damaged" (p. 342). The shift in focus from retribution for past action to responsibility for helping repair damage one has caused "transform[s] citizens through deliberation into being democratically active" (p. 350).

A new sense of being citizens with knowledge relevant to the community is evident in actions by Molly's group. When the county considered building a new jail, the group wrote a letter to the county's Criminal Justice Council suggesting programming initiatives.[9] When the local newspaper sponsored a public forum on opioid addiction, the women submitted written testimony outlining the cost to themselves, their children, and the community of separation from their families. It was published on the editorial page.[10] The group also selects writings from both women's and men's groups for a bimonthly newsletter, giving their words relevance beyond the groups—their writing may inform and move others. And when invited to share reflections on the groups for this essay, many of the incarcerated women in both Molly's and Sue's groups responded out of a desire to contribute to a public discussion of incarceration and rehabilitation. This sense of being a knowledgeable citizen with the responsibility and power to participate in making social change is, for many, a new identity and counters the harm to autonomy and dignity that incarceration causes.

Sue's outside students also are motivated to make systemic change. Angela Davis (2003) observes that people on the outside think of imprisonment as

> a fate reserved for the "evildoers" ... The prison ... functions ideologically as an abstract site into which undesirables are deposited, relieving us of the responsibility of thinking about the real issues afflicting those communities from which prisoners are drawn in such disproportionate numbers (p. 16).

Participating in the group enables outside students to see firsthand the dehumanizing and counterproductive aspects of prisons, and dialogue exposes them to the conditions of the lives of an array of people whom they might not otherwise encounter. That engagement has, over the years, led many to undertake educational projects, pursue internships with advocacy organizations, go to law school, and seek other avenues for making systemic change.[11]

As Lewen (2014) notes, whether writing groups include people from outside or only incarcerated women, "each human encounter changes everyone. It chips away at the dehumanizing layers, it educates and empowers, and it forges alliances" (p. 362). Those alliances, both among the inside participants and among those in the larger community working on an array of issues, are, we hope, "already moving us steadily towards a world in which people get the care that they need, and in which all of us can finally thrive" (p. 362). The writing groups help us envision and begin to create a future in which incarceration is not the preferred response to crime, and in which rehabilitation and the development or restoration of positive relationships replaces punishment in moving towards a just society.

Conclusion

Facilitating and participating in our writing groups has strengthened our understanding of the harms incarceration causes by systematically denying individual dignity and shattering personal, group, and civic relationships. By contrast, the groups foster a sense of agency and positive identity: members move beyond "condemnation scripts" to a focus on future responsibilities and possibilities.[12] Advocating prison abolition, the group Critical Resistance emphasizes the importance of articulating the contours of hoped-for future institutions and relationships:

> we must build models today that can represent how we want to live in the future. [We must develop] practical strategies for taking small steps that move us toward making our dreams real and that lead us all to believe that things really could be different. It means living this vision in our daily lives (Critical Resistance, 2018).

We also see our writing groups as providing a small model of practices, informed by restorative values, that could undergird "how we want to live in the future." Both abolition and more modest prison reform are "not just about closing the doors to violent institutions, but also about building up and recovering institutions and practices and relationships that nurture wholeness, self-determination, and transformation (Bassichis et al., 2011, p. 36). They serve as a modest form of resistance in a much larger struggle against injustice, one requiring concerted action and coalition politics by a wide array of advocates and activists committed to envisioning and establishing

> a continuum of alternatives to imprisonment—demilitarization of schools, revitalization of education at all levels, a health system that provides free physical and mental care to all, and a justice system based on reparation and reconciliation rather than retribution and vengeance (Davis 2003, p. 107).

This approach asks us to imagine a constellation of responses to problems giving rise to crime, including poverty, racism, and unfettered global capitalism, developing institutions and practices that would in the long run replace prisons.

Sudbury's (2009) suggestions to prison scholars on resisting reinforcing the carceral system apply to prison educators as well:

> we must simply learn from and be transparent about our mistakes and limitations, take our cues from inside and outside activists, jump in, and get our hands dirty. Sitting on the sidelines ... is not an option for those of us committed to challenging the complicities of which we are a part. [Rather, we must] constantly recommit our life's work to the radical movements that give it meaning (p. 32).

Writing groups alone are not engines of societal transformation, but these and similar projects have the potential to foster both personal liberation and social change within the confines of prisons and jails and beyond.

We thank Jennifer Tilton, Pamela Wright, and the members of our writing groups for their inspiration and insights, and the prison and jail staff and administrators who facilitate and support our work.

Notes

1 Angela Davis (2003) remarks, "Before the acceptance of the sanctity of individual rights, imprisonment could not have been understood as punishment. If the individual was not perceived as possessing inalienable rights and liberties, then the alienation of those rights and liberties by removal from society to a space tyrannically governed by the state would not have made sense" (p. 44). Individualism runs deep in American political and social thought, but as Virginia Held (2004) has argued, "... we must not lose sight of ... human interdependency and of the need for caring relations to undergird or surround such constructions" (p. 70).

2 During academic years 2010–11 to 2012–13, Rosie Achorn-Rubenstein attended sessions of the Women's Writing Group at the Dutchess County Jail, serving as co-facilitator with Molly Shanley during 2011–13. Her senior thesis, *Old Stories, Fresh Eyes*, contains some writings by women in the group that she collected with their permission and that are included in this chapter.

3 Solitary confinement is the ultimate deprivation of human contact, often producing serious mental illness.

4 The quotation is from an essay written independently of the writing group.

5 Quoted from an anonymous response to a request for feedback on the writing group for the purpose of a public presentation, January 2018.

6 Quoted anonymously with permission from a piece the author wrote for another creative writing group about her experience in the prison writing group, April 2018.

7 Quoted with permission from a written reflection on the writing group by Scripps student Evelyn Gonzalez, December 2015.

8 The sharing of individual life stories as a way to uncover oppressive social structures and practices was a powerful tool used by the Second Wave of U.S. feminism to identify and analyze patriarchy. The writing groups are not consciousness-raising groups, but revealing social patterns emerge as women share stories.

9 Women's Writing Group to Dutchess County Criminal Justice Council, letter of September 2012, received as #78687.

10 "Women inmates add their voices to heroin forum," *Poughkeepsie Journal*, September 21, 2016, 9A.

11 One student received a Strauss Foundation grant to start an organic garden at the prison; students gardened weekly with women inside for several years. Another received a Watson fellowship to visit women's prisons around the world; now a lawyer, she works on death penalty appeals at the Habeas Corpus Resource Center in San Francisco. Another heads a prison education initiative at Tulane University while pursuing a doctorate. Another works with women in a prison education project in Washington. Another works with Critical Resistance.

12 Braithwaite (2010) cites Maruna's discussion of how the transformation of discourse through restorative justice projects teaches participants that the harm done to them that contributed to their criminal behavior does not absolve them of responsibility for their future actions. They must recognize that "I am one of the victims in this room. While I am not responsible for the abused life that led me into a life of crime on the streets, I am responsible for getting out of it and I am also responsible for helping this victim who has been hurt by my act" (p. 343).

References

Achorn-Rubenstein, R. (2013, 8 March). Old stories, fresh eyes: Writing as re-vision in the Dutchess County Jail women's writing group. Thesis submitted to the American Studies Program, Vassar College.

Alicia L. (2017). Untitled. *Voices of DCJ: Newsletter of the Dutchess County Jail*, 1(5), 5.

American Civil Liberties Union (ACLU) (2005). Caught in the net: The impact of drug policies on women and families. Retrieved at https://www.aclu.org/caught-net-impa ct-drug-policies-women-and-families.

Bassichis, M. *et al.* (2011). Building an abolitionist trans and queer movement with every-thing we've got. In E. Stanley and N. Smith (eds.), *Captive genders: Trans embodiment and the prison industrial complex*, pp. 15–40. Oakland: AK Press.

Boudin, K. (2011). Introduction. In J. M. Lawston and A. E. Lucas (eds.), *Razor wire women: Prisoners, activists, scholars, and artists*, pp. xvii–xix. Albany: State University of New York Press.

Braithwaite, J. (2010). In search of restorative jurisprudence. In M. Tonry (ed.), *Why punish? How much? A reader on punishment*, pp. 337–352. New York: Oxford University Press.

Critical Resistance (2018). What is the PIC? What is Abolition? Retrieved at http://critica lresistance.org/about/not-so-common-language/.

Davis, A. (2003). *Are prisons obsolete?* New York: Seven Stories Press.

Davis, S. W. (2013). Inside-Out: The reach and limits of a prison education program. In S. W. Davis and B. S. Roswell (eds.), *Turning teaching inside out: Community engagement in higher education*, pp. 163–175. New York: Palgrave Macmillan.

Dorotik, J. (2011). The prison mentality. In J. M. Lawston and A. E. Lucas (eds.), *Razor wire women: Prisoners, activists, scholars, and artists*, pp. 109–114. Albany: State University of New York Press.

Drabinski, K. and Harkins, G. (2013). Introduction: Teaching inside carceral institutions. *The Radical Teacher*, 95, 3–9.

Foucault, M. (1979). *Discipline and punish: The birth of the prison*. London: Penguin.

Gill, S. (2014). The healing power of narrative: Learning from listening and telling our stories. In I. Goodson and S. Gill (eds.), *Critical narrative as pedagogy*, pp. 193–220. New York: Bloomsbury Academic.

Haney, C. (2002). The psychological impact of incarceration: Implications for post-prison adjustment. Working paper prepared for the "From Prison to Home" Project, U.S.

Department of Health and Human Services. Retrieved at https://aspe.hhs.gov/basic-rep ort/psychological-impact-incarceration-implications-post-prison-adjustment.

Held, V. (2004). Taking care: Care as practice and value. In C. Calhoun (ed.), *Setting the moral compass: Essays by women philosophers*, pp. 59–71. New York: Routledge.

Jacobi, T. (2011). Speaking out for social justice: The problems and possibilities of US women's prison and jail writing workshops. *Critical Survey*, 23(3), 40–54.

Le Guin, U. (2014). Speech in acceptance of National Book Foundation Medal. Retrieved at http://www.ursulakleguin.com/NationalBookFoundationAward-Speech.html.

Lewen, J. (2014). Prison higher education and social transformation. *Saint Louis University Public Law Review*, 33(2), 353–361.

Rafay, A. (2011, April 12). On the Margins of Freedom. *The Walrus*.

Rodriguez, D. (2010). The disorientation of the teaching act: Abolition as pedagogical problem. *Radical Teacher*, 88(Summer), 7–19.

Sherwin, S. (1992). *No longer patient: Feminist ethics and health care*. Philadelphia: Temple University Press.

Solnit, R. (2006, May 14). Welcome to the Impossible World. *TomDispatch*. Retrieved at http://www.tomdispatch.com/post/83153/solnit_on_our_impossible_world_and_ welcome_to_it.

Stanford, A. (2004). More than just words: Women's poetry and resistance at Cook County Jail. *Feminist Studies*, 30(2), 277–301.

Sudbury, J. (2009). Challenging penal dependency: Activist scholars and the antiprison movement. In J. Sudbury and M. Okazawa-Rey (eds.), *Activist scholarship: Antiracism, feminism, and social change*, pp. 17–35. Boulder and London: Paradigm.

13

WRITING FOR REENTRY: A FEW LESSONS FROM TRANSFER THEORY

Maggie Shelledy

Clay[1] tells me that the day he got out of prison was the worst day of his life. At first, I think I must have misheard him, or perhaps he was being hyperbolic. It was hard for me, a middle-class white woman with no personal experience with incarceration, to imagine that this could possibly be true. Not the day he went to prison? I tell him that surprises me, and he insists, yes, that was the worst day of his life. For the final three years of his sentence, he had been training service dogs, and in the days leading to his release, he had been having dreams of taking one of the dogs with him, with whom he had "such a connection." He describes the moment he walked out of the gates after being locked up for twenty-four years, more than half his life: "So these big gates open and my dog's bawling behind me. That's how I walked out. I'm in the parking lot, and this is just horrible. This is the worst thing in the world. I felt like my heart was being destroyed."

I had asked Clay to meet me for an interview as part of a larger research project investigating the experiences of the alumni of various college-in-prison programs across the United States. Clay was one of a dozen individuals I interviewed from five different programs. While my intention was to learn how incarcerated students used academic literacy to gain agency in their everyday lives, stories like Clay's stuck out. It became clear to me that the way I had imagined the relationship between higher education and incarcerated students' futures was not reflected in the actual lived experiences of these alumni.

In this chapter, I argue that students' experiences of reentry must be understood and incorporated into the design of prison writing classes and workshops. Here, I theorize reentry as a form of rhetorical practice of attunement, and I suggest teaching writing and rhetoric that encourage problem-exploring and repurposing through the critical transition of reentry. Drawing on research on the transfer of knowledge from Writing Studies, I offer a few suggestions for incorporating a Teaching for Transfer approach in carceral classrooms. This approach is not meant to be exclusive, to suggest that teaching writing and rhetoric in anticipation of reentry is the only or best approach to teaching writing in prison. The clear limitations of this approach are that it cannot account for the value of literacy instruction for people serving life sentences without the possibility of parole, nor does it count for the immediate uses of writing and rhetoric instruction for incarcerated people. At the same time, it seems to me that for both instructors and students, the future, free lives of the incarcerated students animates literacy instruction in carceral classrooms, from program mission statements to student learning outcomes to student motivation. For this reason, the way those future lives are imagined is crucial and must be grounded in the local context and lived realities of any program's alumni.

Knowledge Transfer as Creating Repurposing across Contexts

Over the last decade, writing transfer inquiry has emerged within Writing Studies to account for conditions under which students successfully apply concepts and practices learned in our writing courses to writing situations in other classes, the workplace, and their everyday lives. Increasingly, scholars (Beach, 2003; Nowacek, 2011; Perkins and Salomon, 1988; Thorndike, 1999) are challenging what is called the "bo-peep" theory of transfer, or the assumption that as long as learning is happening, students will recall and apply this learning to other contexts. Far from simple recall and application, however, many scholars argue that transfer involves an entanglement of social contexts, habitus, and dispositions. King Beach (2003) identifies *generalization* as a more apt concept for describing knowledge propagation:

> Transition, then, is the concept we use to understand how knowledge is generalized, or propagated, across social space and time. A transition is consequential when it is consciously reflected on, struggled with, and shifts the individual's sense of self or social positions. Thus, consequential transitions link identity with knowledge propagation (p. 42).

Building on Beach's theory of generalization, Elizabeth Wardle (2012) invokes Bourdieu's concepts of habitus and doxa to suggest that transfer might better be understood as "creative repurposing for expansive learning." Wardle suggests that as students move from one habitus and its dispositions to another, they experience disorientation, and she argues that when students bring to new situations a "problem-exploring disposition," they may be more conscious of possibilities for creative repurposing of previous knowledge and practices.

This dispositional approach to teaching for transfer is what Anis Bawarshi (2017) refers to as a *knowing-with* approach, which "involves taking the knowledge, skills, or thinking strategies learned in one context and translating/ transforming that learned knowledge, skill, or thinking strategy to accomplish a task in another context" (p. 90). In other words, teaching for transfer means not only teaching skills that can be applied to other, different situations, but also cultivating problem-exploring dispositions, teaching them how to *know-with* what they are learning. Ultimately, Bawarshi argues that the value of teaching writing, specifically first-year composition, should be defined less by the skills students can directly apply to other situations and more by the extent to which it prepares students for future learning. Teaching writing and rhetoric for transfer, then, means not so much instructing students on the conventions of written genres we imagine they are likely to encounter (e.g., professional writing, legal writing), but providing an arena for students to practice bridging and adapting across sociocultural contexts.

If transfer of knowledge is less likely to automatically occur between markedly different situations, like the transition from the classroom to the workplace, then the profoundly disorienting transition from prison to the outside world may seem to pose a significant challenge for the long-term efficacy of higher education in prison. However, I want to argue that the value of higher education in prison generally, and writing and rhetoric instruction in particular, lies precisely in the habitus of the prison classroom and the dispositions it can cultivate, including problem-posing dispositions, with their practices of adaptation and making connections across sociocultural divides.

Reentry as Rhetorical Practice

Clay laughs as he tells me his stories of feeling out of sorts as he navigated the "outside world" for the first time in nearly a quarter century, like when he almost got into an altercation with a gas station attendant over a misunderstanding about the self-serve soda fountain. He goes on to tell me that when he was in the work-release center before he got out, the staff at the facility would tell him to go out and walk around the building for a couple of hours. He guesses they did this because he had been incarcerated for so long, and they wanted him to acclimate to being out in the world.

> And finally it was time for me to go out and look for a job, and I was scared to death to go look for a job. But what was funny was every street, any time I crossed the streets, it didn't matter if there were cars coming or not, it could be a situation where you couldn't see a car anywhere, I had to run across the street [laugh]. Because it was like they would come out of the sewers and run me over. I was super paranoid of cars. But eventually I acclimated, but man, the transition getting out after that, it was just ... and then driving. It was almost a phobia. It still kind of is [laugh]. But I'm getting it. I tell people that I'm now at the level of your average fifteen-year-old. I just got a license.

Though he was laughing, Clay's story reflects a common, though not universal, experience in the lives of the program alumni I interviewed, especially those who have been locked up for a long time: a feeling of disorientation and uncertainty following their release from prison. For Clay, he relates this both in terms of his broken connections with those, human and nonhuman, whom he had come to care for, and in terms of acute feelings of fear and hesitancy in mundane, everyday situations.

This aspect of reentry, the visceral and profound sense of disorientation, ineptitude, and out-of-placeness, is largely unacknowledged in the way reentry is imagined in college-in-prison programs. Here, reentry is typically conceived as a problem of access to basic needs (e.g., housing, employment) or as successful abstention from criminalized activity, but Clay's story underscores how important it is to understand reentry as an unfolding and craggy struggle for attunement between one's identity and the material and social world. This process is not simply the adjustment anyone must make between one social context and another. Rather, as Joshua Price (2015), Lisa Guenther (2013), Dylan Rodriguez (2006), and others have noted, the prison's violence is in the way it works to disarticulate one's identity through attempts to alienate incarcerated people from all meaningful relations: with loved ones, with ideas, and with the physical world of sensation.

In her inquiry into the phenomenology of solitary confinement, Lisa Guenther (2013) writes:

> "[B]ecoming unhinged" is not just a colloquial expression; rather, it is a precise phenomenological description of what happens when the articulated joints of our embodied, interrelational subjectivity are broken apart [...] The very possibility of being broken in this way suggests that we are not simply atomistic individuals but rather hinged subjects who can become unhinged when the concrete experience of other embodied subjects is denied for too long (p. xii).

It seems there is a similar disarticulation that occurs when one moves from the culture and sensorium of the prison to the outside world. Rather than being a relatively simple removal of these barriers, reentry involves a complex shift in habitus that destabilizes orientation and identity. Clay and my other research participants describe reentry as a stripping away of the habitual ways of knowing and being they crafted over several years, as well as the removal of points of meaningful connection that formed the foundation of their identities. The ways of being one develops in prison are often precious modes of survival against "becoming unhinged." It is a practical intelligence shared within the prison as wisdom, but these same habits may not serve one well on the outside, leading one to move swiftly from feeling wise to feeling incompetent and insecure. For many of the individuals I spoke to, the habitus of the prison, and even the prison classroom, did not have direct applicability to the new and unfamiliar situations they found themselves in. This does not mean that these knowledges and practices have no value. Instead, it suggests that greater attention to the cultivation of problem-exploring dispositions through practice with adaptation and boundary crossing might help students to negotiate the process of reentry.

Reflecting on the experiences of formerly incarcerated people, Joshua Price (2015) argues against a liberal notion of freedom defined in negative terms, such as the freedom from socially imposed obstacles, which is based on a conceit of self-reliance and independence. Price argues instead that

> the vulnerability of the social dead belies the viability of this concept of freedom. The outcast lives at the mercy of the society and its members; abandoned, he or she lives not within a social order but rather in a state of socially constructed disorder, of chaos (p. 127).

In other words, freedom, and by extension agency, requires meaningful social and material connections.

Rather than autonomous mastery over an objective world, agency develops through an attunement between the individual and the material and social world. I want to suggest, then, that reentry may be productively framed as rhetorical practice, by which I mean less a process of arguing persuasively for one's full inclusion in the citizenry (though that may be part of it) and more a kind of Burkean consubstantiation, an ongoing process of responsive invention and attunement. The ability to navigate the transition from prison to "the world" depends on an ongoing process of becoming through recursive and reciprocal encounters with new people, institutions, discourses, practices, and things. It is a transition from the habitual ways of being that emerged from attunement to the prison environment through responsive invention of new habits via attunement to the new environment.

My conversation with David, a research participant who, at the time of our interview, was attending college after six years of incarceration, illustrates this difficult transition in habits of being. We met on the campus of the community college where he both works and goes to school, sitting at a table outside a cafe. He tells me that he always had a good heart, but in prison, "having a good heart will get you late, and by late, I mean out back." So when he got out, he "still had that penitentiary state of mind":

> That was the hardest thing for me. I struggle with it even to this day. I'll give you an example. I asked if you wanted to sit inside or outside. You chose outside. You took that seat. I was gonna go for that seat. I don't like my back to the entrance or exits. That's why I keep looking behind me, in case you're wondering. But it's penitentiary habits. I pay attention to things like that, always. There's certain things you have to turn on and off.

This intrusion of the habitus and disposition of the prison into everyday life on the outside is, according to David, a struggle, one that contributes to the layers of disorientation and disconnection experienced during reentry. I do not mean to suggest that obstacles such as the legal discrimination against people with felony convictions in employment and housing do not significantly contribute to exclusion from full citizenship. But these stories indicate that reentry can be profoundly disorienting, and a humanist approach to intentional agency by autonomous subjects through rhetorical virtuosity fails to account for what appears to be a more entangled process of becoming. It is also worth noting that while David's "penitentiary habits" may be experienced as a struggle for him in this moment, his ability to "turn on and off" this disposition could be precisely the kind of creative repurposing Wardle describes, if those penitentiary habits, knowledges, and ways of being can be adapted for new situations as they arise. College-in-prison programs that aim to increase students' participation in democratic citizenship, then, should engage in rhetorical education based in the emergent and ecological nature of rhetorical practice.

Casey Boyle (2016) argues against rhetorical education that focuses on making students aware of affordances and constraints, because this approach reinforces an orientation that focuses on individual agency in choosing appropriate responses. While this orientation has its usefulness, it does suggest that one's rhetorical success or failure lies in one's ability to correctly discern the available means of persuasion, and this may not be as useful for those facing the social stigma and legal discrimination a felony conviction brings. In other words, a focus on individual agency and rhetorical savvy may not be adequate for individuals with significantly constrained agency. While I agree that higher education in prison can and should aim to increase inclusion and participation in democratic life for currently and formerly incarcerated people, we must be attentive to the unique barriers to participation they face. My worry is that our well-intentioned concern for increasing autonomous agency for incarcerated students is focusing on increasing individual rhetorical savvy, especially through strategic deployment of personal narratives, rather than addressing the systemic exclusions that individual action may mitigate but is unlikely to transform. If we do not inquire into the lived experiences of reentry and incorporate this into the design of college-in-prison programs and curricula, there is a danger that our pedagogy merely produces a *sense* of increased agency within the classroom, rather than substantial empowerment and change.

Instead, Boyle advocates for a shift from humanist reflection to posthuman rhetorical practice, which he connects to rhetoric's ancient connection to the body and exercise. This repetitive production through practice is a process of attunement of the self-in-world, writing as a way of not only being but *becoming*. Boyle suggests this rhetorical practice through serial encounters develops not humanist autonomous agency but sensitivities, or sense-abilities. It could almost be imagined as a kind of rhetorical orienteering. Patrick Berry (2014) similarly calls for prison educators to attend to the lived realities of incarcerated students. He suggests that rather than focusing on some imagined future in which students' constraints will vanish and they can put their academic skills to use, educators can use classroom space to address the everyday problems of the students and increase their capacities to act in what he calls the "contextual now" (p. 155), by acknowledging the values of literacy even for currently incarcerated students. I agree, and I also suggest that this same attention must be paid to our students' experiences of reentry if we are to craft programs that are as attentive to our students' futures as to their present circumstances.

By attending to the rhetorical challenges of reentry, including formal and informal exclusions from social life, prison educators may craft curricula that more directly address the rhetorical complexities our incarcerated students must navigate in order to successfully integrate into the outside world. In what follows, I suggest three literate practices that might be emphasized in the writing classroom to foster rhetorical resilience in the transition from prison to the outside world.

Creative Repurposing and Making Do

Wardle's concept of creative repurposing, which encourages not direct application of prior knowledge but a kind on inventive reconciliation of the individual and the activity system she is entering, invokes Michel de Certeau's (1998) concept of "making do," a sort of bricolage in which rhetors seize the affordances of a given moment and place to create spaces of freedom. Further, Wardle's notion of "problem-exploring" disposition resonates productively with Boyle: "Yagelski claims this privileging [of humanist sense of distinct self] occurs through a critical regimen of reflective practices that exacerbates our dispositions as subjects empowered to control an objective world" (p. 537).

This disposition may be unhelpful, even harmful, for students with little control over the mechanisms of their own disenfranchisement. A problem-exploring disposition encourages comfort with uncertainty and emphasizes the processes of attunement and acclimation to the unknown, rhetorical practices that may better serve incarcerated students in the critical transition of reentry.

"Creative repurposing" is something with which incarcerated people are intimately familiar, from inventive uses for ramen noodles to complex social codes of conduct, or politics, that provide a sense of stability and agency in an otherwise chaotic environment. Inviting students to bring their out-of-class rhetorical and literate practices into the writing classroom establishes a foundation on which to build, and it also provides students with opportunities to practice and reflect on adapting prior knowledge, identities, and practices for new rhetorical purposes.

Boundary Crossing

For far transfer, or transfer of knowledge between contexts that are dissimilar, students need practice in creative repurposing through crossing boundaries between genres and writing situations. In his exploration of transfer and business and technical writing, Doug Brent (2011) suggests that mentorship and apprenticeship support critical transitions between the activity systems of the classroom and the workplace, thus mitigating disorientation and promoting creative repurposing. In other words, just as students should be encouraged to make connections between past knowledge practices and present rhetorical situations, they also need to be able to project future contexts where their academic knowledges, dispositions, and practices may be adapted for nonacademic purposes. For Brent, this means traditional forms of mentorship and apprenticeship, in which someone with intimate knowledge of the context the student is hoping to occupy helps bridge the boundary between these contexts.

This attempt at boundary crossing is evident in Patrick Berry's (2014) account of his incarcerated students' first writing assignment. When asked to write a traditional cover letter, Berry's students produced cover letters that had fabricated work experience for positions they did not believe they would ever realistically obtain ("Don't you know that many of us are going to have to flip burgers?" (p. 137)). While I do not think writing instructors should resign themselves to the notion that incarcerated students will necessarily have menial employment, if any employment at all, when they are eventually released, I do think it is important for incarcerated students to have some mentorship that is informed by the lived experiences of returning citizens. This mentorship happens in all kinds of formal and informal ways outside of the classroom, but for the dispositions and rhetorical practices to transfer, this mentorship should happen in the context of the classroom itself. So, in addition to knowledge of the genre conventions of the cover letter, incarcerated students also have to be able to imagine the affective economy in which that future writing will take place. This includes mentoring in not only the realities of discrimination and stigma, like how to address a criminal background or lack of experience in a cover letter, but also the affective and embodied experience of disorientation, alienation, and ineptitude that can come with this critical transition.

Of course, this form of mentorship is especially fraught for incarcerated students. As Cavallaro et al. (2016) argue, this kind of boundary crossing is in direct opposition to what they term the *carceral communications framework*, the ways in which the prison constricts communication as a method of control by dividing incarcerated people from each other and the outside world. In other words, the prison regime surveils and punishes boundary crossing, particularly by means of communication between those currently incarcerated and those experiencing reentry. Promoting deliberate practices in boundary crossing and mentorship in the experience of reentry will require inventive methods in this restrictive context.

Hope as Critical Rhetorical Practice

In *Writing Across Contexts: Transfer, Composition, and Sites of Writing*, Yancey et al. (2014) argue that the extent to which students see connections between the writing classroom and their imagined future significantly affects their transfer of writing knowledge and practices, as well as their motivation to invest in the work of the class. While motivation may not be as much of a concern for incarcerated students, the ability to imagine their future may well be. In his study of the phenomenology of prison life, Thomas Meisenhelder (1985) argues that in the modified life-world of the prison, time takes on an important salience. Here, time is a problem to be managed. One's sentence "hangs ominously over every prison experience. Every action is affected by the ubiquitous sense of having to wait for world time to pass so that one can finally return to the 'outside'" (p. 44). This split between "prison time" and "world time" is reflected in one research participant's feeling that his life was "on pause." Time was passing, but it was not his life. Perhaps more than violence, my research participants describe boredom as the biggest threat in their everyday lives in prison.

Meisenhelder, drawing on the work of Husserl and Heidegger, argues that a human being is "temporally structured through and as a casting of oneself toward the future" (p. 42). But one of the ways that the prison produces a distorted life-world is by degrading incarcerated people's ability to attain or imagine a viable future. This futurelessness is created in part by the unthinkability of the future for incarcerated people, for looking towards one's life in the free world just makes time inside the prison pass more slowly, making one's sentence that much more difficult. Further, Meisenhelder suggests that there may be a psychological withdrawal from a future that is uncertain or unavailable. "Even if the [incarcerated person] has conventional goals for his life, he may reasonably conclude that there exists no connection between his present situation and those future goals outside the prison" (p. 46). So, by detaching oneself from the outside world, incarcerated people find some relief from "watched pot syndrome." Without a meaningful connection to a future in the real world, investment in a future-oriented pursuit like education becomes meaningless.

Through explicit bridging of current and future writing situations, prison writing classrooms can, I argue, provide practice in the production of hope. As Ben Anderson (2006) puts it in his theory of affect, because hope anticipates the *not-yet become*, it "enacts a future as open to difference" (p. 734), while at the same time revealing the present to be unfixed and partial. Higher education programs, in their potential for new affective attachments and, thereby, future-being, produce new ways to counter, in tactical and fleeting ways, the materialization of hopelessness and dehumanization in everyday life for incarcerated students. Hope, then, is a critical rhetorical practice, a method for making meaningful connections that keep open possibilities for future change. By producing potential for future-being, hope is the method by which transfer of knowledge is possible as well as a practical knowledge that students will (hopefully) adapt and repurpose as they navigate reentry.

Conclusion

Producing participatory democratic agents is the raison d'être of most higher education in prison programs. But as these case studies suggest, the normative functions of higher education do not necessarily lead to increased inclusion, nor does academic literacy necessarily translate to successful rhetorical practice and attunement in the process of reentry. For composition scholars and practitioners, this suggests a need to, as Wan (2014) suggests, directly confront unequal access in our pedagogy and acknowledge the limits of personal volition in achieving full citizenship. "In order for writing classrooms to enact citizenships that matter, we need to recognize the ways that our idealized notions of citizenship are complicit in the citizenship that already exists" (p. 178). With an eye towards to the realities of reentry, we might begin to develop ecological, adaptive, boundary-crossing writing pedagogies that encourage creative repurposing.

Note

1 All research participants are identified by pseudonyms.

References

Anderson, B. (2006). Becoming and being hopeful: Toward a theory of affect. *Environment and Planning D: Society and Space*, 24(5), 733–752.

Bawarshi, A. (2017). Economies of knowledge transfer and the use-value of first-year composition. In B. Horner *et al.* (eds.), *Economies of writing: Revaluations in rhetoric and composition*, pp. 87–98. Logan: Utah State University Press.

Beach, K. (2003). Consequential transitions: A developmental view of knowledge propagation through social organization. In T. Tuomi-Grohn and Y. Engstrom (eds.), *Between school and work: New perspectives on transfer and boundary-crossing*, pp. 39–61. New York: Pergamon.

Berry, P. (2014). Doing time with literacy narratives. *Pedagogy*, 14(1), 137–160.

Boyle, C. (2016). Writing and rhetoric and/as posthuman practice. *College English*, 78(6), 532–554.

Brent, D. (2011). Transfer, transformation, and rhetorical knowledge: Insights from transfer theory. *Journal of Business and Technical Communication*, 25(4), 396–420.

Cavallaro, A. J. *et al.* (2016). Inside voices: Collaborative writing in a prison environment. *Harlot: A Revealing Look at the Arts of Persuasion*, 15. Retrieved at http://harlotofthearts.org/index.php/harlot/article/view/323/188.

De Certeau, M. (1998). *The practice of everyday life*. Minneapolis: University of Minnesota Press.

Guenther, L. (2013). *Solitary confinement: Social death and its afterlives*. Minneapolis: University of Minnesota Press.

Meisenhelder, T. (1985). An essay on time and the phenomenology of imprisonment. *Deviant Behavior*, 6(1), 39–56.

Nowacek, R. (2011). *Agents of integration: Understanding transfer as a rhetorical act*. Carbondale: Southern Illinois University Press.

Perkins, D. N. and Salomon, G. (1988). Teaching for transfer. *Educational Leadership*, 46(1), 22–32.

Price, J. (2015). *Prison and social death*. New Brunswick: Rutgers University Press.

Rodriguez, D. (2006). *Forced passages: Imprisoned radical intellectuals and the U.S. prison regime*. Minneapolis: University of Minnesota Press.

Thorndike, E. L. (1999). *Principles of teaching: Based on psychology.* London: Routledge.

Wan, A. (2014). *Producing good citizens: Literacy training in anxious times.* Pittsburgh: University of Pittsburgh Press.

Wardle, E. (2012). Creative repurposing as expansive learning: "Problem-Exploring" and "answer-getting" dispositions in individuals and fields. *Composition Forum*, 26. Retrieved at http://compositionforum.com/issue/26/creative-repurposing.php.

Yancey, K. B. *et al.* (2014). *Writing across contexts: Transfer, composition, and sites of writing.* Logan: Utah State University Press.

14

UNTIMELINESS; OR, WHAT CAN HAPPEN IN THE WAITING

Anne Dalke with Jody Cohen

Wasting Time

For seven years now, you have been travelling, weekly, to a range of different jails and prisons.

Then waiting.

Wasting time.

It feels personal.

And political.

You hop in the van with your students and are waved through by guards onto the grounds of a local women's jail. Stow belongings in a metal locker, except your state-issued ID which you hand to representatives of the state. Put your papers, pencils, books through the electronic scanner (all inside the transparent plastic bag, until they disallow this, before they again allow it, sometimes), walk carefully through the body scanner. Hands out to the sides, step closer for a pat down, shoulders arms torso legs, oddly gentle. Get your hand stamped. Are buzzed through the first heavy-duty metal door, along with your compatriots and others in uniform—an officer, black-robed chaplain, heavily veiled woman who runs Muslim services. And you can still see back to the waiting room and glimpse the outside door beyond that.

You are situated between these two, the outside and the inside, visible to shadowy uniformed figures in a glassed-in techni-tower above and before you. You might get buzzed quickly through the second heavy door, then move into the hallway and the next pat down and ultraviolet before the elevator takes you up. Or you could wait in this linoleumed square, maybe 5' x 5', for some immeasurable time, smelling a lunch of fish and something starchy mixing with ammonia and, faintly, cleaning products, and it is during this time that you lose your capacity to speak lightly to your colleagues and to think of anything really except confinement.

> Waiting is an articulation of structural inequality ... made ever more insufferable when fused with a sense of inferiority that percolates beneath the unmistakable impression that ... you inhabit a time and space in which other lives are more valued than your own (Brendese, 2014, p. 103).

A friend who is a web developer identifies an "attribute to waiting" that has to do with agency and choice. Where you grew up, in the rural south, folks spent a lot of time hunting and fishing, a lot of time waiting that did not seem to them like time wasted.

But you left that slow pace long ago. On the fast track now, an academic with lots to do, you get impatient. Have few ways to prepare for slow-downed time in prison. No guidelines on how to handle it. No prescriptions for dealing with the inconsistencies.

One day you are not waved through, pointed instead through a windowless door into a narrow visitors' waiting room, where family members mill around, sit in hard plastic chairs. In this timeless space, this limbo between the surveilled outside and the promise of contact within, you shift uncomfortably, think to use the time to engage with the college students who accompany you. Then you see the line of books hiding their faces: just now doing the reading for today, since their own time is always pressed and compressed with the rush of becoming, the promise of position, of impact.

Once, twice a semester, you spend the entire class time in the waiting room, watching the hour hand spin you all out.

"A prison is a trap for catching time" (Gopnik, 2012).

Sarah Shotland, a contributor to this volume, describes the experience:

> There will be so much time for you to think, undistracted. There will be nothing useful to say. There will be nothing to occupy yourself with; you will know time is moving but you have little proof that you were in it (Shotland, 2017).

Another semester, you are co-teaching a course, not far from your home, at a community jail for men. It's minimum security, "a joke," say those who are incarcerated here, close to reentry, also close to home.

What do they mean? Do they think the rules here should be tougher? That they can outsmart them?

You go in on Tuesdays with ten outside students, back alone on Wednesdays to tutor the inside guys on their writing. The rules here may be lax. But they are also more unruly in application than at the medium- and maximum-security prisons where you also work.

Maybe because there are so few real checks and guards?

Sue Castagnetto, another contributor to this book, muses that prison staff members "have little to do. They watch over others. Enforce the rules. Fiddle with them" (Castagnetto, 2017).

The fiddling costs you time—and the prison can take as much of your time as it wants. That is its power, a smaller-scale version of taking the time of those living inside. It is the price you have to pay if you want to enter.

This is Wonderland, where Alice sighs wearily:

> "I think you might do something better with the time," she said, "than wasting it in asking riddles that have no answers."
>
> "If you knew Time as well as I do," said the Hatter, "You wouldn't talk about wasting IT. It's HIM."
>
> "I don't know what you mean," said Alice.
>
> "Of course you don't!" the Hatter said, tossing his head contemptuously. "I dare say you never even spoke to Time!"
>
> "Perhaps not," Alice cautiously replied: "but I know I have to beat time when I learn music."
>
> "Ah! that accounts for it," said the Hatter. "He won't stand beating. Now, if you only kept on good terms with him, he'd do almost anything you liked …" (Carroll, 1963).

You are not included on the memo. Get a revised memo. Bring in a copy. The CO insists on locating her own. Can't. Pages through the folder. Again. Inefficiency? Again. Stupidity? Again.

Thank you for bringing your supplies in a see-through bag. It's not on the memo. You may not take it inside. Remove your scarf. Your watch. Not listed on the memo. Which has now been found. Your co-teacher must remove a tissue from his shirt pocket. You may only take in golf pencils. Which are on the memo. But you may not take in the plastic bag holding the golf pencils. A college student is refused admittance, her jeans too tight. They have a hole. She has worn them inside for weeks now.

Another student is told to remove her earrings. Says she can't: just got them pierced; the studs are to stay in for a month.

Take them out. Or you can't come in.

Like Alice, you fret and fume your way through the obstacles.

Your co-teacher smiles. "We get off easy. Those pat downs are a joke."

Again: the language of flippancy, of humor. A way of managing frustration in a situation where you have no agency, no choice but to comply.

In preparation for a large event, you bring in 100 empty folders. The CO at the gate. Opens. Every. Single. One.

This takes some time. It is no joke.

You are assigned to volunteer training for a restorative justice project at a maximum-security prison a long, hard drive away. It's been three months since you applied to work with this project, three months spent waiting for a letter of notification.

Due to some clichés there will be no letter sent out (Clerk Typist, Department of Corrections).[1]

The cliché of the glitch.

This is the expression of a powerful bureaucracy, designed to control—presumably to protect—you and your outside students, as well as those inside.

Your "training"—a litany of offensive descriptions of those who are incarcerated—includes the repeated assurance of how valuable your work is. Thank you for volunteering. You need to return for TB tests. Make another trip, before 4 p.m., to get your photo ID.

"Sorry about the added coordinating and trips," writes your outside supervisor. "Welcome to the world of prison work!"

> ... the question of who has the prerogative to tell whom to "wait" ... who gets to "keep time"—and who has the prerogative to "mark time" ... reveals potent tools of power ... the long-term wasting that comes from ... being forced to wait indefinitely ... time is used as a vehicle through which power is leveraged (Brendese, 2014, pp. 82, 84, 85).

Escaping Time

Why do you wait? Why waste your time?

Counter-wise, and curiously (a central dimension of Wonderland), this likely has to do with the slowing of time in prison, the absence of the usual measurements of its usefulness, its forward motion. Time inside the walls actually seems to you more spacious, capacious, more inviting of attentiveness. Outside, "continuous partial attention" is the order of the day, exacerbated by multiple online marketing tricks designed to snag you all (Lewis, 2017).

The main reason you really like teaching in prison, you now realize, is because you find fewer distractions there, including those increasingly insistent electronic ones, which make so many demands on your time.

You are "acutely aware" that prison is your "only unplugged time/space" (Shotland, 2017).

You've been teaching college classes for thirty-five years, have spent your life wanting and trying to be in serious conversation with people who seem, increasingly, to be drawn elsewhere, have calls to answer, meetings to attend, children to fetch and feed. On your first trip into prison for Inside-Out training, you enter a huge auditorium, walk down the sloped floor. One of the men walks up briskly, shakes your hand, greets you warmly: "Hello. How are you? What are your thoughts about the prison industrial complex?"

Why has it taken you so long to offer courses inside? In these windowless rooms, shut off from the world, it's easier for you to be present, available to those who make themselves available to you. More able to connect. With them. And to connect them. With books and ideas.

When you are inside, time seems to operate more in the way physicists and philosophers think of it: without "pass or flow," "laid out in its entirety—a time scape, analogous to a landscape—with all past and future events located there together" (Davies, 2006).

Several of your outside students luxuriate in an expansive sense of inside time. They tell you how much they look forward to their Friday afternoons in prison. A student in her first semester with your program says she feels "relaxed" in prison, much more so than at the college, where she's losing a power struggle with a professor. A friend with decades of experience teaching inside says similarly that she "loves being in jail," where the expectations are lower than in the academy.

Less pressure.

No push to perform, no reach for the future.

The jail itself feels like a kind of limbo, a state of in-between, as during shift change when everyone freezes in place. Time stands still. All events simultaneous.

You read together a passage in *Bodega Dreams* about how school is utterly alienated from the lives of the characters, then veer into a discussion of parents' roles in their children's education. A student says she tries to—but often can't—be there to check her children's homework. Another jumps in: "You have to be!" "But I am working three jobs to put food on the table—and my father always checks that homework anyway, no matter what!" "You got to have priorities!"

In this moment, no one is checking children's homework. And yet. You are all in more than one place, time, both here and there, now and then, sitting in this circle and at home.

"… how is one to be untimely when our own time seems to be so many times at once?" (Euben, 2003, p. 15).

In this moment, your splintering voices creating a cacophony of guilt and accusation, longing and regret.

And time is up.

"Time is the culprit" (Einstein, as cited in Petersen, 1985, p. 427).

But inside time bleeds out. You carry home with you a more capacious sense of phenomenological time, one in which past, present, and future are intertwined.

You and your co-teacher acknowledge to each other those drifting dream-thoughts just before sleep: you are here on your own soft sheets with your bathroom down the hall, meds to take if needed, and yet, just as you fall asleep, you imagine yourself there, in that bunk, risking a flush in the night that might wake your cellie. What are these walls separating in from out, you from me, so real—and yet are they?

When you are inside, you are still out; when you are outside, you are still in.

Serving Time

And yet. Of course.

What happens inside when you, your colleagues, and students visit, differs profoundly from what happens again and again, every day, for those who do not walk out of the prison at the end of each class session.

> ... visits and looking forward to visits ain't the real thing. The real thing's the time I got to do ... Everybody leaves ... then I got to start all over again, working myself up to deal with being alone. The stopping and starting's too hard. Better to let visits go (Wideman, 2010, p. 55).

Your speculations about the capacious nature of time, your own capacity to revel in the ability to be "present," fail to acknowledge the enormous pain of being confined in a place where there is no forward movement, where what is happening is coeval with what happened long before—not just across individual life spans, but through centuries of history: "the complex temporal echoes of past practices of convict leasing and outright slavery are creatively tethered to the projected future ... of segregated time" (Brendese, 2014, p. 94).

Sue Castagnetto again: "The split second in which you commit a crime may relegate you to prison for years" (Castagnetto, 2017).

In solitary confinement, especially: nothing to do to "fill the time"—for days, weeks, months on end. No one to share the time with.

One of your students reports that he spent his time there studying Maria Mies's *Patriarchy and Accumulation on a World Scale: Women in the International Division of Labour*—which he recommends. A student in another class says she spent her time in solitary learning to distinguish the sound of the footsteps of each of the correctional officers. A discipline she also recommends.

What seems to you the luxury of endless time is, for your students in prison, the essence of their punishment. The absence of a future. Segregated in a space and time where there is no movement.

> ... one day typically stretches out for decades. It isn't the horror of the time at hand but the unimaginable sameness of the time ahead that makes prisons unendurable ... Time stops ... the presence of time [is] something being done to you, instead of something you do things with ... time becomes in every sense this thing you serve (Gopnik, 2012).

Your attempts to give an account of this difference, here, are endistanced, oblique. Direct testimony is scarce.

In Jesmyn Ward's novel, *Sing, Unburied Sing*, a ghost named Richie describes his entrapment at the infamous prison farm that is Mississippi State Penitentiary:

> I didn't understand time … when I was young. How could I know that after I died, Parchman would pull me from the sky? How could I imagine Parchman would … refuse to let go? And how could I conceive that Parchman was past, present and future, all at once, that the story and sentiment that carved the place out of the wilderness would show me that time is a vast ocean and that everything is happening at once? I was trapped Parchman had imprisoned me again (Ward, 2017, p. 186).

In the prison landscape—that slowed time scape, closed time space—everything that was, is, will be is already present. There is no change to come.

Those students monitoring their children's homework manage prison time by speaking of life at home in the "now"; they experience being in two places at once. Others focus only on one, insist that they are "living where they are and experiencing what's here, being here." Romarilyn Ralston, a formerly incarcerated student and contributor to this volume, stakes a different claim: whatever the institutional structures, "change happens through the passage of time. Although the system may tag me forever as 1988, it's 2018, and I am no longer my crime" (Ralston, 2017).

Thirty-five years ago, Thomas Meisenhelder actually graphed successive stages of "prisonized time" (Meisenhelder, 1985, p. 51). More recently, Sarah Shotland similarly charted the ways in which the speed of time shifts, depending how much of it her students have been assigned:

> Time doesn't really *stop* in prison once you have an indefinite amount of it. Students who are lifers are absolutely engaged in the work. For those who aren't going home, *right now* becomes very important to do something with. Others, whose sentences come to a close, disengage from the class. The most difficult classes I teach are the ones in which everyone has a sentence of less than a year (Shotland, 2017).

The jerkiness of prison time, Sarah adds, means she

> never knows if a student will have one class with me or two years of classes with me, which makes classes a very strange thing to plan, and makes the actual time spent in class seem super high-stakes. I don't feel the comfort of "we can continue discussing this next week," because I have no idea if that's true (Shotland, 2017).

In prison, constrained by interrupted and uncertain time, you are somehow freer to experiment with the unstable time you do have.

You find yourself suddenly needing to prove something before shift change. The intensity of opposing perspectives making the circle smaller, the time tighter.

You do this with students who are defined by their pasts. With futures withheld.

Bryan Stevenson writes of the many juvenile lifers "matured into adults who were … now nothing like the confused children who had committed a violent crime" (Stevenson, 2015, p. 266). PastPresentFuture. "Aged out" of criminal behavior. Marked always for what they have outgrown.

And assaulted, in between, by the unpredictable irruptions of prison time.

Another writer in this volume, Anna Plemons, observes that her own teaching

> experiences inside are bound and regularly disrupted by chronological time. There is clearly a profound disrespect for people's time, and poor stewardship of chronological time in prison, but I can't get past the fact that my class is always, without fail, interrupted by an officer needed to take count, and rushed because folks need to get back to their houses by a certain time (to again make count) (Plemons, 2017).

Another semester, another prison. Co-teaching a very different class with three others. Accompanied, with lots of back-up, lots of hands on deck. You spend hours meticulously planning: propose, design, and—well past midnight—send one another revised lesson plans. Laugh with deep pleasure at how co-generative it is to work together, revel in all the energy a-brewing. Eagerly enter prison for your first class. On time. With an agenda.

> 12:15—Depart.
> 12:45—Process class into facility.
> 1:20—Moment to center.

The room now bubbling with the voices of students, working together in small groups, you suddenly realize that—having followed instructions to leave your cell phones in your cars—not one of the instructors has a watch. There is no clock on the wall. Not laughing now. You've got a hard stop, must be out before count. You borrow a wristwatch from an inside student.

Carefully get yourselves back on track.

Disrupting Time

Daniel Karpowitz celebrates the capacity of universities to offer the most marginalized people access to the best education. The Bard Prison Initiative, where he serves as director of policy and academics, is committed to replicating, inside, the classes that take place in "a high quality, selective college" (2017, p. xiii):

> The college that establishes itself inside the prison without disrupting the prison as experienced daily by its students inside has failed. [Only a] disturbance of the normal modes of operation … can lead to the alteration of

the daily experience of the time and space of incarceration upon which everything envisioned and narrated here depends (2017, pp. 172–173).

Anything less, Karpowitz argues, accedes to the degrading assumption of incapacity, a "bigotry of low expectations" and "low ambitions" (Karpowitz, 2017, pp. 24, 170).

In sharp contrast, Robin Kelley dismisses the college classroom: not a place for profound personal or social change, merely "a performative space, where faculty and students compete with each other":

> universities are not up the task ... of social transformation ... By definition it takes place outside the university ... the formal classroom was never the space for deep critique ... struggle cannot occur solely inside the refuge we call the university. Being grounded in the world we wish to make is fundamental (Kelley, 2016).

Elsewhere in this volume, Raphael Ginsberg enters the charged landscape staked out by Karpowitz and Kelley. Offering a "corrective to higher education in prison's triumphant transformational narratives," Raphael argues that conceptualizing "the prison classroom as a space of transformation reduces and ultimately exploits the students on whose behalf the pedagogue works": "incarceration's degradation increases instructor–student power disparities," making the "abject category" of prisoner "impossible to deconstruct ... and reconstitute ... in liberated form" (this volume, p. 63).

Your own experiences with what college in prison can do are deeply entangled in these debates. One of your students muses that prison is where they put people who "just don't understand life." His learning to read, he explains, has become a mode of "understanding how to understand," a form of political activism that now enables him to begin to see how he once "found the gun in his hand." Juxtapose this account with that of another student, who finds the class stimulating, and is serving wonderfully as a mentor to the younger ones. Rather than thank you for raising his political consciousness, however, he asks lots of sharp questions about the aims, goals, methods of your class, charges you with being "in collusion with the prison industrial complex." Another student is similarly frustrated with all your philosophizing: "Our focus here is to survive. We have no time or space to intellectualize; to sit here and ask questions is wasting our time. We need an immediate stop to this thing."

You want to say: No. Slow down.

Although the programs in which you work are both pro-student and anti-institutional, none of you who go in to teach can really be overt about this latter political agenda.

But in offering a space for deep relationship, examination, and critique, you are deliberately enacting the paradox of teaching against the prison, inside the prison.

In her essay in this volume, Tessa Hicks Peterson puts it this way: "Practicing a healing and liberatory form of teaching and learning together in this shared educational journey, inside one of the world's most dehumanizing and violent settings, itself becomes an act of resistance" (this volume, p. 178).

Prompted by your students' critiques—their insistence that your course isn't wrestling with the larger issues, is all theory, no practice—you replace the conventional final paper with small group proposals for "Think Tanks," in which course alumni and faculty might meet regularly after the semester ends, to work together on local interests and systematic issues.

It is the claim of this paper that, in both the short- and long-term, teaching inside can assist in disturbing the order of the prison industrial complex. Margo Campbell, a colleague in restorative justice work, calls these kinds of practices "abolishing prison from within" (Campbell, 2018).

The workshops to which you and Margo contribute are part of an "accountability" project, which focuses on the needs of those who have been harmed, and asks who is obliged to meet such needs. Many of the men who have designed and are teaching the workshops are serving life sentences in a maximum-security prison, and do not anticipate parole. They are offering a variety of sessions to those who may be getting out: ten-week-long classes introducing restorative justice; ten-week-long advanced classes; weekend versions for those who will not be in prison for ten weeks; and just recently: a six-week pilot course specifically targeting reentry and reintegration. During an alumni event, open to anyone who has completed any version of this course of study, one man testifies that while he was out, he was riding the subway with a pocket full of cash, en route to pay off a licensing violation. A group of young people entered the train, started shaking down the passengers.

A few years ago, he says, he would have gotten into a rumble. Instead, guided by what he'd learned from the workshop, he got off at the next stop, far from where he was heading. Stepped away from violence. His being out there, making a choice to move away, has been impelled by your shared work in this room.

And now: parole violation. He's back again. His being here, testifying to this experience, animates your reunion, circled up, leaning in, hunkered down together in this closed-in space.

Disrupting things as they are.

Integrating Time

Over fifty years ago, James Baldwin illuminated the paradoxical space where you work, in which the process of being educated leads to the "right and necessity to examine everything" that you are taught: "The paradox of education is precisely this—that as one begins to become conscious one begins to examine the society in which he is being educated" (Baldwin, 1998, pp. 686, 678).

You are joined—both in this volume and in prison classes around the country—by educators ("themselves abolitionists") who share an "uncompromising commitment to the disenfranchised," and see a role for radical prison education in "undermining the effects of incarceration" (Scott, 2014, p. 413).

Your class gatherings also include, profoundly, the writers whose work you are reading together. You are all untimely contemporaries, together creating a different "reality of time," "cultivating solidarity with asynchronous others" (Brendese, 2014, pp. 98, 85).

P. J. Brendese has written, powerfully and extensively, about the long history of segregation that has shaped the current carceral project. In offering alternative experiences of presence and attentiveness, both to one another and to the texts you share, your classes attempt to counter that history. One of your co-teachers in prison, Joel Schlosser, suggests that you call this practice "time integrated" (Schlosser, 2017).

Present in such multiply time-crossed ways, students in your class are repeatedly, if temporarily, released from what Angela Davis (2003) calls the "computability of state punishment in terms of time—days, months, years" (p. 44). In this essay, you represent such computations of prison time as real-life versions of Lewis Carroll's dream world: distorted, exaggerated renditions of the world outside, where not less, but more, rules apply.

You ask the exuberant superintendent, leading you and your fellow tutors through the light-filled hallway of the medium-security prison, what draws her to this work. "Well," she says, "for starters, I like the structure."

Prison life *is* intensely structured—an oblique intensification of what's outside—*and* it is filled with rules that keep getting changed, or are inconsistently applied. Not an alternative you'd think anyone would choose.

As Gillian Beer observes, "Alice can walk away" from Wonderland; "she is not imprisoned" in the "rumpled and energetic" forms of time underground (Beer, 2016, p. 41). Her story ends in "the nightmare atmosphere" of a courtroom, where "there are rules but no order, voices but no listening, and assertions but no evidence" (Beer, 2016, p. 202). Alice resists the disorder, and the injustice it perpetuates, by "wreaking total destruction" on the court; she thus ends its power over her (Beer, 2016, p. 208).

Unlike Alice, who departs from her dream, you continue coming in, going out, coming in again. Not shrugging off what happens in between. You remain in continuous, complex negotiation with the prison apparatus, acceding repeatedly to various changes in protocol (*remove your earrings, your scarf, your watch, your tissue, your see-through bag*) in order to get inside.

Your co-teacher begins each class with a moment of centering, of gratitude and reflection on all that each of you, driven by a desire for human connection, has done to get here.

In that classroom, you find ways to disrupt the (dis)orderly patterns of the prison, offer something "outside" its jumbled, Alice-in-Wonderland-y, law-and-order, lawless, disorderly structure.

Staying present with yourself, colleagues, students, texts, shared thoughts—filled with the exchanges possible not just in the present, but past and future, too.

Time integrated.

Note

1 We are keeping this citation purposely vague in order to protect our relationship with the Department of Corrections.

Acknowledgements

In deep gratitude to all who gave attention to this project. Jody Cohen, there in the beginning and still here now: co-teacher, co-author, who wrote some of these inside stories. Multiple other co-teachers, with whom you continue to work out all the details: Benjamin Berger, Margo Campbell, Miguel Glatzer, Janice Lion, Margaret O'Neil, Keith Reeves, Emma Sindelar, Barbara Toews, Katherine Walden. Members of the writing collective, who offered careful readings of this essay, and accompanied you in producing this book: especially Susan Castagnetto, Rebecca Ginsburg, Tessa Hicks Peterson, Anna Plemons, Romarilyn Ralston, Sarah Shotland. And those beyond these circles, who have for so long supported, and continue to sustain, your work, inside and out: Jeff Dalke, Kristin Lindgren, Joel Schlosser (who first named time as your topic). Last and first: your granddaughter Naima Belle Dalke-Gupta, who colored and gave to you a bookmark of "A Mad Tea-Party," which supplied an early scene.

References

Baldwin, J. (1998). A talk to teachers. In T. Morrison (ed.), *Collected essays*, pp. 678–686. New York: The Library of America. (Original work published 1963.)

Beer, G. (2016). *Alice in space: The sideways Victorian world of Lewis Carroll*. Chicago: The University of Chicago Press.

Brendese, P. J. (2014). Black noise in white time: Segregated temporality and mass incarceration. In R. Coles *et al.* (eds.), *Radical future pasts: Untimely political theory*, pp. 81–111. Lexington: The University Press of Kentucky.

Campbell, M. (2018, February 28). Personal communication.

Carroll, L. (1963). *Alice's adventures in Wonderland*. Retrieved at http://www.alice-in-wonderland.net/resources/chapters-script/alices-adventures-in-wonderland/. (Original work published 1865).

Castagnetto, S. (2017, December 27). Personal communication.

Davies, P. (2006, February 21). That mysterious flow. *Scientific American*. Retrieved at https://www.scientificamerican.com/article/that-mysterious-flow-2006-02/.

Davis, A. (2003). *Are prisons obsolete?* New York: Seven Stories.

Euben, P. (2003). *Platonic noise*. Princeton, NJ: Princeton University Press.

Gopnik, A. (2012, January 30). The caging of America. *The New Yorker*. Retrieved at https://www.newyorker.com/magazine/2012/01/30the-caging-of-america.

Karpowitz, D. (2017). *College in prison: Reading in an age of mass incarceration*. New Brunswick, NJ: Rutgers University Press.

Kelley, R. D. G. (2016, March 7). Black study, black struggle. *Boston Review*. Retrieved at http://bostonreview.net/forum/robin-d-g-kelley-black-study-black-struggle.

Lewis, P. (2017, October 6). "Our Minds Can Be Hijacked": The Tech Insiders Who Fear a Smartphone Dystopia. *The Guardian.* Retrieved at https://www.theguardian.com/technology/2017/oct/05/smartphone-addiction-silicon-valley-dystopia.

Meisenhelder, T. (1985). An essay on time and the phenomenology of imprisonment. *Deviant Behavior,* 6(1), 39–56.

Petersen, C. R. (1985). Time and stress: Alice in Wonderland. *Journal of the History of Ideas,* 46(3), 427–433.

Plemons, A. (2017, December 12). Personal communication.

Ralston, R. (2017, December 9). Personal communication.

Schlosser, J. (2017, November 30). Personal communication.

Scott, R. (2014). Using critical pedagogy to connect prison education and prison abolitionism. *Saint Louis University Public Law Review,* 33(2), 401–414. Retrieved at http://law.slu.edu/sites/default/files/Journals/robert_scott_article.pdf.

Shotland, S. (2017, December 15). Personal communication.

Stevenson, B. (2015). *Just mercy: A story of justice and redemption.* New York: Spiegel & Grau.

Ward, J. (2017). *Sing, unburied, sing.* New York: Scribner.

Wideman, J. (2010). *Fanon: A novel.* New York: Mariner Books.

15

TEACHING AMERICAN HISTORY IN PRISON

Margaret Garb

In September 2014, just one month after Michael Brown was killed by a police officer in Ferguson, I began teaching American history in a medium-security prison in Pacific, Missouri. The prison is about an hour's drive from Ferguson along highways that snake through affluent, largely white suburbs and past rural towns that are little more than gas stations and strip malls. The students came from throughout the state, one from Chicago and another from rural Virginia, and many were raised in St. Louis; all seemed familiar with Ferguson. That was all I asked the students on the first day of class: where they were born and raised.

That fall, I taught the survey of American history in prison, where I had fifteen students, men ranging in age from early twenties to early fifties. I taught the same course on campus where the ages of sixty men and women spanned eighteen to twenty-two. The campus students, it would turn out, were better writers; they had been drilled in the five-paragraph essay throughout high school. The prison students, more than half of whom had earned a high school degree through the prison GED program, were weak on writing skills, strong on analytic skills. We read the same books and primary source materials in prison and on campus. The prison students quickly learned to tear into a text, target key terms and phrases, and rip open a bundle of meanings. They were starving for ideas and opportunities for debate in ways the campus students were merely hungry. Despite vast differences in the ages, life experiences, and education of the two groups, their responses to American history, or at least my version of a U.S. history survey, were fairly similar.

By the first day of class, protesters had been in the streets of Ferguson and downtown St. Louis for nearly a month. They demanded the prosecution of the police officer, Darren Wilson, who shot Brown. The protesters' broader demands included a restructuring of the policing and bail systems, police training, and the firing of the police chief and mayor of Ferguson, both of whom were white.

What became clear (to those of us living outside low-income black communities) after Brown's killing was that the more than two dozen tiny municipalities north of St. Louis—and many towns in America—were using traffic violations and housing court fees to generate revenue. African Americans living in or driving through Ferguson entered an authoritarian regime where minor infractions of traffic rules or housing code violations could land them in jail for weeks or months. A bail system with a series of ever-multiplying fees meant that someone stopped for a broken taillight or fined for a damaged front porch could sit in jail, losing a job and amassing such large fees that payment, and an escape from the carceral system, was impossible. Misdemeanors and minor infractions could grind out tens of thousands of dollars in fines and prison costs from citizens least able to pay. Poverty was criminalized.

The protests—the nightly battles with police who used tear gas indiscriminately and arrested hundreds of people—hovered just beyond my classrooms. On the college campus, some students were participating in the protests and the activists regularly brought their politics to class, offering comments about how history helps explain the police killing and protests on St. Louis streets. I let them talk without injecting my views. Students in prison also wanted to talk about the police shooting but I tried to limit those discussions. The incarcerated students that fall were under heavy Department of Corrections scrutiny for expressions of support for the protesters or opprobrium for the police. I did not want to put them in an awkward position, especially as the CO (Corrections Officer) sitting outside our classroom often listened to our discussions. In any case, teaching American history offers many opportunities to talk about white supremacy, state-sanctioned violence, social control and intertwined histories of race, crime and poverty.

We were studying American history as history was being made not far from our classrooms. Yet, I pushed the students to look beyond the present to work through the very specific contexts of past struggles, past forms of oppression, past techniques of violence and control. Over the course of the semester, events in the streets and discussions in the prison and campus classrooms came together and sped apart. Like tracks on a railroad map, the classroom conversations and protesting crowds were contained within the same intellectual and political landscape even as they often moved in different directions. What became clear week after week was that oppression takes new forms and violence takes new meanings as political and social circumstances change. Yet connections between past and present often were too obvious: slavery, lynching, mass incarceration, police murders of black Americans seemed part of a three-centuries-long continuum. With each outburst of protest and police violence—and each time I walked through the maze of security to enter the prison—I was reminded that cruel subjugation cuts through American history into the present moment.

I always open the first class of the American history survey with a question: When does American history begin? Or, I add, when should this course begin? I present the students with some options: 30 million years ago when the first people crossed a land bridge from Asia into the continent of North America; millions of years before that when a retreating glacier formed the grasslands, plains, mountains, and lakes that would provide the material conditions out of which humans would build societies; early European contact with Columbus or the Vikings; 1619 with the first slave ship to land in Virginia; and on and on, hitting crucial moments of change in lands and peoples. I remind students that their chosen originary moment reveals something about what America is and who is an American, or what counts as American identity. Origin stories, I tell them, shape understandings of the present.

The incarcerated students responded by turning, almost immediately, to the writing of the U.S. Constitution. With laws, government, and a document defining the nation, America as we modern citizens know it began. I reminded them that the Constitution treated enslaved people as three-fifths of a person and that the eighteenth-century states denied women the right to vote and required men to own property to exercise the franchise. A student then suggested the end of the slave system or when women got the vote. Another student commented, "Freedom is not the point of America." (I did not write them down, but have not forgotten some of the phrases my students used that fall.) Others in the class pushed backward, arguing that the arrival of Europeans and Africans on the Atlantic coast marked the nation's beginning. To the prison students, it was society—people and laws—that make a nation, free or not.

On campus, the students focused on the physical environment and the making of a territory inhabitable by humans. To the campus students, the retreating glacier, the sweeping plains, grasses, northwestern forests, lakes and rivers defined America. The landscape, the organic material out of which humans build societies, marked the beginning of the American nation. The students were environmentalists and, to my and their surprise, more concerned with the material stuff used to make communities than the ideas that validated a social order. America was a place and many peoples, not an ideal. Freedom, equality, and all the grand ideals of the founding documents had little to do with the making of the nation. Here, at the semester's start, the prison and campus students converged.

The most raucous classroom debate that fall was among the incarcerated students when we discussed the slave narrative written by Harriet Jacobs (a pseudonym for Linda Brett). Jacobs, born into slavery in North Carolina, fled her plantation home when her owner attempted to rape her. She ultimately made it to Massachusetts where she was reunited with her children, settled in a house, and wrote a memoir of her life, which she and her abolitionist friends used to publicize the horrors of slavery.

In the prison classroom, our discussion quickly turned to whether incarceration was similar to slavery. It is, and it isn't, we concluded. I nudged the conversation back to the book by asking what freedom meant to Jacobs. It meant owning herself, someone said. Freedom meant having a home, another student said, adding that at the end of the memoir Jacobs said she still needed a "hearth and a home." He read the passage out loud. But she had to leave her home in the south to find freedom, another student said. She left her grandmother behind. A plantation is not a home to a slave, someone commented, and the debate continued until a quiet, skinny, twenty-something black man said, "Michael Brown was shot right outside his home." True, I said and asked if home meant something different in the mid-nineteenth century. Did home mean something different to men than to women? Maybe someone said, but there were still slave catchers looking for Harriet in Boston. Just like the police "go after us in our neighborhoods," he said.

What is home, I asked. The place where you were born, where you were raised, where you live, where you feel you belong? And now I, who have read and written a lot about nineteenth-century housing and domesticity, was feeling my way forward. Prison isn't home, a middle-aged white guy said. The black nationalist student, a middle-aged black man who liked to inject a comment and then retreat to watch the debate, noted that in most states, the U.S. Census counts incarcerated people as residing in prisons, which means that when district lines are drawn for electoral purposes, the incarcerated add bodies to the districts surrounding the prisons. Most prisons are in rural areas far from the urban neighborhoods where incarcerated men have families and homes. And, he noted, people locked in prison cannot vote. That sent us off on an exhilarating discussion about the relationship between race and "home" and citizenship in nineteenth- and twenty-first-century America.

That debate guided my discussion of Jacobs' slave narrative with my students on campus. Those students, unlike my incarcerated students, had answers to the questions about home and belonging. Even the students who had moved around a lot with their families could name a home. When I told them of the very different views of the men in prison, of the incongruity of counting incarcerated people in districts far from their home communities, the students on campus were surprised and saddened and, in some cases, wanted to find ways to fix this uncomfortable situation. (That was one difference between the classes: students on campus typically sought solutions to social problems while those in prison often emphasized causes like racism or poverty.) Where you were born is not necessarily where you end up, one bright young woman said. Look at Jacobs, born into slavery, then years later living as a free woman. True, I thought. But not always. Jacobs, I noted, was among a small portion of enslaved people who were able to reach free states. Most people enslaved in the American south could do little more than dream of freedom.

Michel-Rolph Trouillot, drawing on the work of Pierre Bourdieu, calls the Haitian revolution "unthinkable." The slave insurrection in late eighteenth-century San Domingue was, Trouillot writes, outside the realm of possibility in the writings of French thinkers and Haitian planters, who had convinced themselves that people of African descent were biologically inferior and that slavery served a social good (or at least a necessary economic purpose). The French elite—the politicians, intellectuals, and propertied classes—had no "conceptual frame of reference" through which to imagine or articulate a slave uprising ending in an independent nation governed by the formerly enslaved. They simply could not imagine a society, a well-ordered and productive nation, where black people ruled (Trouillot, 1995, p. 82).

College-in-prison is for many Americans unthinkable. Millions of Americans have experienced incarceration or know someone who has spent time inside a prison. According to the U.S. Census, approximately 16 million students are enrolled in college while more than 2.2 million people are incarcerated in prisons or jails. Federal statistics do not track the overlap; there is no official count of incarcerated college students. Trouillot writes that the Haitian revolution had to happen before French intellectuals could imagine black people governing a country. Practice proceeded discourse. People in prison have long read books and educated themselves. But it took news stories about imprisoned scholars and formerly incarcerated lawyers, poets, scientists, and social workers to give a slight jolt to the American imagination. There is a growing body of literature about the experiences and achievements of college-in-prison programs around the nation. Yet when I have been interviewed by reporters about college-in-prison, the first or second question always is about the need for "remedial" courses and then shock and awe that our incarcerated students can complete demanding college courses.

Teaching the survey of U.S. history in one semester is a mad dash from fourteenth-century indigenous societies (the Mississippian people based in southern Illinois and eastern Missouri) to Watergate. In late November, we got to the Civil Rights movement in post-war America. We read the Civil Rights Act of 1964 and Bayard Rustin's essay, "From Protest to Politics," and talked about the movement's origins in labor organizing in the 1930s and in black veterans' experiences in World War II. We talked about the courageous legal team of Charles Hamilton Huston, Thurgood Marshall, Pauli Murray, Spotswood Robinson, and others who argued a series of cases before the U.S. Supreme Court, culminating in the Brown decision overturning legalized segregation in American schools. We talked about the movement's heroes and its foot soldiers, the strategy of civil disobedience and the era's tremendous violence.

Later that week, I sent a request to the warden asking if I could show a segment of "Eyes on the Prize," Henry Hampton's beautiful and award-winning documentary series on the movement produced in the 1980s. The warden, who is about five-feet-two in heels, smart, funny, and a strong advocate for prison education, denied my request, saying a film screening was "not a good idea right now." The warden was, she said, concerned the film could whip up anger and incite new tensions. I could see her point. The prison felt unusually jumpy that fall; there were lockdowns, fights, expanding gangs, anxious rumors. Anger over the police shooting in Ferguson and rage over the police's military-style response to public protests seemed to surge through the prison, even as few people spoke openly about it.

From the documentary, I wanted to show the segment about the lunch-counter sit-ins, which began with college students sitting at the segregated Woolworth's counter in Nashville in 1960. The film shows the students dragged from their stools and beaten by mobs of white men, who burned the college students with cigarettes, poured ice water and ketchup on them, and slammed fists into bodies curled on the floor, covering their heads and nonviolent. The film shows the Nashville police arriving at Woolworth's where they arrest the bruised and beaten students. I wanted my college students on campus and in prison to see that college students could be the central actors in a movement for social justice. In the film, they would see the generational shift from the older court room-oriented activism to a protest movement in the streets.

The film includes old news footage of the parents of several of the black college students expressing concern that their children's arrest records will impede their education and limit their career opportunities. Their children were, through college, moving socially upward; an arrest record could prove a barrier to the students' and the family's aspirations. Yet, towards the end of the segment, an activist (I think it was John Lewis) talks about his many arrests and says that a prison stay became "a badge of honor." An arrest and time in a southern jail was both terrifying and a mark of the courage of white and black college students in the movement. For those students, the movement transformed the meaning of prison. I wanted students in both classrooms to see that. But I could not argue with the warden, whom I respect.

This was not the Haitian revolution. The incarcerated students surely could imagine mass protests and mob violence. They watched the Ferguson protests every night on the TV news. The difference between the scenes of Woolworth's in Nashville in 1960 and Ferguson's streets in 2014 was that we knew that the lunch-counter sit-ins culminated in the passage of the Voting Rights Act and the Civil Rights Act, and the transformation of protesting college students into national heroes. The nation had not been ripped apart by the mid-twentieth-century struggle, but rather had, in many ways, been sewn back together. We—the students in both classrooms and I—were part of and living within that unfinished struggle of the civil rights movement. We did not know how the Ferguson protests would end. A breakdown of the police state in black neighborhoods and suburbs, and an end to police shootings of unarmed black men and women were beyond imagining.

The week before Thanksgiving, as class in prison ended, I asked the students about Thanksgiving in prison. They got turkey and mashed potatoes for lunch and a couple hours off from work, they said. They reminisced about Thanksgivings at home. Green bean casserole, an aunt's brown-sugar sweet potatoes, thick salty gravy.

Over Thanksgiving week, despite an unusual cold front descending on St. Louis, the protests over police shootings continued. The county prosecutor had refused to indict Darren Wilson; in mid-October a young black man, eighteen-year-old Von Derritt Myers, had been shot by an off-duty police officer. Change seemed impossible. Justice, or simply an unprejudiced judicial system, for black Americans and low-income St. Louisans seemed far away. The protests, which eventually would become the foundation for a national movement challenging white supremacy, seemed largely ineffective, unable to pierce the walls of a powerful police state. That fall, discouraged by the scenes of police driving military tanks through city streets and confronting protestors with full-on riot regalia, I saw the prison, much more than the college campus, as America's future.

I am writing this essay in the fall of 2017, three years after the events described and in a different political moment. We are living under a new (corrupt and mendacious) president who ran on a law-and-order platform and encourages racism, xenophobia, sexism. This semester I am again teaching in the prison and on campus, though this course is called "America in the Age of Inequality." It's a study of the Gilded Age and the Progressive Era, intended to explore industrialization, urbanization, mass immigration, and the other dramatic changes in American society in the late nineteenth and early twentieth centuries. But as we near the end of the semester, I realize that I unconsciously taught a course on utopian thought; I emphasized the reformers who worked to end poverty, writers like Edward Bellamy who imagined a classless society, women's rights activists who called for kitchenless houses to allow wives and mothers to earn a living outside the family home, an anti-lynching crusader like Ida B. Wells believing she could halt lynching by investigating and publishing the horrible facts, socialists like Eugene V. Debs pushing for nonviolent revolution and anarchists using dynamite to eliminate Wall Street. The characters who wandered through my prison and campus classrooms imagined the impossible. At a time in American politics when all paths for improving society seem closed, perhaps utopian visions become political strategies.

In her utopian novel, *The Dispossessed*, Ursula Le Guin (1974) describes an anarchist society established on the moon hundreds of years in the future; there are no possessions, no private property, and no central government. It's a world without prisons. In Annares all people are expected to work, but individuals are free to choose their labor, choose their lovers, and choose their families. There is no inequality as all are provided with adequate shelter, food, and education, though the dormitory-style housing and cafeteria-style food seem grim. Early in the novel, Le Guin describes children in a history class, learning about prisons in past societies. The children are fascinated and confused, and finally sneak away to try out this strange institution by locking a friend inside a cement cave for two days. The boy emerges from his cement cell frightened, hungry, and covered in feces. The boys are so disturbed by what they have done that they never discuss the incident again. They find this ancient penal practice unimaginable.

Prison education—at least, the program where I teach—aims to transform the prison into a university campus. We work to colonize space within the prison walls. We add books to the library, claim sections of the community room for tutoring sessions, take over cinder-block rooms for classrooms. We launched our education program with two for-credit college courses; within four years we were teaching six courses per semester, along with sponsoring academic talks, writing workshops, peer-tutoring, and an array of programs that would appear in a college catalogue. It is a gradual process of peaceful though often aggressive conquest, slowly replacing the carceral with college spaces. As Truillot suggests, something extraordinary—almost unbelievable—happens with the mundane practice of distributing course books and syllabi, leading seminar discussions, and arguing over grades while standing in a prison.

College and prison stand at opposite ends of the American social landscape. The terms do not even belong in the same sentence. One is an expensive reward for diligent school work and, too often, economic privilege; the other is an expensive consequence of poverty, poor education, and a grossly inadequate health care system, among the many causes of mass incarceration. My aim is not to entrench that binary, but rather to crush it. In bringing college to prison we are, I believe, gradually making prison impossible.

The distance between Michael Brown's home in Ferguson and the prison in Pacific, Missouri, was, in many ways, just a step. More people from Ferguson spent time in prison or jail than in college, though many did both. Brown, when he was killed, was preparing to go to college. There is significant social science research that contends that the zip code where you were born determines your future health, education, and life-time earnings. People born in poor communities like Ferguson are more likely to be stuck in prison; those born in the wealthy suburbs just west of St. Louis head to elite colleges like Washington University and to well-paying careers. Geography, like history, is a story of origins.

The earliest American prisons were built in the early nineteenth century as penitentiaries, designed for the penitent to contemplate their sins and regenerate their souls. Prisons quickly became institutions used to control the poor, supply cheap labor, punish political deviants, and harden the structures of white supremacy. Numerous scholars have written about the significance of mass incarceration, the steep rise in prison populations from about 1970 onward. Most agree that it is tied to the rapid loss of decent-paying industrial jobs, the use of federal dollars to tear down urban neighborhoods, weak social safety nets, and self-serving, racist political rhetoric that framed black men as dangerous and, in effect, redefined poverty and joblessness as crimes. Prisons, Ruth Wilson Gilmore writes, serve as "catchall solutions to social problems" (Gilmore, 2007, p. 2). What's worse, prisons became brutal warehouses for people designated as "social problems."

At the end of my course in 2014, I said goodbye to the students, told them how much I enjoyed working with them, how much I had learned from them. I am a middle-aged, middle-class white woman, small-boned and well-educated and, by the numbers, the demographics, have little in common with my students in prison. We had come a long way from that first class in September. We had grappled with serious questions about what America was and is. Men who had never before met told me that they had found themselves arguing about the course readings while working out in the make-shift prison gym and discussing their papers over meals. We had become a tiny community of scholars.

As they gathered their books and left our classroom, several students thanked me and shook my hand. One, a talkative young black guy who was always ahead in the reading, always giving me drafts of his papers a week before the due dates, shook my hand and walked with me out of the classroom. This class had been really important to him, he said. He was grateful for it. "You shook my hand," he said. "No one has touched me like that for almost eleven years." It was not clear if he meant that in metaphorical or literal terms, but, standing next to the floor-to-ceiling chain-link fence that separated the education annex from a beat-up ballfield, I felt a sudden surge of joy.

Studying history reminds us that nothing in the past was inevitable, nothing was set in stone. It reminds us that societies change and that humans, with all their inadequacies and inequalities, change worlds. History can bind us to the past, give us a sense of belonging and of being part of a larger narrative. At the same time, history's ruptures and erasures can leave us excluded, marginalized, forgotten, homeless. But we, as scholars, can fill those gaps by uncovering the social and political processes that erased the lives of some, marginalized others, and rewarded a small group with power and wealth. The philosopher and prison abolitionist Angela Davis calls prison education a path to "autonomy of the mind." She cites Malcolm X as an example of "prisoners' ability to turn their incarceration into a transformative experience" (Davis, 2003, p. 56). Malcolm, while in prison, read widely in politics, philosophy, literature, whatever books he could find. No doubt, prison scars the mind and raises powerful barriers to the imaginations and aspirations of incarcerated and formerly incarcerated people. But education whether inside prison walls or on a lush university campus is, for most people, intellectually freeing.

That fall, as protesters filled city streets night after night, what happened in my prison history course and in my course on campus was, I think, a rebuilding of connection, a shedding of light on forgotten people and events. It was a process of linking Harriet Jacobs' search for a home to Michael Brown's shattering death just outside his home, and a breaking open of the political processes that made both Michael Brown's death and my college course in prison possible. It occurred to me that as I drove the highway between the campus and the prison classrooms, I became the string that linked the students to each other, the present to America's heart-rending past, standing in the ever-shifting space of imagined possibilities.

References

Davis, A. Y. (2003). *Are prisons obsolete?* New York: Seven Stories Press.
Gilmore, R. W. (2007). *Golden gulag: Prisons, surplus, crisis, and opposition in globalizing California.* Berkeley: University of California Press.
Le Guin, U. K. (1974). *The dispossessed: An ambiguous utopia.* New York: Harper & Row.
Trouillot, M. (1995). *Silencing the past: Power and the production of history.* Boston: Beacon Press.

16

THE PRISON OPPRESSES: AVOIDING THE FALSE US/THEM BINARY IN PRISON EDUCATION

Victoria M. Bryan

This chapter is perhaps primarily useful for someone who is very early in their experience of teaching in jail or prison. If you are brand new to this movement, welcome. Please know that there are many steps to get through and many barriers to the work you are trying to do, and you will likely want to do a lot of research to ground yourself in the movement that has come before you. Do not lose hope. A few years into my experience teaching in prison, I had a mentor tell me, "We cannot afford to leave people behind in this movement," and I have come to thoroughly believe that. With all of that said, if you have not yet found a program to work with, please make use of the listings of college-in-prison programs that are available through the Education Justice Project website (www.educationjustice.net) or the research coming out of the Research Collaborative on Higher Education in Prison at the University of Utah.

Perhaps you have already found a program with which you plan to teach and you are in a preparatory phrase, reading a great deal about the environment you are about to walk into. You are likely finding a lot about practices and policies that led to mass incarceration, the injustices inherent in the system under which the criminal justice system currently operates, definitions of phrases like "carceral state," "prison abolition," and "prison industrial complex," and the dealings of big business that make prison so profitable and therefore so difficult to change. Perhaps you have begun your class already, and all of that reading was helpful in conceptualizing what you were taking on but utterly useless when you step into the actual classroom and encounter the tensions and challenges that in some ways are very similar to classrooms you have been in before, but in some ways are inherently different. In my experience, one of those inherently different tensions was that which came with dealing with COs and prison administration.

When educators are new to this kind of activist teaching, it becomes all too easy to seek out the "bad guy" in your new environment. It is true that while doing this work we see prison workers do horrible things to incarcerated people. That is a heinous reality that we should be aware of. It is created by the unfair power dynamics that the system has set up. It is facilitated by policy that does not value the humanity of an incarcerated human being and the practice of disappearing human beings rather than dealing with structural inequalities. We have an obligation to push against those actions when we see them.

What I hope this chapter will convey is that if we are looking for a "bad guy," some evil person driving the trauma and inhumane treatment that characterizes the U.S. prison system, we aren't going to find it. That force is bigger than the person patting you down or walking you to your classroom. If we see education in prison as a kind of activism, as a small piece of the effort to abolish the oppressive prison industrial complex (PIC), we have to recognize that the force we are working against oppresses our students and the incarcerated people who never make it to our classrooms, and also acts on the prison workers and the communities that they come from. As incarcerated writer Lacino Hamilton (2018) argues,

> The consequences of caging people cause damage to both jailed and jailer. This is a point that has to be emphasized more often—all who exist or work in this environment are affected. Prison solves no social problem; it merely creates new and more complicated ones. It is a descending spiral ending in emotional and psychological harm for all.

The work of abolition is complex and the goals are long-term. Our goal is not merely to unlock all of the cells. Doing so would not eliminate the forces that disproportionately incarcerate people of color and people of poor socioeconomic status. The goal of prison abolition is to eradicate the forces that lock the cells in the first place, and doing so requires a complex understanding of all individuals oppressed by the PIC.

We cannot—and should not—ignore the fact that prison workers are often barriers between the curricula we want to teach and the students who sign up to engage with them. On a day-to-day basis, ignoring this fact would certainly interfere with our ability to do the work we have set out to do. In my experiences, they were the people checking my bags when I arrived, patting me down after I went through metal detectors, walking me to the classroom and talking about how disrespectful the incarcerated individuals are, and turning me away because my clothes were too revealing (even though the same outfit was completely acceptable the week before). In many interactions, they acted as opposition. But they were also the people asking about how expensive college is, why I wanted to drive several hours each week to teach the class, if other professors are as dedicated to their work as I was, standing up for me when other COs or prison administration got too oppositional, telling me how important opportunities like this were for the people I was there to work with. Though I have my fair share of stories about opposition from prison workers, I have also had several interactions with prison workers who have demonstrated curiosity, kindness, and advocacy for education in prison. The people who work in jails and prisons are a diverse group who have come to their work for a variety of reasons and have been affected by their time working in jails and prisons in a variety of ways.

In fact, prison workers often demonstrate competing understandings of what prison is supposed to do, what their role in that system is, and how education plays into it. Often these understandings are not critical interrogations of the PIC. Being critical of a system is difficult when the system in question provides your paycheck. Interestingly, though, these competing understandings of how prison workers fit into a vast system of incarceration do not just vary from person to person; often they compete within single individuals. For example, several years ago I walked through the doors of a prison library to begin an English composition course, and found a group of students who were obviously frustrated with something, but I was unaware of what it might be. The very kind administrator who walked me to the classroom had given me a brief history of the program, had talked about how supportive he was of programming like this, had offered me his cell phone number and email address in case I ever ran into any trouble. All things considered, I was thinking that this would be a much better experience than some I had had at other facilities.

However, when one of the students in the library asked the administrator why they had been pulled to the cafeteria two and a half hours ago and whether that was going to be the case every week, he replied that today had been a rough start to the class, and that they were working on a better system. When the same student offered a suggestion for addressing this issue, the administrator barked,

> Do you want an application to work at this facility? Do you think you're qualified for that? We work sixty hours a week doing what we do, and we know what we're doing. We'll get you where you need to be. Why don't you just leave that to us?

His diatribe went on for less than a minute, and his voice got kinder over the course of his response—as if he realized that his response had been unnecessarily aggressive—but the class tensed up and the vibe did not lighten all evening.

I was stunned and angry. I thought, "So much for being hopeful." However, during an in-class writing assignment about fifteen minutes later, the prison worker took the opportunity to whisper "There's another guard in here, so I'm going to go. I can tell that I put the class on edge, and I want this to go well." His outburst and his private recant illustrates something really important for us to keep in mind as we approach prison education: prison workers are trained on an us/them binary. They are taught to interact with incarcerated people in oppressive and degrading ways. Though the language of training is often couched in terms like "protection" and "control," it pits these men and women against incarcerated people. This binary often leads them to default to mistreatment as a kind of self-protection.

The prison industrial complex is a vast system of oppression that not only maintains, but creates, segregation and hierarchy among the people it contains. Among incarcerated people, the PIC systematizes racial separation in its housing choices, often creating and enforcing the racial hierarchies that these policies supposedly control (Noll, 2012, pp. 851–857). Multidimensional identities a person has built in the free world "are reframed and reduced to Black, White, Hispanic, and perhaps 'Other,'" (Noll, 2012, p. 854), a system that many researchers have suggested perpetuates the racial violence it supposedly exists to control. The system relies on categorization that is indisputably unreliable—not surprising when the categories are built on unreliable and reductive social constructions that do not account for multidimensional identities.

These categories, the racialized system of segregation on which many prisons rely, make it easier to control people, and just as the prison does not discourage racialized gang activity because a group pitted against itself is easier to control, the PIC cannot operate without having a group that is unrelentingly in power over the incarcerated. It is not built on an understanding of individual potential or identity. It is built, as Angela Davis argues, as a "first resort" in dealing with many of the problems that burden our society by "disappearing vast numbers of people from poor, immigrant, and racially marginalized communities" behind walls and into cages "to convey the illusion of solving social problems" (Davis, 2003, p. 683). In general, the people who work in our country's jails and prisons have, like most of our country, been sold the narrative that prisons are what keep our communities safe. They, like most of our country, have been indoctrinated by the media on a daily basis to believe this version of the story. While there may be many working within the profession who see the problems within the system, who lament the high recidivism rates and the violence within jails and prisons, who may say "this system is not working," who may recognize that what separates them from the people they have been put in charge of may be just a few different decisions or circumstances—in order to continue the work they have signed up to do, they have to maintain their belief in the hierarchy between prison worker and incarcerated individual. That systematic and hierarchical belief—despite any amount of personal awareness or willingness to interrogate the system—maintains the system.

In the story detailed above, I saw a man who consciously supported efforts to educate incarcerated individuals and, in a stressful moment, defaulted to what has been instilled in him as normative behavior and was taken aback by his own actions. He could not actually walk back something aggressive and disrespectful, so he walked away instead, and in doing so, he saw himself allowing class to proceed as productively as possible. Unwilling to examine his role in an oppressive system, he continues to do that work today. He, like so many others, is an agent of the problematic control over human beings that the PIC perpetuates.

On a macro level, his work is degrading and contributes to the decay of individual lives and entire communities. On a micro level, he was rude to one of my students, but he tried to do what he could to make sure the class went smoothly. If I have conveyed a version of myself that was not immediately enraged with this prison worker, then I have not represented myself fairly. However, as I drove home angered by the prison worker's actions, I realized that I was more than willing to understand my students' current position in light of troubling, abusive, violent pasts marked by various kinds of physical, emotional, and economic trauma, but I was not willing to extend those efforts to the prison worker who had shown me such kindness that afternoon.

Similarly, in another teaching endeavor in a different facility, I watched helplessly as one of my female students was berated, goaded into a fight, forced into her cell, and maced as she yelled "You can't take away my books." I had been distributing books when a member of my reading group walked to the book cart before it was her turn. Basic conflict resolution would have eliminated the need for this kind of altercation, and I was angry at the female guard for not allowing me to take care of things and for defaulting to anger and violence instead of asking respectfully if my student could just step back in line. The guard got maced pretty badly herself, and as she ran from the pod coughing and crying, I thought, "Maybe she won't do that next time," but again, I thought nothing of her struggle.

The following week when she apologized to me for having gotten in the way of my work, I told her it was fine and asked if she was okay. She looked at me as if the question was a confusing one, and said, "Yes. Thank you for asking." I don't know why my asking that question was so odd to her. I know nothing of her personal life. I know only that she is young, small in stature, and the least liked CO in that facility. I can speculate that she struggles with feeling like she has earned her place in the facility's workforce and trying to establish a sense of control over a population decidedly older and larger than her.

I tell these two stories to illustrate that the prison oppresses all it touches, but we should recognize the humanity among any group we work with. As Doran Larson (2015) has argued, corrections officers are, in a sense, "doing time," as well. Our economic structure is such that we are outsourcing jobs to other countries and cutting out lucrative work opportunities for blue collar workers. As jobs that do not require a college degree have disappeared, the cost of a college degree has skyrocketed. More and more individuals working in rural areas are funneled into CO positions that do not require these expensive degrees, and in these jobs, they will experience higher rates of PTSD, alcoholism, hypertension, heart attack, and suicide than any other area of law enforcement. E. A. Paoline's research shows that the life expectancy of a corrections officer is nearly twenty years shorter than that of the average American (Paoline et al., 2006, p. 183).

Less dire than lower life expectancy and high rates of terminal illness is the reality facing any workplace that individuals experiencing high rates of stress and burnout "have the potential to show a lack of commitment" and "increased counterproductive attitudes and behavior"—a trend we certainly see in COs in the jails and prisons across our country (Finney et al., 2013, p. 2). Their connections to the prison system are limiting and traumatizing in different ways than the connections our incarcerated students have had, but they are limiting and traumatizing all the same. We could argue that the prison guards could choose to work elsewhere, but people regularly make the same argument about our incarcerated students. They could have chosen not to commit a crime. If our response to the latter is going to be to insist that it is more complicated than that, it seems that we should have a comparable response to the former.

Though the PIC clearly oppresses the incarcerated in much more damaging ways, it also oppresses the COs and wardens and other staff with whom we often find ourselves at odds. It oppresses the teachers who walk through the gates. It oppresses the nurses and doctors who offer medical care. It oppresses the town in which it is built. The PIC is far-reaching, and its history of slavery, violence, and emotional and mental trauma extends beyond the incarcerated population.

That is the crux of the connection between the oppression felt by those who work at the prison and those who are imprisoned there: the same forces of capitalism and financial insecurity that keep the prisoners oppressed keep the COs, the administrators, and the town in which the prison is built oppressed, too. Ruth Gilmore (1998) writes in "Globalisation and U.S. Prison Growth: From Military Keynesianism to Post-Keynesian Militarism" that the expansion of the prison system was sold to rural America as a "geographical solution to socioeconomic problems" (p. 174), and ties much of this to a rapidly changing economy juxtaposed with a political message that suggested that more widespread incarceration would allow more safety among communities terrorized by drugs and crime.

A few decades ago, as the United States' population and subsequent demand for food continued to rise, small family farms became financially unmanageable, and many folded under economic pressure. Around the same time, factories in rural areas closed and big business sent the work overseas where they could find cheaper labor. These two changes in economic structure in small-town America meant that individuals without a college education were hard-pressed to find employment. Rather than invest in access to education and job training or commit to protecting these industries, the state and/or federal government bought the devalued land in these small and economically depressed towns and began to build prisons. They were far from city centers and therefore removed from much attention.

As Angela Davis (2003) writes in *Are Prisons Obsolete?*, the people who lived in these small towns, now deprived of ample opportunities for gainful employment, were assured by the state "that the new, recession-proof, non-polluting industry would jump-start local redevelopment … People wanted to believe that prisons would not only reduce crime, they would also provide jobs and stimulate economic development in out-of-the-way places" (p. 114). Of course, economic development was not stimulated by the increase of prison infrastructure in rural America. Businesses and housing developers do not want to build near sites of incarceration because, as a society, we like to keep these things out of sight. The work of a CO is so demanding, the training so minimal, the pay so slight, and the stress so high that the likelihood of getting an advanced degree while working is low and the opportunities for advancement limited. In short, the only thing stimulated by the increase of prison infrastructure was the rate of incarceration.

I do not mean to suggest that the corrections officer is in any way not responsible for his or her actions, or that we should not be aware of the problematic draw of control and hierarchy that attract some people to the job. Take, for example, the recent revisiting of the Stanford Prison Experiment conducted by Phillip Zimbardo in 1971. Zimbardo orchestrated a mock-prison dynamic among graduate students that has commonly been read to suggest that when ordinary people are put into positions of all-consuming power over other ordinary people, violence and mistreatment abound. During the six days that the experiment was allowed to persist, about one-third of the students put in positions of power exhibited sadistic and violent behavior towards those positioned as prisoners.

A study conducted by Thomas Carnahan and Sam McFarland out of Western Kentucky University in 2007, however, suggests that selection bias may have been at work here in ways that we have not examined before. These researchers studied the ad Zimbardo used to recruit participants and attempted to reproduce the selection process. They used two different ads, one that included references to "prison life" and one that did not, and a comparison of the volunteers those ads attracted indicated that selection bias may have influenced Zimbardo's study. In short, Zimbardo's ad likely attracted people with a grotesque interest in the dynamics between guards and the incarcerated (Carnahan and McFarland, 2007, p. 603). Combined with studies that suggest that the violent, sadistic, narcissistic, and authoritarian personalities are often drawn to positions in corrections at high rates (Carnahan and McFarland, 2007, p. 603), it becomes clear that addressing the problem of violence in prison is much more complicated than simply giving corrections officers the benefit of the doubt.

With that said, we are all working to come out of various kinds of intersectional oppression, whether that oppression be gendered, sexually normative, racialized, criminalized, etc. The PIC certainly does not oppress all people *equally*, and my struggle as a teacher is not at all comparable to the struggle of my students or to the COs who stay long after I have left. I only mean to suggest that the oppression exists, as many of us know, in nooks and crannies that we may not expect or examine fully unless we have experienced the oppression ourselves. It is our responsibility as educators and as administrators of education programs within jails and prisons to be cognizant of those intersectional forms of oppression, to examine our interactions carefully, and to provide our fellow teachers with resources and community to express their frustrations and identify the root causes of these inequitable interactions. If education in prison is to be a radical endeavor, if it is be truly abolitionist in nature, if it is to be a piece of what will eradicate the PIC, we must look beyond the people who are harming others and be actively aware of the bigger forces allowing for (and in many cases facilitating) that harm.

In prison education programs, we strive to offer higher education to the incarcerated for various reasons, including the understanding that education should be seen as a basic human right. This work requires a willful ignorance of the wrongs committed by our students. In offering educational opportunities in jails and prisons, we insist that someone's past, decisions, and/or allegiances have no bearing on their right to the information offered in our classrooms. In other words, their engagements in criminalized activity do not intersect with their status as a student.

As a result, we often find ourselves at odds with the prison staff. Corrections officers and wardens enter our classrooms as interruptions and sources of tension for our students and interfere with our ability to help them empower themselves through knowledge and skills. These workers, however, are increasingly more and more often sucked into prison jobs—not as a personal calling for which they are highly trained and carefully prepared—but as an afterthought as factory and labor work leaves rural or underdeveloped areas leaving very few choices for those without college degrees. While this country sees high rates of violence enacted on the incarcerated by prison workers, we also see high rates of depression, hypertension, and suicide in prison workers—evidence that the PIC damages those who work within it. If we believe that part of our job is to provide the means for restoring or regaining humanity for the incarcerated in this nation, and if we believe that one of the biggest challenges to our civil rights is the PIC, then we must work to understand—and to keep readily in mind—how the prison oppresses the prison worker so that we can work in conjunction with these human beings to offer as much assistance to our students as possible.

When this willingness to critically examine the forces behind an individual's actions or decisions extend beyond those we teach and to those who challenge our work, we do not have to kowtow to them. We do not have to excuse their behavior or decisions. We do not have to side with them over our students because, as with any binary, it is socially constructed. If our work is going to feed into the goals of prison abolition, we cannot leave anyone oppressed by the PIC behind.

I issue a challenge to educators to see the humanity in the prison workers just as we see the humanity in the students we serve. Far from arguing that the prison system is benign or that prison education programs should not challenge the prison as an oppressive entity, we must keep in mind the oppression this entity enacts on those who find themselves doing time within it in various capacities.

Education in jails and prisons does not come easily, and engaging our students in educational programming is often a struggle—a form of resistance. As David Coogan (2015) argues, "[e]ach year in America millions of prisoners and college students are blocked … from giving and receiving intellectual and creative gifts" because of the very structure of the PIC and the people who have stepped up to administer its oppressive policies.

However, Coogan goes on to argue,

Ignorance of the other benefits no one. Unchecked it just may fester into thick indifference or hostile incuriosity. It makes us vulnerable to reductions of reality that make conceivable an "us" and a "them," the incarcerated and the free. It denies solidarity. It disables a collective imagining of change.

We all default to this us/them mentality sometimes—when a CO shuts down our classes early for no clear reason or when the facility bans certain reading material. We are angered or discouraged. We want someone to blame, someone at whom to direct our anger.

We must know, however, that blaming a CO or a member of the administration would not make the situation better. It would create a larger schism that we have to overcome to work with our students—those we know are thirsting for education and those invested in "giving and receiving intellectual and creative gifts" (Coogan, 2015). We should not ignore that, with the rising cost of education, the fear of college debt, and the flight of factory and labor jobs from rural areas in recent decades, the COs are often thirsting for education and opportunity, too, and are part of a system that also leaves them in need of rediscovering something about their own humanity.

Bibliography

Carnahan, T. and McFarland, S. (2007). Revisiting the Stanford prison experiment: Could participant self-selection have led to the cruelty? *Personality and Social Psychology Bulletin*, 33(5), 603–614.

Coogan, D. (2015). Public life through a prison/university partnership. *Organizing. Culture. Change*, 3. Retrieved at http://public.imaginingamerica.org/blog/article/94-2/.

Davis, A. (2003). *Are prisons obsolete?* New York: Seven Stories Press.

Davis, A. (2013). Masked racism: Reflections on the prison industrial complex. In Paula S. Rothenburg (ed.), *Race, class, and gender in the United States: An integrated study*, pp. 683–688. New York: Worth Publishers.

Finney, C. *et al.* (2013). Organizational stressors associated with job stress and burnout in correctional officers: A systematic review. *BMC Public Health*, 13(82), 1–13.

Gilmore, R. W. (1998). Globalisation and U.S. prison growth: From military Keynesianism to post-Keynesian militarism. *Race and Class*, 40(2–3), 171–187.

Hamilton, L. (2018). I am buried alive in a Michigan prison. *Truth-Out*. Retrieved at http://www.truth-out.org/opinion/item/44007-i-am-buried-alive-in-a-michigan-prison.

Larson, D. (2015). Incarceration's witnesses. Massive Open Online Course. Hamilton College, March–April, 2015. Web. December 1, 2017.

Lisitsina, D. (2017, December 1). Prison guards can never be weak: The hidden PTSD crisis in America's jails. *The Guardian*. Retrieved at http://www.theguardian.com/us-news/2015/may/20/corrections-officers-ptsd-american-prisons.

Noll, D. (2012). Building a new identity: Race, gangs, and violence in California prisons. *Miami Law Review, 66*(3), 847–877.

Paoline III, E. A. *et al.* (2006). A calm and happy keeper of the keys. *Prison Journal, 86*(2), 182–205.

17

LEARNING INSIDE-OUT: THE PERSPECTIVES OF TWO INDIVIDUALS WHO HAD THE OPPORTUNITY TO PARTAKE IN THE SOUL JOURNEY OF HEALING ARTS AND SOCIAL CHANGE

Jerrad Allen and Osvaldo Armas

Introduction

How can one even begin to explain what the Inside-Out Project Prison Exchange is? The difficulty does not lie in the format of the project, because it is quite simple, but in bringing our experiences as inside students to life. This experience holds a sacred place in our hearts and our aim is to do it justice. We find it a tall order to fill, but we hope this piece serves as a springboard for action, or at least opens up dialogue.

We lay before you this crazy idea, called the Inside-Out Project, which was formulated and put into action in 2014 at the California Rehabilitation Center in Norco, CA. The California Rehabilitation Center is located about fifty miles east of Los Angeles, CA, and about fifteen miles southeast of Claremont, CA. We only mention this because there are over thirty prisons in California and most are located hours away from civilization. It is rare for a prison to be set in the middle of suburbia. We believe this is the precise reason why the California Rehabilitation Center was chosen to be as one of the first prisons on the West Coast to be involved with the Inside-Out Project.

The Inside-Out Project initially began at the Dallas State Prison in Pennsylvania. The idea was formulated by Lori Pompa, a professor at Temple University in Philadelphia, PA, and Paul Perry, who was serving a life sentence at the Dallas State Prison. At the time, Ms. Pompa taught courses for the Criminal Justice Department at Temple University, and took her students to visit jails and prisons in Pennsylvania and New Jersey.

In 1995, she took a group of students to the state prison in Dallas, PA, where they did the usual tour of the facility, followed by a conversation with a panel of men serving life sentences. The discussion ventured into matters such as crime and justice, race and class, politics and economics, as well as connecting the dots on how they are all interrelated. At the end of that discussion, one of the men on the panel, Paul Perry, approached and asked her if she had ever thought about doing this as a regular course instead of it being a one-time event. After having the idea kick around in her head for a few weeks, Lori eventually created a syllabus for a course aptly titled "The Inside-Out Prison Exchange Program: Exploring Issues of Crime and Justice behind the Walls." She realized that the typical didactic, hierarchical methodology of teaching often used in higher education would be ineffective in a prison setting, so she created a liberating learning experience through a dialogic pedagogy format, where the class is held amongst equals in an open and safe space, where ideas and thoughts are shared freely. More important than an open space, is the community building process, where solutions and dialogue can flourish.

This might seem impossible, especially in a prison setting, but it really is not. We speculate that the hardest part was acquiring all the right approvals due to logistics, security reasons, and because of the bureaucracies involved. It is uncommon in daily prison life to come in contact with civilians, let alone college students, or anyone who is concerned about the issues stemming around prison and prison reform.

Almost twenty years later, on September 25, 2014, the first Inside-Out class at the California Rehabilitation Center, "Healing Arts and Social Change," began. Entering the room, we noticed there were twenty-two desks placed in a circle. They were arranged this way so that every inside student sat next to an outside student. If it was not set up in this manner, the room would have probably looked like a seventh grade dance—boys on one side and girls on the opposite end. The class consisted of eleven inside students (incarcerated), ten outside students from Pitzer College, and one instructor, Tessa Hicks Peterson, a professor at Pitzer College. All the inside students were extremely nervous and felt out of place.

The instructor asked if we had any concerns and one inside student responded that he feared being looked down upon or judged for being an inmate. The instructor made it abundantly clear that during class we were no longer inmates, but students in a class of equals, no one superior or inferior.

The first day of class began with the traditional "name and introduction" followed by creating ground rules, to create a safe and respectful space. On a dry-erase board, the instructor wrote the acronym R.E.S.P.E.C.T., for which every letter had a corresponding rule for communication that the class chose and agreed to abide by. The instructor handed out a giant pile of articles for us to read for the upcoming class sessions. Along with the assigned readings, we received a syllabus outlining the entire course, and the required written assignments. Next, we went into an icebreaker exercise. As mentioned before, we (inside students) were extremely nervous on the first day, so the icebreaker exercise was vital and necessary. We had no clue that the outside students were just as nervous as us.

For the icebreaker, the outside students formed a circle facing out, and we, inside students, formed a circle around them facing inward, the person you faced was your partner for that moment. The instructor began to ask us random questions, and we were allotted about forty-five seconds to discuss each with our partner. She asked questions like, "If you were a superhero, who would you be?"; "If you didn't know your age, how old do you think you are, or feel?"; and "How do you describe yourself socially, geographically, and ethnically?" These questions came at such a fast pace and the content was so unusual that there was no time to think them out or be nervous about what you were going to say, leaving us momentarily vulnerable. And after every question, the outer circle rotated clockwise, allowing everyone to have a chance to interact with everyone else.

After the icebreaker, the classroom ambiance went from being able to hear a pin drop, to chatter, laughter, and smiles. The exercise allowed us to open up and see the commonalities that we all shared, as well as the differences that were between us. However, those differences did not set us apart, but brought us closer. We then sat down, and the instructor asked us to jot down what we thought prison felt, looked, and sounded like. After that, we broke off into small groups and shared our descriptions of what prison, education, social change, and healing, sounded, felt, and looked like. All of our answers sounded like a free form poem. This is a sample of what one of us scribbled down on that nerve-racking first day.

Prison

Cold loud solitude

With an influx of overcrowding;

Many faces sharing one identity

Osvaldo Armas

My name is Ossie, a lifelong student of Healing Arts and Social Change, and this is the view from my lens. I am a first-generation Mexican American. I was born in Bellflower, CA, and raised in the lower middle-class city of Ontario, located about thirty miles east of Los Angeles. I wouldn't consider my upbringing as affluent by any means, but we never went without. Being I was the youngest out of three boys, all my clothes were hand-me-downs. That helped me learn very early on in life that it was best to appreciate what was given to me and to work with what I had.

Growing up, my father fell ill, causing my mother to venture off into the working world to supplement my father's income. This gave me independence and caused me to raise myself, as she worked nights. I spent most of my time alone, drawing, or with my nose in a book. I lost interest in school at an early age, since most my classes failed to keep my interest. I liked the concept of education but disliked the education system. I was tired of waiting for the school system to teach me how to read in English, so I took it upon myself to teach myself.

I eventually dropped out of school; I was more interested in hanging out with friends, making money, and helping my family out. In 2013, because of my bad decisions, I stumbled, fell, and caught myself a three-year prison sentence. And as I have always done in the past, I made the best out of a bad situation.

As luck would have it, I ended up being one of the twenty-two students that was involved in this Inside-Out experience. I cannot speak for everyone else, but I can tell you about how this unique opportunity has influenced me, and the way it has transformed the way I see the world and myself. All the theories, practices, and coping mechanisms I have learned in class have forever changed my conduct and the way I interact with others.

The assigned readings were no easy task—the sheer number of pages was a feat in itself. Not to mention the academic difficulty of some of the theories we read about. There were many nights that I found myself up until 3 a.m., reading and rereading the materials we were assigned. I must admit some of the topics gave me difficulty wrapping my mind around, due to the intellectual content and wordiness. I became nervous, thinking that I had bitten off more than I could chew, until I got to the class and was able to discuss the readings, only to find out that the outside students were just as confused as I was. This was where the dialogic educational format came into play, for we were able to discuss and break down the different theories and together gain a better understanding of the topics, as we all had picked up different insights. At times we arrived at more questions than answers, which was okay, since those questions ended up being my ammunition for my critical reflection papers.

The critical reflection papers were biweekly, three-page written assignments, where we were asked to discuss the previous week's topics, theories, and discussions. Initially, when I saw the number of pages required for each critical reflection paper I thought to myself, "Mrs. Tessa is nuts, that is way too much writing!" As life would have it, I was the one who was nuts for thinking that I would not have anything to say. See, for most of the critical reflection papers, three pages was not enough for all my rehashed questions and newfound thoughts. These papers made me think in ways I had never thought before. At times, I could feel my brain become exhausted. My thought patterns took on a metamorphosis from convoluted selfish prison bullshit and elevated them into deeper meaningful thinking. I began to think about the problems of the world as well as those in my community. And when I say community, I speak of the community that I am momentarily a part of (prison), and of the community that I am currently detached from (society). I began to strive for the answers on how I or we could bridge the gap between the two, and how to alleviate the problems that exist within them.

I was not the only one feeling this way; the rest of my fellow students were experiencing this same mental alteration. The Inside-Out Project was the only thing we talked about. We'd huddle in circles and talk about theories and why they would work or why they were flawed. It came to a point where other inmates got tired of listening to us "*drone*" on about "*that class.*" They would ask, "What's so great about it?" and I would try to explain to them that it was not just a simple class; it was a cathartic journey, a schism in what the prison complex is, or what it could be. Then they would say, "What the hell are you talking about? Let me guess, I bet you really think you could go to that school (Pitzer) when you parole?" And I would respond, "Of course, I could and you could too, as long as you set your mind to it. Trust and believe we can do anything."

It's about a year later, and I still find that to be true. Yet, I still have trouble putting this voyage into words. The irony is that without this class, I would not have found my voice, and I would not be writing, or pursuing what I once thought were far-fetched dreams. I would not be doing many of the things that I now do. One of those things is practicing mindfulness and heartfulness, which I learned about from one of our guest lecturers, Alane Daugherty. I practice the breathing exercises and meditation that she taught us whenever I begin to feel stressed or overwhelmed by my surroundings. Her book has also taught me to quit being scared of achieving, and to embrace myself to function at my full potential. Art and writing are my calling and my source of inner peace, healing, and sanity; I credit this class for that. There is nothing in the world that can detour me from accomplishing this. No prison, no person, or no dogma can keep me from achieving success, because I—no *we*—have already achieved what we set out to do, so I know that it can be done again. We focused on change and community building and thus we did. We built a community of twenty-two within the drudges of oppression, barbwire, and watchtowers. Little did they know, they overlooked what was really going on, a schism in the prison complex. With their big binoculars they could not see the essence of what was truly transpiring—social change, in its purest form.

Jerrad Allen

My name is Jerrad and I grew up in a dysfunctional, lower class-borderline-middle class African American household. I come straight outta Compton, CA. As a child, I witnessed friends murdered and was surrounded by gang activity, drug dealing, and domestic violence, which usually involved my father getting drunk and then assaulting my mother.

I was born the middle child of three, all boys, to two broken young adults. As my father has always said, I was always a very mischievous child, the type that was always into something. I would poke foreign objects into electrical wall sockets. I learnt a lot from just living life. Once, I fell off of a second story apartment balcony because I chose not to listen to my parents and continued to play around an opening; I even allowed my curiosity to lead me into doing some foolish things like shaving off one of my eyebrows, super-gluing one of my eyelids shut, and getting a popcorn seed stuck in one of my ears.

Growing up, it was hard not to be influenced by the gangs, pimps, and drug dealers, especially when that is all you see on a day-to-day basis. I had no role models to look up to; however, my uncle was someone I idolized, even though he happened to fall into all three of those categories. He always kept it real with me, my brothers, and all my cousins. If we asked him for anything, he would go out of his way to get it. He was what you would call a hustler, a jack of all trades; he would sell just about anything, from baby clothes, to toys, to drugs, and even women. There were no secrets with him and for that, we all respected him. We would do anything for him and he would do anything for us. On numerous occasions my cousins and I would chase down grown men, putting hands and feet on them, all because they refused to pay my uncle the money they owed him.

As I got older and developed a desire to start making money, I landed a job at a Carl's Jr's Restaurant. It was part-time because I was still in high school. At first, I loved it; I was doing something positive and productive, while helping my mother with the monthly bills, which made me feel good. However, I got sick and tired of it quickly. I had saved up some money and wanted to "flip it." So, I went to my uncle and told him, "Man, Unk, I need to flip this change I got saved up." To which he responded, "What ... how? Are you sure?" I just nodded my head. With that we both understood how serious I was. Deep down, I was really hoping he was going to say, "Hell nawl, what's wrong with you? You should do something better with yourself." But he did not.

He taught me everything there was to know about selling drugs and stressed that should I never use them. I must admit, I was attracted to the allure of the fast money, cars, and women. If I only knew all of that was just as addictive as drugs. Once I was introduced to that lifestyle, everything started to spiral out of control, except for school. Learning always came easy to me. That is why, as soon school ended in the afternoon, I was out on the streets up to no good. In my short-lived young adult life, I managed to do everything under the sun at least twice, maybe three times. Money has a way of making you feel invincible and above the law and I was really getting my feel of it.

Despite the circumstances in which I was raised, I still managed to excel in school and graduated at the top of my class. I always believed that education was my key to success. Then, after making some very foolish decisions as a young adult, I found myself locked up. I believe it was by divine intervention that I was also blessed to be one of those twenty-two individuals who were afforded a ticket to ride along that scenic road of creating change within an environment filled with individuals that most people have already written off as a lost cause.

It's ironic to consider that in a shadow society, such as prison, one would desire to venture into higher learning. I initially thought that this Inside-Out class was going to be something similar to a social experiment, where we, the inside students, were the test subjects and the instructor and outside students were the researchers. Even though on the first day of class Mrs. Tessa stressed that was not the case, I was convinced otherwise. Prison taught me to be very observant, and as I soaked in the theories and techniques that were being introduced to me, my eyes became wide open and I slowly allowed my mind to be more open and accepting. Maybe we weren't their lab rats after all, but partners on this ever-changing path of social transformation.

Still to this day, the one thing that rings loud in my head was when Mrs. Tessa stood up and said to me, "Now, you may look at this blonde, skinny, blue-eyed girl and immediately think you two have nothing in common." Honestly, when I heard that, I was thinking in the back of my mind, "You damn right! What could we possibly have in common?" But the first time we had the opportunity to break off into groups to discuss the assigned readings, I was left dumbfounded, because one of the outside students began to speak about discrimination within the education system and I could not help but be amazed at what she was saying. She spoke about the issue from the same perspective that I identified with, because growing up I faced my share of discrimination within the educational system. I was shocked that we had that in common. What I learned from that situation is that I need to change the way I initially view people, and the way I perceive them, before getting to know them.

I have been incarcerated for over ten years and throughout my experience within the system, I have not encountered many individuals from the outside who possess a desire to help change the dynamics of the prison system or just simply understand what prison is actually all about, until I took this class. Throughout all my years of incarceration, I have often asked myself, "How am I actually being rehabilitated?" I was sentenced to eighteen years in prison at the age of nineteen and sent off to sit in a hole in the wall, only to sit and think. Yet, thinking could make an individual worse, especially, if he or she only knows how to think and function in a negative manner. In my opinion, that is not rehabilitation.

From the teachings, techniques, and theories of the "Healing Arts and Social Change" class, I learned that social change is not always a movement composed of groups that desire to change something specific. It is also single individuals whose minds and hearts are in the right place to see that things are aligned along the moral spectrum of society. The ability to have a heart and to be mindful of others and their plights, despite the mishaps and misfortunes you may be experiencing—this is the key to creating social change.

The educational material that was introduced to us ranged from *Preventing Violence* by James Gilligan; *Empowering Education: Critical Teaching for Social Change* by Ira Shor; *The Better World Handbook: Small Changes that Make a Big Difference* by Ellis Jones, Ross Haenfler, and Brett Johnson; "Humanizing the Other in 'Us and Them'" by Tessa Hicks; *Pedagogy of the Oppressed* by Paulo Friere; and much more. Many students thought that this was a massive undertaking of intellectual material to ingest in such a short period of time, but as I reflect, it was actually the right amount for the journey we went on, week after week.

Dialogue plays a major role in understanding people and through it we were able to learn from each other. The many different perspectives allowed us all to see the topics of discussion from different points of view. Most of the assigned readings gave me a different outlook on my own view of life and how I deal with people, because prison has a tendency of skewing one's way of thinking. The most amazing realization I grasped from the readings was identifying that I had the ability to put into action the many techniques discussed in those readings, even while I was still in the process of reading them. Overall, the material gave me room to self-reflect and develop a desire to transform and to rehabilitate myself.

From the topics and theories that we covered in this course, I learned to be more forgiving, not only of others, but of myself. I began to see myself and the world around me in a different light. I developed an understanding that you cannot blame others for their shortcomings, especially, if they know not what they do. I would recommend this type of class to anyone who is willing to allow themselves to be open and vulnerable, and to those who are hungry for change. This course is what rehabilitation feels, looks, and sounds like.

Over the eight-week period, the instructor, Mrs. Tessa, would ask us from time to time to improvise poems on the spot. Some of these poems we shared out loud, others were kept to ourselves. On the second to last day of class, she asked us to free write our thoughts about the class. Then we stood up one at a time to read a single line from what we wrote and formed this joint poem:

Welcome to our own little world

Something happens that significantly impacts my reflection of what has become of my life today

Has it been life that I've been craving or a phantom of its sweet, deceitful brother?

Because I will embrace the world even if it throws me a punch

It feels like discomfort as I begin to pick apart parts of myself that have always, without question, compromised me

But I have become the all-seeing I, once a shaky unfocused lens now I'm more like a tight panoramic view

The shackles are removed and my mind is now free

Oh, the readings! Where's Webster when you need him?

Waves of energy splashing on the shore

The cawing of crows, and lines reaching to embrace

Then look up and share the taste of a smile

A beautiful tapestry of interwoven narratives

Assumptions turned inside-out. Hope competes

Life opens like dawn

We have made ripples in the ocean that is social justice and the sea of self-healing

It feels like creating a space for confrontation of hopelessness. I just want to stay in this space for a while.

The energy in this room is positive and warm

I learned how to escape for a few hours each week, in a constructive way.

Near freedom

Compassion for self

Feeling free by releasing the crutches that have taken hold of me

The Inside-Out Project has continued at the California Rehabilitation Center with much success. Following the "Healing Arts and Social Change" class, Professor Andre, a history professor at Pitzer College, taught a course entitled "History as Autobiography" in the spring of 2015. That opened the door to twenty-two more students into this journey. This work is not yet finished. Future students, as well as past students, can continue to add on to this work and to be components of change.

18

HEALING PEDAGOGY FROM THE INSIDE OUT: THE PARADOX OF LIBERATORY EDUCATION IN PRISON

Tessa Hicks Peterson

Introduction

It's been five years since Osvaldo and Jerrad gave me their essays with the charge to craft my own reflection and get them published together because, they claimed, "people out there have to know what kind of revolutionary transformation we are making in here!" At the time, I was fired up, just like them, and wrote a sentimental piece about how the activities of our class birthed a level of healing, critical consciousness, and bridge-building I could never have imagined cultivating inside a prison.

But, over time, I have begun to wonder how revolutionary that transformation really was.

I know that, like them, the class moved and changed me deeply, and that it also upended my previous understanding of our "injustice" system and manifested a resolve to teach within while working against this system. But what has happened since that class ended has also made me question the endurance of a liberating and healing education, within the oppressive and violent realities of prison and the collateral damage inside students invariably face once they get out. In addition, living at the intersections of prison education and prison abolition causes me increased moral and political friction, even as my absolute commitment to teach inside deepens. And so, I revised my essay, in an attempt to match Jerrad's and Osvaldo's honest and heart-opening work, offering a candid engagement with the convictions, paradoxes, and personal commitments I have related to promoting liberatory education in prison.

Healing Pedagogy

When I was invited to teach our college's first Inside-Out Prison Exchange class, I was quite certain the school must not be aware what my class was about. My flagship course, "Healing Arts and Social Change," engages a praxis of healing arts as a vehicle for self-realization as well as a "rehearsal for revolution" (Boal, 1985). It employs a critical analysis of our educational, political, and justice systems while simultaneously exploring internal landscapes (identities and values, personal strengths and wounds). It does so while studying theories and cultivating tools for disrupting, transforming, and uplifting the political and the personal. Beyond engaging in typical critical readings and class discussions, the course also includes group meditations, "theatre of the oppressed" activities (Boal, 1985), music, movement, and shared poetry practices, thereby merging intellectual and creative explorations with intimate and embodied learning that is rare in academia and even rarer in prison.

I believe firmly in meshing critical, as well as compassionate, learning about ourselves, each other, and the systems that bind and divide us. This is a form of resistance against the unjust systems we are a part of as well as our own tendencies to isolate ourselves from and judge others we feel are too politically or culturally distant from us. It is also an affront to the inordinate amount of time and energy many in academic and activist circles spend participating in the "woke Olympics," critically over-analyzing every word, intention, and outcome of every reading, comment by a peer, or attempt at change or self-reflection. Creating space to expand consciousness around our values, biases, and positionalities is critical, but learning to be allies in learning rather than competitors on "the battlefield of woke" seems to be an exception these days.[1] I find that shedding a performativity of political knowledge, consciousness, and cool seems harder for the outside students (still finding themselves on the college campus battlefield), than for the inside ones (who are more likely unabashedly enthusiastic for this opportunity to learn, grow, and connect).

I also find that both inside and outside students face challenges (as well as a deep longing) to pierce through their external personae and look at intimate wounds and traumas of injustice that are carefully lodged where they cannot be disturbed. Yet creating the space to get to know this inner landscape, as they do the political and intellectual ones, invites them into dialogue with their own shadows, as we simultaneously wrestle with our collective shadows: inequity, oppression, injustice. They begin to reimagine the traumas they have experienced not as personal deficits but as, more often than not, the consequences of poverty, violence, illness, inequity, and/or oppression that they and their families have often faced for generations. I am convinced that social change and community building cannot be divorced from healing the individuals and the collectives we are a part of that are hit hard by institutional, intimate, or spiritual violence and alienation. I am also convinced that this healing can be done as part of our political praxis, with joy, creativity, and a commitment to liberation arts.

This conviction is my impetus for approaching prison education from a lens of engaged and liberatory pedagogy. Liberatory (critical) pedagogy mobilizes critical consciousness around the power structures that dictate opportunity, power, access, and resources for different individuals and groups in society (Freire, 1970;

Shor, 1992); engaged pedagogy occurs when "diverse forms of contemplative practice become conduits to elicit deep awareness, focus, compassion, social change, transformation, creativity, and inspiration, as well as intellectual understandings" (Rendón, 2014, p. 134). When classroom learning is both liberatory and engaged, both critical and contemplative, it can "highlight an 'embodied reflexivity' in which participants learn to reflect on their own ideologies and experiences, question their ways of thinking, and imagine alternatives" (hooks, as cited in Berila, 2015, p. 15). This form of pedagogy recognizes that engaging within is a critical component of creating just and effective partnerships in community. Laura Rendón (2014) reminds us that "introspection, or deep involvement in the critical examination of one's beliefs, assumptions, and worldviews" is a form of engagement that must accompany community work (p. 136).

> Faculty and students must be willing to confront their own fears and biases and the extent of their participation in maintaining the status quo. Self-reflexivity can serve as a means for faculty and students to probe more deeply into what they are learning and how the learning is transforming them (Rendón, 2014, p. 137).

These particular approaches are rooted in reciprocal learning where respect, humility, and dialogue are centered in the classroom, where discerning power structures in society is equally valued with discerning one's own internal experience. It is an intentional approach to community building and democratic education in the classroom, disrupting notions of traditional "service-learning" and the paternalistic notions of charity that can often be embedded therein.

It not only creates resistance to the traditional hierarchy and banking model of conventional classrooms but also creates an affirmation of community engagement and consciousness raising that extends beyond the boundaries of the classroom (as referenced by Osvaldo in his discussion of he and his peers wrestling with theories of social change after class, on the prison yard). In this way, critical and contemplative learning becomes the building blocks of personal and social change, resulting in a classroom connection that pierces through the isolation generated in prison, as well as, ironically enough, that which exists on college campuses, supporting both sets of students' sense of worth, awareness, and hope.

For inside students, raising political consciousness and brokering "brave spaces" to acknowledge personal wounds and the impacts they have provides an educational experience that supersedes most initial interests in our class (for credit, for milestones, for connection, for intellectual advancement). I believe that the knowledge, tools, and relationships forged in the classroom are just as important to successful transition out of the system as knowing how to craft a marketable resume and cover letter. As Osvaldo and Jerrad testify, students inside insist that this kind of learning is a critical form of survival,[2] one that enables them to manage the life-threatening existence inside while developing a critical analysis of the system they are a part of.

For outside students and professors, becoming proximate in this way to people and procedures of the criminal "injustice" system prevents us from leaving class and (for those who had the luxury to begin with) resuming the comfortable experience of "not-knowing" the pain and suffering that exists in the system. After teaching in this program for a number of years, I believe firmly that cultivating critical consciousness, empowerment, and connection with a combination of inside and outside students is key to propelling a social change movement against the prison industrial complex. Gathering inside and outside students together for a shared journey of critical learning and "radical openness," we create an actual lived experience of the "global vision wherein we see our lives and our fate as intimately connected to those of everyone else on the planet" (hooks, 2000, p. 88). Practicing a healing and liberatory form of teaching and learning together in this shared educational journey, inside one of the world's most dehumanizing and violent settings, itself becomes an act of resistance.

The Liability of Vulnerability

My inside students say again and again that this kind of shared course is a lifeline for their intellectual and personal growth as well as their survival. I believe that is true during the duration of the course and can only hope it continues to be true thereafter, though I cannot know for sure, given the strict state prison rules that forbid my being in touch with them after the class concludes. I also worry about the risk involved in facilitating a short-term project that excavates individual and collective wounds. There is obviously a risk for opening up this kind of work with individuals who have suffered from great acts of trauma, even as we highlight strengths and strategies of resilience as part of the healing trajectory. This is true whether inside or outside, but, in particular, I know that this work carries with it a liability in prison that is far different than that of the typical on-campus college classroom. My inside students leave the brave space of our classroom at the end of the two hours or the semester, and return to the oppressive and violent spaces of prison, where this newfound self-awareness and personal work is usually unwelcomed and unsafe. The liability of vulnerability inside creates a cost to this work that could threaten its worth.

One inside student, S., confided in me that the class offers the only two hours of light and hope in an otherwise totally intolerable and violent existence. He went on to say that it is *almost too much to bear* having to return to that reality after our two hours is up, *almost too painful* to feel that sense of freedom, connection, and healing, only to have it ripped away. He thought about this a long time, weighed whether it was actually worth it, and decided it was.

Yet after our class ended, I learned that he tried to escape on two separate occasions and ended up in the hole.

The enormity of this tension cannot be easily resolved.

It emerges directly in this essay, too. I have not been able to be in touch with one of my co-authors, Jerrad, since he was transferred to another prison 300 miles away. I have no idea how he is faring, but I don't believe his transfer was made under good circumstances. He used to write me regularly, but given the strict rules that prohibit me from maintaining any contact with him while he's still inside, our communication has been irrevocably fractured.

My other co-author, Osvaldo, was released a year or so after our class ended. Soon after his release, he came to visit me on my home campus and I felt relieved to see him so upbeat as he navigated the many hurdles of reentry. He came back to campus soon after to be a guest speaker in another Inside-Out class. We wrote back and forth a bit about our elation that our three pieces had been accepted into this anthology, and our dismay at not being able to work some more with Jerrad in person on this writing. But within the next year, Osvaldo lost touch with me almost completely. I wrote him repeatedly in hopes that we could begin a process of shared reflection and editing on these collective contributions but he failed to respond. Finally, just weeks before a gathering of our anthology contributors, I received word from him. He had run into a rough patch, felt embarrassed to go "MIA," but was just trying to negotiate what he called "a weird head space" and potential self-sabotage.

Internal Transformation against a Backdrop of Systemic Oppression

The fractured relationships with my students after our classes have concluded exemplify the repercussions of incarceration and reentry—and these represent only a fraction of the challenges faced by those mired in these systems. I can't help but wonder if the deeply transformative nature of the class we shared was only momentarily so. Perhaps it was as profound as Osvaldo and Jerrad describe, but this personal transformation couldn't withstand the monumental challenges they faced after class concluded, both inside and "on the outs." Healing and transformation are not finite destinations at which we arrive; they are processes of becoming that must be nurtured over time, both internally and within whichever structures and social settings we find ourselves in. While ever powerful, when the community we build inside the classroom dissolves, individuals are left alone to battle structures that have not made the same transformations they have. This illuminates an age-old argument about the limits of internal transformation against a backdrop of systemic oppression.

Given these tensions that exist in a short-term transformative education class, I recognize potential problems to teaching in this way. I also recognize the risks of not doing so. Too often this kind of work is squelched because it involves all that which occurs below the shoulders: matters of the heart, spirit, and body are rarely given space in classrooms, especially in prison. Yet time after time, inside and outside students ask for more support on issues of their own emotional, intellectual, and political development. They ask for safe spaces to heal from the repercussions of oppression, injustice, abuse, disease, violence, loss, low self-esteem, and the variety of emotional distresses they ignite. When we do crack open this area, I find that, again and again, students are empowered to navigate the difficult terrain that arises, especially within the embrace of support that the class community provides.

I have asked inside students directly if they feel it is a disservice to raise consciousness both about personal wounds and the injustices of the prison industrial complex—and then leave them in a setting in which they may face repercussions if they enact either vulnerability or agency around these topics. They tell me fervently that, while the tensions are real, they absolutely need this kind of education: it creates a level of freedom and personal empowerment that no cage can touch.[3] It may not change the realities they face inside nor the challenges they'll face once out, but it ignites a sense of personal power and knowledge that creates at least one more buffer against the forces that might break them down. It also allows them fuller understandings of the fix they are in, the conditions that led to it, and how their voice and experience can be a critical component of the movement to change it.

And so, I try to heed the keen warning to not "throw people into the deep end if they can't swim back to shore," providing a variety of tools such as writing, meditation, community-building exercises, and strategies for social change that will enable my students to continue to navigate what comes up long after the class is done. I hear from them, long after classes, graduations, or release dates, that this class helped them learn how to question, analyze, survive, thrive, and transform. Maybe I don't hear from the ones who have different experiences. And maybe those who celebrate this work on the inside do so out of pressure to show gratitude and minimize critique, because of the power dynamics inside or because of their own desire for more credit-bearing college courses. Again, it is hard to know.

As such, I hold the paradox that two things may be true at once: that this work is deeply transformative, as well as risky and limited.

Prison Education and Prison Abolition

Another paradox I straddle in this teaching is that of trying to attend to the immediate needs of those trapped in this system while working towards the long-term aim of dismantling it. I am deeply disturbed by the violent and oppressive nature of the prison itself that I must repeatedly befriend in order to get inside. The stance of many prison workers I've met is a punitive one; eyes roll at the notion of "rehabilitation" that has been thrust upon their operations in the last few years. Walking through the administrative offices with my outside students one day, we met a high-ranking prison administrator who shared a litany of horror stories about what "really" goes on inside, emphasizing that inmates are worthless manipulators who are getting what they deserve, and finally, that "the only things those guys can teach you is what not to do." Likewise, the guards at the gate repeatedly intonate to me, implicitly and sometimes explicitly, that they do not understand the point of trying to teach the students inside, and only see our program, and others like it, as creating unnecessary additional work for them.

The warden and the community resource manager at the prison are kind, smart, strong African American women who hold the primary positions of power that allow us in. Building necessary and authentic relationships with these gate-keepers deepens the paradox of my work. These women have worked hard to make it to where they are today and intervene diligently, in a culture of indifference, to create programs offering education, job training, drug recovery, arts, and more. They understand the importance of these Inside-Out classes, and fight hard to ensure the support and expansion of our program. Yet, they are also the ones upholding the very system my students and I study, critique, and advocate for dismantling. I cringe at the fact that our credit-bearing liberal arts college class makes the prison "look good," and so upholds the very system I want no part of. But in order to maintain the fragile relationships that allow us to continue this unprecedented program, to keep it alive and growing, to offer whatever transformation it may bring to those who are incarcerated, I must keep my critique to myself, follow the rules, and hope to get in and out with as little fuss as possible. And so, I, too, become a cog in the wheels of this industry, support its structure in order to get inside and teach about how we might dismantle that very structure through personal empowerment and systemic change.

I also know that I am complicit in upholding the prison industrial complex whether I teach inside or not. The cell phone in my pocket, the college furniture I sit upon, and the Starbucks drink I am enjoying as I write this are all products of prison labor (which, for my inside students, can be as low as 0.7 cents per hour). As an obedient tax-paying citizen, I also contribute to the *$80 billion tax dollars* spent this year on corrections by federal, state, and local agencies (Committee for a Responsible Federal Budget, 2015).

But through the Inside-Out model, I am also complicit in alerting those who may not understand the realities of this unjust system (my outside students) to what is going on inside, in introducing them to peers they are accountable to inside, and in guiding all towards a sense of our shared agency to be actors in a movement for change, both inside and out. Recently a prison abolitionist activist came to give a guest lecture in our class about the legislation her grassroots coalitions have helped to create; those that have passed are making significant shifts in the policies that uphold this system. Asked, in light of her abolitionist convictions, what she thought of our work inside, she said that through spending the two-hour class with us she could sense the vibrancy of the Inside-Out student relationships, the absolute agency students felt in their newfound knowledge about the prison industrial complex and commitment to activism around it. She was convinced that classes like this were a critical piece in building the consciousness, will, and solidarity necessary to change this system. Other abolitionist colleagues have not been so generous in their support of teaching inside, critical that anything that helps keep the system going is impossibly at odds with its dismantling.

I somehow agree with both.

Working for Change Inside and Out

S. is in the hole, Jerrad has been transferred 300 miles from home, and Osvaldo is lost amid the myriad rules and regulations that actively deter his "successful reentry." Where am I? As a middle-class, white woman with twenty-three years of formal schooling and correlating credentialing (BA, MA, PhD), I have gainful employment, live in a safe and beautiful part of Los Angeles, and am asked repeatedly, by a number of publications, to share my experience as a prison educator. The discrepancy between my students and me, in terms of institutional power, opportunity and access, is highly problematic. It is also not at all unusual, as I find that well-off white women make up the majority of prison educators, predominately in institutions housing men of color. Is this just the newest iteration of "savior behavior"? It can sure look that way, which is why I have been so reticent to speak publicly both about my deep commitment to this work and my critiques and honest reflections around it.

After twenty years of working in social justice organizations and community engagement centers and five years of teaching inside, I am under no illusion about my ability to "save" anyone, nor any desire to enact the long lineage of charity-based work done under this assumption. But there are multiple reasons and ways I engage in this work which seem important to name, as I find critical reflection on one's positionality and motivations to be crucial aspects of conscious activism. In part, I actually do this work to save myself—to renew my own sense of hope and inspiration by participating in the powerful shared learning and humanizing experience that unfolds again and again in the Inside-Out classroom. This work also saves me from rage and despair by providing direct means to push back against the prison industrial complex, from the inside out.

As a white woman doing racial justice work, I also know that both my family's gains and losses in the racial, cultural, and political systems of this country tie me to the struggle. Like many, I have intertwined ancestral experiences of both oppressed (as persecuted Jews who lost their land, language, and livelihood in Eastern Europe and as blacklisted activists who lost their vocation and dignity in America's McCarthy era) as well as oppressor (as homesteaders whose fortunes were built in part on the land and backs of numerous communities of color in the wild, wild West). These diverse identities and experiences of my grandparents and great-grandparents implicate me in various ways as I navigate power dynamics and injustice in today's world. While my current social location is steeped in privilege, I feel that my own wholeness and humanity is greatly diminished by my complicity in this intersection of unjust systems. I am called to this work out of solidarity with and accountability towards those persecuted today because I know that it is about what we all lose, to monumentally uneven degrees, by participating in these dehumanizing systems.[4]

I also know that my whole community is diminished by the myriad factors creating, supporting, and resulting from mass incarceration, including the poor schooling and unfettered school-to-prison pipeline that disproportionately impacts low-income children of color in our city and the near-erasure of black and brown men (sons, fathers, partners) as contributors to the common good. Despite the fact that crime rates continue to fall (Krisberg and Marchionna, 2013), California intentionally chooses to spend $11.8 billion on corrections in 2018–19 — up from $11.4 billion in 2017–18 (Californians United for a Responsible Budget, 2018)—diverting desperately needed funds towards prisons and policing instead of investing more towards equitable education, restorative justice, environmental justice, affordable housing, and quality healthcare. Teaching inside is one tangible way to push back against these racialized political decisions that so clearly devalue and discriminate against mass portions of our society under false proclamations around security and justice.

I also do this work because I have been asked to. My students have charged me with their hopes that I keep teaching this stuff and that I get others to come in and teach other stuff (the best request I've received yet was for a class on acoustical physics!). Aside from my role as a professor I also carry the title of Assistant Vice President, focusing on community engagement at my college—and I take seriously the charge by these community partners to fulfill my work as a leader in my institution. I have used whatever power and access afforded me in that position to greatly expand the Inside-Out Prison Exchange program and ensure that any class taught in the future is credit-bearing and guided by the requests of the students therein. As an institution situated in Southern California's infamous "Prison Valley," we are not divorced from the realities and fates of those inside and are accountable to working to change them.

While most of the work I do to push back against the system occurs through the act of teaching inside, I am also committed to working consistently on the outside to disrupt the policies that uphold it and ignorance and prejudice that exist to support it. This involves learning from and collaborating with organizations led primarily by the formerly incarcerated or systems-impacted individuals in ways that they believe will have the greatest impact on changing the fundamental problems of prisons and policing. For me this has meant working with abolitionist organizations (such as Critical Resistance[5]) to host general trainings and workshops for students across our campuses about what the prison industrial complex and abolition mean and are all about, to speak about abolitionist movements for social change in my other, non-prison related classes, and to present "dis-orientations" about the prison system to counter the mandatory prison orientation for the faculty and students participating in the Inside-Out program.

It includes building partnerships with organizations organizing campaigns to change laws related to prisons, probation, and parole (such as Californians United for a Responsible Budget and Anti-Recidivism Coalition[6]) and includes creating assignments in my classes that involve inside and outside students co-authoring letters to elected officials on related legislative topics.[7] It involves developing community–campus partnerships with programs that advocate for grassroots and policy change on mass incarceration while also participating in their reentry services for formerly incarcerated individuals who live and work in our region (such as Riverside All of Us or None[8]).

It also means contributing tangible resources to many of these organizations (such as meeting space, office space, fiscal support, and semester-long interns who provide community-directed research and service), utilizing the assets of our institution to support the radical work these organizations do against these systems. Lastly, it means providing guidance, advocacy, and letters of recommendation to formerly incarcerated students as they advance their college-going trajectories.

Through these multiple threads, I attempt to enact the accountability I have as a result of my identities as a "free," middle-class, white teacher, activist, and community member. I also attempt to enact the gratitude I have to my inside students for how they teach me, inspire me, and forward in me and my outside students a renewed consciousness around a system that was previously invisible to many of us. Aside from the critically important advocacy work that can occur on the outside, as a result of this Inside-Out project, I am deeply committed to address state persecution and violence by affirming the rights, access, and knowledge of those on the inside, creating educational communities within that resist this system of domination through personal affirmation and intellectual liberation.

Conclusion

In response to the urging of our "think tank" (a group made up of Inside-Out students and faculty alumni who participate in a process of shared governance to decide how this program should continue to grow and unfold), and through advocating with both campus and prison administrators, I have helped secure a commitment from the consortium of the five Claremont Colleges to offer fifteen Inside-Out classes annually.[9] This marks a monumental advancement in shared credit-bearing learning inside.

I hold the multiple truths presented in this essay as one paradoxical whole: the program recognizes the beast it's up against, and then marches on, hoping to ignite connection, critical awareness, and change, on individual and institutional levels. As such, prison education can weave together solidarity activism, transformative education, and personal and collective healing, not only as acts of resistance but also as acts of affirmation and transformation.

Epilogue

In a desperate attempt to maintain my commitment to my co-authors prior to this shared publication, I managed to locate where Jerrad had been transferred and decided it was worth the risk to initiate contact in order to confirm that he still was interested in getting our essays published and to see if he had any edits for his work or for my own (which he had never seen). He wrote back immediately, with great enthusiasm to be back in touch, appreciation for the truth telling in my story, and to share an updated version of his piece. Inspired by this last-minute success with Jerrad, I initiated contact again with Osvaldo, hoping to pierce through his state of isolation to likewise share my work and confirm his interest in going forward. Just prior to our deadline with the editor, I received the following email, which, with his permission, I decided to include as our epilogue, as it so poignantly captures the paradoxes of our beautiful and complex shared journey.

Saturday, March 31, 2018, 2:23 AM
Tessa,
!Hola! Feliz Viernes Santo and the commencement of Passover, Shabbat Shalom, hermana. I have received your correspondence, even in the shadows I've been hiding in. I've read your new rendition of your offerings towards our efforts and, as uncomfortable as I may find some of it, I like it. It is the truth and nitty grittiness this experience has been. I can only imagine the path you've travelled to make this all happen. I am only one of many that you've made a connection with and exposed yourself to in a very real way.

I am doing better than when we last spoke. At the time, I was great on the surface but battled with my own inner struggles and plight of parole and the restrictions that come along with it. Plus, my own manias that, at times, get the better of me. But, so is life and so is me. I find myself here, not quite lost but perhaps a bit hidden. My own inner sanctuary of what was. I hold the class deep and dear and perhaps feel inadequate to describe what it was or perhaps I may feel as I have failed you, myself, and all those bright minds that took part in it. I also question the validity of my intentions. What proactive steps am I taking to put the praxis we so dearly spoke about into action? What am I doing? Was I true to myself and those promises I made to myself on those late nights on my bunk? I share some of the sentiments you feel; are we dissidents or did we become cogs in the machinery that keep it going? You to the prison industry and me to society. Does a decent salary deserve to muffle the yells of revolution that I once chanted? But is it all truly lost now that I am out here? We built a community in there, the foundation to the success of that first class. The answer is no, I haven't lost that.

As I meld back into society I have the blessing to do so in Downtown Los Angeles. With that comes a plethora of interactions with all walks of life.

From Legacy Record producers that have to worked with Aretha Franklin to young men down on their luck, scraping enough change to get back to Las Vegas, where everything will be fine, who thank me for the cigarette and brief interaction. After receiving your most recent email, I have randomly encountered writers (a poet and essayist) that encouraged me to leave it all on the leaflet, yet I was reluctant to do so until now. I could go ahead and blame it on sixty-hour work weeks or lack of self-discipline or, as I mentioned before, self-sabotage. But here I am, pressing away at these keys, making sense of the now. I am very grateful for what you have done and continue to do. My sincerest apologies for my lack of communication. Please do not give up because no matter how grim things get, here I am and there you are, flourishing in our own ways. I say, thank you.

Best Regards,
Osvaldo Armas

Notes

1 I am grateful to be a part of a community of practice with Nadinne Cruz, Kathy Yep, Erich Steinman, and Susan Phillips, colleagues and comrades with whom I can have difficult and honest conversations about our engagement with injustice as it relates to mass incarceration, settler colonialism, immigration, and community engagement/activist scholarship. Special thanks to Nadinne for articulating so beautifully that the classroom is not the battlefield and we must nurture our students to be allies in learning.
2 A fellow contributor to this anthology, Anne Dalke, offers these expanded interpretations of such survival: "Vizenor offers the term 'survivance;' 'an active sense of presence … not a mere reaction … renunciations of dominance, tragedy and victimry.' Others have analyzed the term as a portmanteau of 'survival + endurance,' and 'survival + resistance.'" This conglomeration and reconfiguration of notions of survival reflect what I see my inside students embody on a daily basis.
3 This brings to mind the beautiful Albert Camus quote: "The only way to deal with an unfree world is to become so absolutely free that your very existence is an act of rebellion."
4 Lila Watson and her aboriginal activist colleagues in the 1970s so artfully express this point that has become so central to my own work: "If you have come here to help me, you're wasting your time. But if you are here because your liberation is bound to my struggle, then perhaps we can work together."
5 http://www.criticalresistance.org
6 http://www.curbprisonspending.org and http://www.antirecidivism.org
7 I am proud that my most recent Inside-Out class won the Project Pericles Debating for Democracy Letter to an Elected Official Competition for their letter regarding Bill 3356, supporting transitional housing for the formerly incarcerated: http://www.pro jectpericles.org/projectpericles/programs/section/debating_for_democracy_d4d_/
8 https://nationinside.org/campaign/all-of-us-or-none-riverside/
9 I am grateful for the vitally important work that I have had the opportunity to engage in with my colleagues at the Claremont Colleges to support and expand prison education. I especially appreciate that alongside our shared commitment to this program is also a shared commitment to question how we can do it most respectfully and critically while simultaneously forwarding advocacy on the outside. Special thanks to Pitzer's

Dean Boyle and the Community Engagement Center, as well as the Claremont College's Office of Consortial Academic Collaborations, the Justice Education Working
Group, and the Center for Teaching and Learning.

References

Berila, B. (2015). *Integrating mindfulness into anti-oppression pedagogy*. New York: Routledge.

Boal, A. (1985). *Theatre of the oppressed*. New York: Theatre Communications Group.

Californians United for a Responsible Budget (2018). Overview of 2018–2019 corrections budget. Retrieved at http://www.curbprisonspending.org/2018/05/16/over
view-of-2018-19-corrections-budget-may-revision/.

Committee for a Responsible Federal Budget (2015). Does the U.S. spend $80 billion a year
on incarceration? Retrieved at https://www.crfb.org/blogs/us-spends-80-billion-year-inca
rceration.

Freire, P. (1970). *Pedagogy of the oppressed*. Translated by M. B. Ramos. New York:
Continuum.

hooks, b. (2000). *All about love: New visions*. New York: William Morrow.

Krisberg, B. and Marchionna, S. (2013, April). *Fact sheet: Police, prisons, and public Safety in
California*. Berkeley, CA: University of California, Berkeley School of Law.

Rendón, L. (2014). *Sentipensante (sensing/thinking) pedagogy: Educating for wholeness, social
justice, and liberation*. Sterling, VA: Stylus Publishing.

Shor, I. (1992). *Empowering education: Critical teaching for social change*. Chicago: University of
Chicago Press.

19

SCHOOLS, PRISONS, AND HIGHER EDUCATION

Romarilyn Ralston

Corporal Punishment in Schools

My earliest experience of educational discipline was in the first grade. It was recess and I was on the swing when a white classmate ran in front of me. Since I was holding on to the swing chains I was okay; except for a wild shift in my direction, all was fine. However, my classmate hit the ground and skinned her knees. She got up and headed right for the white teacher supervising the playground, screaming, "she kicked me." I apologized and explained that we collided by accident. The teacher decided that explanation was unacceptable, and I was aggressively pulled off the playground by my shirt collar. I tried to pull the teacher's hand away, but she was too strong. Since she would not let me go, I bit her on the hand. I would spend the remainder of the school year in the principal's office.

Attending public school in St. Louis was brutal and left emotional scars that would not heal until after I received therapy, many years later, while serving a life sentence in a California prison. Ironically, it would be the carceral system's attempts to simultaneously punish and rehabilitate me that would teach me to interrogate the "prison industrial education complex"—in particular, the ways in which corporal punishment in the educational process desensitizes poor children from urban areas to accept state violence, conditioning them for a life lived in cages.

President Johnson signed H.R. 9567, the Higher Education Act of 1965, into law on November 8, 1965, at his alma mater, Southwest Texas State College (now Texas State University) in San Marcos, Texas. It was there, Johnson said, that

> the seeds were planted from which grew my firm conviction that for the individual, education is the path to achievement and fulfillment; for the Nation, it is a path to a society that is not only free but civilized; and for the

world, it is the path to peace—for it is education that places reason over force (Johnson, 1965).

Not always! In elementary schools in Missouri it was common practice for teachers to paddle students for disciplinary reasons, whether for low-level classroom disruptions or for more serious acts of violence. Teachers used paddles ranging from twelve-inch rulers wrapped in layers of tape to oversized, handmade, square-shaped, quarter-inch thick boards with handles among other instruments of power and pain to wield authority and fear.

As a young student, I remember being lined up in the classroom or hallway with the other students and told, "Bend over or touch the wall," then wacked any number of times by the teacher. Students would scream, jump into the air, or remain silent for fear of being teased by other students. Regardless of our participation in the incident or behavior deemed "unlawful," we were all held accountable, criminalized, and punished. Being treated this way as a young girl left me feeling humiliated and confused, especially when school had become "a place of refuge" from the abuse I was experiencing at home and the gun violence present in the community. Many days, school was a refreshing break from the turmoil of home life, but on other days it was just as chaotic and painful.

The use of corporal punishment resulted from the biases, biographies, and epistemologies of teachers and administrators. For many reasons, teachers believed in spanking and used corporal punishment as a teaching method and means of classroom control. Corporal punishment was then legal in many Southern states, including Missouri, which still continues to use spanking as a tool to control students.

Corporal punishment, as a mechanism of control in the classroom, has traumatic consequences for the student long after school is out. For me, those consequences manifested as low self-esteem, isolation, and self-doubt. Once internalized, the effects of corporal punishment continued to produce self-criticism, a collateral consequence of school discipline.

Higher Education in Prison

My first college course was in a prison classroom in 1990. I was so excited! When I saw my name on the list I knew my life was about to change. Acceptance into the college program elevated my self-esteem and gave me hope that maybe one day I would be released. Finally, I had something good to share with my grandmother during our fifteen-minute calls. What I didn't know was that access to higher education in prison would be short lived. I would not earn an accredited degree inside.

These classes were part of a *carrot and stick* system of privileges and punishments. Access to college-in-prison is a privilege. Instructors are few, space is limited, resources are scarce, and college is something you do in addition to your work assignment and many other required programs. Squeezing college into an already demanding schedule of prison life when the evening ends at 8:30 p.m. is intense and stressful. And the privilege could be given and taken away by correctional staff based on one's conduct in the prison. Any number of rule violations—such as fighting or possessing contraband—could get me kicked out of the college program.

However, I ultimately lost access to college because the federal government decided incarcerated people did not deserve higher education programs.

Two weeks into the elementary algebra class we had our first test. Walking into the classroom I could feel the anxiety in the air. Having studied and been tutored by my cellmate I felt confident I would do well. The following week the professor seemed agitated as he passed back the test results. Although I had done well, most of the class had not. Reviewing all the missed questions seemed to frustrate the professor tremendously. The more questions were asked, the more frustrated he became. During the break, he called me over to say, "Well done." When I asked if he was alright, he revealed that he had thought he was coming to teach at the California Institute for Women, a place for scholars and higher learning. Instead, he was dismayed to realize that he had signed up to teach in a prison. The rest of the semester was tense and hostile.

Three semesters into my college studies, the program was discontinued. We later discovered this was because of a federal law that made people inside prisons ineligible for Pell Grants. Congress made this decision while directing billions of federal dollars towards building more prisons. Prison education scholar Daniel Karpowitz explains,

> Pell grants had made a huge impact inside American prisons. Higher education quickly became the most efficient, affordable, and effective "program" in American corrections, consistently associated with the lowest rates of recidivism—meaning people who went to college while incarcerated almost never came back to prison again. It was stunningly cheap: at their peak, in 1994, such programs nationally cost a total of one half of one percent of all Pell spending (Karpowitz, 2017, p. 6).

Twenty years would pass before I would have the opportunity to finish what I started in prison.

Impostor Syndrome

After I was released from prison, education was my reentry practice. I was privileged to have the support of Pitzer College, a small private liberal arts college in Claremont, California. I started there as a second-year student, fresh out of prison, still on parole, and very nervous. I remember my first mid-term and needing to purchase a "blue book." I had no idea what a "blue book" was and was too embarrassed to ask. A day before the mid-term a classmate had her course materials spread out on the table and I looked over and saw the infamous blue book. I could not believe how silly and ashamed I felt because I spent days stressing over how to get a blue book for the mid-term.

After the mid-term, I told my professor what had happened. She responded with compassion and support. I finished that semester with increased confidence in my present and decreased fear of my past. Pitzer faculty were not the only professors that supported me in the classroom and forgave my past. Several Scripps and Pomona faculty had been long time advocates and mentors of mine. In fact, it was prison where I met professors from Scripps, Pomona, and the Claremont Graduate University. They had come in at the request of the warden to partner with an inmate self-help group that I co-founded, the Young Adult Networking Group, that provided mentoring to our 18–25 population. Although I had a history with these professors as an organizer in the prison, I was now their student and felt as though I had to be perfect to gain their trust, respect, and acknowledgement.

To my surprise, I was wrong. But it took me a few more semesters to liberate myself from the "impostor syndrome" created by decades of prison conditioning and shaming.

The "impostor syndrome" simply means "feeling like a fraud." For me and many students in Project Rebound at Cal State University, Fullerton, where I am now program coordinator, overcoming the impostor syndrome is our biggest challenge and oftentimes leads to relapse and placement on academic probation. A 2013 article, "Feel like a Fraud?," illustrates this phenomenon with graduate students who feel as though they don't belong in PhD programs (Weir, 2013). The stories in the article strikingly correlate with what I have witnessed working with undergraduate students with an incarceration experience. The impostor phenomenon and perfectionism often go hand in hand. So-called impostors think every task they tackle must be done perfectly, and they rarely ask for help. Formerly incarcerated students see asking for help as a weakness and deficiency. Prison conditions and "convict codes" that must be followed for one's own protection foster the impostor syndrome post release. That perfectionism can lead to two typical responses, impostors may procrastinate, putting off assignments out of fear that they won't be able to complete them to high enough standards. Or they may over-prepare, spending much more time on tasks than is necessary.

Weir explains that "impostor phenomenon occurs among high achievers who are unable to internalize and accept their success. They often attribute their accomplishments to luck rather than to ability, and fear that others will eventually unmask them as a fraud" (Weir, 2013). For many incarcerated students, remorse and the need to prove ourselves worthy of parole and higher education drive our need to be successful. It could be said that our achievements are not our own: they belong to our victims, the state, and our families. We are more appreciative of the teachers who come to provide the classes than we are of the sacrifices and hard work we ourselves contribute to becoming accomplished students. Although our success is not due to luck, but to commitment, determination, and effort, we unfortunately don't see it this way. Teachers who teach in prisons should instill in their students that their success is their achievement, not that of their teachers or of the prisons.

Weir also notes that although the impostor syndrome doesn't appear in the Diagnostic and Statistical Manual of Mental Disorders (DSM), "psychologists and others acknowledge that it is a very real and specific form of intellectual self-doubt. Impostor feelings are generally accompanied by anxiety and, often, depression" (Weir, 2013). Moreover, people with it tend to keep feelings to themselves and don't talk about it. Brady Heiner, Director of Project Rebound at Cal State University, Fullerton, coined this decision to suffer in silence "the Rambo Complex." Since we launched the program in the fall 2016 several students have refused social and academic support, claiming they were doing well when they were overwhelmed, missing classes and/or failing tests. I believe certain types of punishments and discipline, from arrest to conviction, foster the impostor syndrome. Many incarcerated people, including myself, were told they were never getting out of prison or would suffer dire consequences for our actions: the death penalty or life without the possibility of parole.

Project Rebound

Project Rebound is an admissions and support program for students transitioning out of the carceral system. It has helped hundreds of formerly incarcerated individuals earn Bachelors and graduate-level degrees since 1967. The number of Project Rebound students who return to prison is just 3 percent, compared to a California state average of 61 percent. The program has maintained an extraordinary 95 percent graduation rate, with more than 180 students achieving a bachelor's or master's degree since 2005 (Schock, 2016).

I am one of the many formerly incarcerated scholars who, after serving decades in prison, now work in the field of higher education through Project Rebound. It is a privilege to assist incarcerated and formerly incarcerated students apply to college from inside prisons, jails, and community colleges. *College is for everyone* is a phrase I heard during my first week on the job at Cal State University, Fullerton, and I believe it! After all, I am one example of the benefits of a higher education.

Programs like Project Rebound do more than support the formerly incarcerated reintegrate into a college setting. These programs create safe and brave spaces where students with incarceration experiences can breathe and relate with peers and administrative staff who not only understand their positionality but who have challenged it, earn degrees, and contribute to academic scholarship. The lived experiences and knowledge held by students with incarceration experiences are as valuable as any textbook. But large state colleges and universities often ignore students who have past involvement in the criminal punishment legal system. They don't know we are there and many don't want to know! Fly under the radar, get your degree, and get out. Many formerly incarcerated students don't feel welcome on campus and are afraid of coming out for fear of rejection and possible harassment. Yet formerly incarcerated students are an asset to the classroom.

Conclusion

Teaching in prison and learning in prison are both rewarding and challenging. The prison as a system of oppression makes it hard for teachers to access incarcerated students and students are subjected to a number of rules and regulations that can lead to being pushed out or removed from the class. However, if both teacher and student are allowed to bring their full hearts and minds into the classroom, magic happens. Incarcerated students become aware of their agency, intellectual power, and critically use the knowledge they are acquiring to set themselves free!

Nelson Mandela put it best, "Education is the most powerful weapon which we can use to change the world" (Mandela, 2003). Spending exorbitant amounts of tax dollars on weapons of mass punishment (i.e., prisons and jails) is costly and ineffective. The cost of incarceration in America is over one trillion dollars, when we take into account the social costs borne by families and communities (Schoenherr, 2016). It's time to invest more in educating than incarcerating. It appears President Johnson had it right fifty years ago. As stated in *Don't Stop Now*, a document that celebrates California's recent investment in higher education in prison and support for formerly incarcerated students on campus, "we can no longer consign incarcerated and formerly incarcerated men and women to ending their education with a GED … [We all] deserve the opportunities that hard work and a college degree create" (Mukamal and Silbert, 2018, p. 3).

References

Johnson, L. B. (1965, November 8). Remarks on signing the Higher Education Act of 1965. Retrieved at https://www.txstate.edu/commonexperience/pastsitearchives/2008-2009/lbjresources/higheredact.html.

Karpowitz, D. (2017). *College in prison: Reading in an age of mass incarceration*. New Brunswick: Rutgers University Press.

Mandela, N. (2003, July 16). Address by Nelson Mandela at launch of Mindset Network, Johannesburg, South Africa. Retrieved at http://www.mandela.gov.za/mandela_speeches/2003/030716_mindset.htm.

Mukamal, D. and Silbert, R. (2018, March). *Don't Stop Now*. Retrieved at https://correctionstocollegeca.org/assets/general/dont-stop-now-report.pdf.

Schock, K. (2016, June 16). University joins statewide effort to expand college access for formerly incarcerated men and women. *Fresno State News*. Retrieved at http://www.

fresnostatenews.com/2016/06/16/university-joins-statewide-effort-to-expand-college-a
ccess-for-formerly-incarcerated-men-and-women/.

Schoenherr, N. (2016, September 7). Cost of incarceration in the U.S. more than $1 trillion.
the SOURCE. Retrieved at https://source.wustl.edu/2016/09/cost-incarceration-u-s-1-
trillion/.

Weir, K. (2013, November). Feel like a fraud? *gradPSYCH Magazine,* 11(4). Retrieved at
https://www.apa.org/gradpsych/2013/11/fraud.aspx.

INDEX

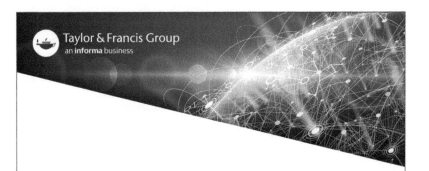

Milton Keynes UK
Ingram Content Group UK Ltd.
UKHW020719240124
436584UK00010B/95